Technology, Literature and Culture

Alex Goody

polity

First published in 2011 by Polity Press

Polity Press
65 Bridge Street
Cambridge CB2 1UR, UK

Polity Press
350 Main Street
Malden, MA 02148, USA

ISBN-13: 978-0-7456-3953-6
ISBN-13: 978-0-7456-3954-3(pb)

A catalogue record for this book is available from the British Library.

Typeset in 10.5 on 12 pt Bembo
by Toppan Best-set Premedia Limited
Printed and bound in Great Britain by MPG Books Group Limited,
Bodmin, Cornwall

The publisher has used its best endeavours to ensure that the URLs for external websites referred to in this book are correct and active at the time of going to press. However, the publisher has no responsibility for the websites and can make no guarantee that a site will remain live or that the content is or will remain appropriate.

Every effort has been made to trace all copyright holders, but if any have been inadvertently overlooked the publisher will be pleased to include any necessary credits in any subsequent reprint or edition.

For further information on Polity, visit our website: www.politybooks.com

Contents

Acknowledgements   vii

1. **Introduction: The Twentieth-Century
    Technological Imaginary**   1
    Victorian technoculture   2
    Uncanny technology   7
    Victorian Science Fiction   11
    Technology in the twentieth century   14

2. **Writing Technology: Literature and Theory**   22
    Mechanical reproduction   23
    The question concerning technology   30
    The medium is the message   34
    Technology and postmodernism   37
    Desiring machines   41
    Media technologies, theory and the human   43

3. **Media Technologies and Modern Culture**   48
    Modernism and the cinema eye   50
    Talking across distances: radio modernism   60
    Beckett and broadcast media   73

4. **Cold War Technologies**   78
    Electric death   79
    Machine-war and poetry   82
    Total War, information and the spy   86
    Nuclear culture and counterculture   96
    Postmodernism, media and the death of the real   101

5. **Technological Texts: From Typewriters
    to Hypermedia**   109
    Type-writers and texts   110
    Typing, poetry and spontaneity   114
    Digital writing and hypertext   119

6. **Robots, Cyborgs and the Technological Body**   136
    'I would rather be a cyborg than a goddess'   137
    Machine-age man   140
    Robots, automation and the future of the human   146
    Technology, identity and the cyborg subject   152
    Screens, bodies and late twentieth-century culture   160

    Notes   168
    Select Bibliography   171
    Index   186

Acknowledgements

I would like to express my thanks to all my colleagues in the English department at Oxford Brookes University for being great people to work and talk with. I am grateful especially for the departmental sabbatical that enabled me finally to finish this project. I would particularly like to thank Steve Matthews, who continues to be a mentor as well as a friend, Simon Kovesi, who is a great boss, and Eric White, who shares several of my enthusiasms in modernism and technology. I am grateful also to my students, particularly those on my third-year 'Literature, Technology, Culture' module, for discussing many of the ideas and questions that govern this book and for giving me new ways of thinking about them. I would also like to thank Edward Plowman for conversations about James Bond, Antonia Mackay for getting me interested in the Cold War, and Niall Munro for letting me talk about this book when we should have been discussing his PhD thesis.

I have presented my ideas on technology at various forums, including the *Flesh Made Text* conference in Thessaloniki in 2002, the *Technology Media and Culture in the Space Between* conference in Montreal in 2005, the *Modernist Studies Association* conferences in Nashville in 2008 and Montreal in 2009, and the *Intercultural Humanism* conference in Oxford in 2010. I would like to thank all the organizers of these conferences for the opportunity to expound, discuss and refine my ideas. I would also like to thank Rod Mengham for the opportunity to write this book, the two anonymous readers for their useful comments on the draft manuscript, and Andrea Drugan and Lauren Mulholland at Polity, who have helped to make the process of producing this book as painless as possible.

This book has been completed during a very difficult time and I would like to say thank you to all those who have offered support and sympathy, including Sue Ash, Jo Esra, Harriet Irvine, Gail Marshall, Charlotte McBride, Catherine Morley and Nicole Pohl. My family continues to be my source of strength and comfort and I give my ultimate thanks to them – to Inge Goody, Steph Ashworth, Vicki Goody, Trevor Ashworth, Alex Cook, Jake and Olivia – and dedicate this book to the memory of my father Peter Goody. Finally, I express my great love and gratitude to Dan and to Jasmine.

1 Introduction: The Twentieth-Century Technological Imaginary

Technology is a key defining factor in twentieth-century culture. From the early Fordist revolution in manufacturing to computers and the Internet, technology has reconfigured our relationship to ourselves, each other and to the tools and materials we use. A technological imperative emerges as the driving force of the century, impelling societies and individuals to a ceaseless invention and advancement of new machines and machine methods. Under this imperative, it seems, natural processes were superseded by artificial ones and technological development took humanity further and further from the limits of their biological organism. As the dominating episteme, technology impacted on all aspects of human existence and, as will be explored, had profound implications for what it means to be human. Technology in the twentieth century was not a neutral force or objective apparatus, but a material practice that necessarily had political and social causes and effects; as the following pages disclose, technology cannot be examined as discrete from human culture. Rather than simply being the outcome of human invention and resourcefulness, technology needs to be considered as a generative cultural intensity that makes us just as much as we make it.

Just as technology is inherent in human culture so, as the twentieth century revealed, is technology inherent to human nature. Freud argued that all technology (from writing to houses, motors to microscopes) is an extension of the human, 'removing the limits' to make man 'a kind of prosthetic God' (1929: 37–8), but it is possible, in the light of actual developments in the twentieth century, to go beyond Freud's perspective and argue humanity is never distinct from the technologies that it generated and that underpin its civilizations. What the twentieth century reveals about technology is its profound fusion with the human; as the century progressed it became impossible to maintain an absolute distinction between the organic expressions of human nature and the technological processes, forms and devices which recorded and communicated those expressions as culture. Similarly, the nature and limits of human experience in the world (and even beyond it) were overwhelmingly configured through some form of technology. But what becomes apparent in an examination of the literature of the twentieth century, and what this study is concerned to highlight, is that technology does not ultimately release humankind from the material burdens of being. Instead, it binds us ever closer into the physical processes and substantial connections that constitute our existence in the world.

The following pages will explicate how Anglo-American texts across the twentieth century have represented and explored the inescapable presence and progress of technology. Looking at media technologies, textual technologies, technologies of destruction and the cyborg or technologized subject, this book considers the technological imagination of different decades, movements and cultural phenomena. Drawing on theoretical perspectives on technology, the continuities and contiguities as well as differences and changes across the century are considered, as the discussion ranges from the early years of the century to the millennium. The picture that emerges is one in which technological innovations and the increasing technologization of human culture and existence have had an inevitable impact on the literature of the twentieth century in terms of its thematic concerns, its formal innovations, and in what that literature is held to be. As the human relationship to machines becomes more and more complex, literature can fruitfully be considered as a transcription of that complex relationship and the literary work cannot, by the end of the twentieth century, be viewed simply as the natural expression of an isolated, organic individual. Literature is firmly inserted into the machinic interconnections of a technological world of production, destruction, replication, malfunction, communication, transmission and reception.

VICTORIAN TECHNOCULTURE

The destabilizing of a liberal-humanist conception of self and art by technology begins a long time before the networked age of global communication; the many innovations that mark the great expansions of the Victorian era, and that the twentieth century inherited, served profoundly to disrupt conventional notions of the human and human culture. With the invention of the telephone (1876), the commercial typewriter (1873), the phonograph and microphone (1877, 1878), the cinematograph (1895), the wireless (1896), and the modern internal combustion engine (1885), the technologies that were to transform the culture of the twentieth century had already arrived, but what subsequent generations inherited from the Victorians were not only specific machines, objects and processes, but also attitudes to, and ideas about, what technology was and what it did in the world. The figure of the cyborg, ideas about the posthuman, and various examinations of the interactions between 'meat' and 'data' in the world of wireless communication and digital culture are all prominent features of contemporary academic discourse. These specific features of the late twentieth century would appear to set us apart from preceding generations and cultures and far remove us from the materialist, humanist world of the Victorians. However, as Herbert Sussman points out, there is a 'new sense of technoculture . . . the stirrings of a new project in Victorian studies', in which the nineteenth century is seen as the 'birthplace of the information age' (2000: 288). Friedrich Kittler's account of late nineteenth-century recording technologies in *Discourse Networks* (1990) has been very important in generating this sense of Victorian technoculture. Kittler examines how, with the advent of visual- and sound-recording technology (phonography and film), the material signifier replaces the transcendental signified of previous (Romantic) ideologies of the word. These new technologies enabled non-literary data processing, and the differentiation of data streams (aural, oral, visual), in which language and the signifier, like the machines for recording images or sounds, are reduced to 'mechanisms'. At the same time, Kittler points out, the typewriter was also a form of standardizing writing, making its mechanisms apparent, disconnecting it from a universal point of origin and meaning, rendering it incapable of authorizing a coherent and stable self. He serves to demonstrate that the discourse networks of the late nineteenth century – 'the network of technologies and institutions that allow a given culture to select, store and process relevant data' (1990: 369) – and their effects on ideas of the subject were not so different from our contemporary 'wired' world of data and digital communication.

In recent examinations of the relationship between science, technology and culture in the nineteenth century, the network technologies – the telegraph, undersea communication cables, the railway telegraph and Charles Babbage's proto-computers, the Difference and Analytical Engines – have been given precedence over the more manifest technological advances of the nineteenth century such as steam engines, railways, bridges, manufacturing machines. Thus, as Roger Luckhurst and Josephine McDonagh highlight, 'studies of the imbrication of telegraphs, typewriters and gramophones with re-configurations of modern subjectivities have stretched from ventriloquy, via spiritualism and automatic writing, to the emergence of the serial killer as an exemplary subject-position of a newly saturated machine culture in the late nineteenth-century' (2002: 7). This new idea of Victorian technology, and its links or indeed similarity to our own information age, is explored in both fiction and theory. William Gibson and Bruce Sterling's 'steam-punk' novel *The Difference Engine* (1988) imagines an 1850s world radically altered by Babbage's computer engine, while in *Zeros + Ones: Digital Women + the New Technoculture* (1998) Sadie Plant focuses on the Victorian woman Ada Lovelace, the self-proclaimed 'High Priestess of Babbage's Engine'. She uses Lovelace's explanation that Babbage's planned 'Analytical Engine' would 'weave algebraical patterns just as the Jacquard loom weaves flowers and leaves'[1] as the starting place for her theorization of the affinity between women and the nets and webs of digital culture.

Our present-day concerns about what it means to be human, and what the impact of the networked world of data and communication might be on human culture, may not mark an absolute rupture with previous generations, but our predecessors did have their own distinct concerns and enthusiasms about technology. It is vital to acknowledge the specifics of what the Victorians bequeathed the twentieth century in terms of a technological imaginary – a set of ideas, articulations and metaphors – and not simply assume the Victorians were like us. The technological advances of the nineteenth century did mean an increase in manufacturing productivity, in the speed of travel and communication, and in the amount and quality of leisure time and amusement, which fundamentally transformed the landscape and urban environments of the Western world. Leo Marx's study of nineteenth-century America, *The Machine in the Garden*, characterized the period as one in which the fascination with technology gave rise to a 'rhetoric of the technological sublime' which celebrated the 'unprecedented harmony between art and nature, city and country' this technological development would enable (Marx 1964: 195). Such unfettered technophilia, a utopian faith in technology, was not unchallenged and was certainly made more complex by various discoveries and movements of the late nineteenth century. As Nicholas Daly points out, the anxieties about industrialization and machine culture that permeate the novels of 1840s and 1850s England do not disappear in the later years of the century. For Daly, the industrial accident as a concern of the early Victorians is recast in the popular railway rescues of the stage dramas of the 1860s, which 'thrill[ed] audiences on both sides of the Atlantic, and at both fashionable and cheap houses' (2004: 12). Using large amounts of lighting effects, smoke and other illusions, dramas such as *After Dark*: *A Tale of London Life* (1868), *Under the Gaslight* (1867–8), *The Engineer* (1863) and *The London Arab* (1866) presented the spectacle of a bound victim on the railway tracks in the path of a train approaching at full speed, only narrowly missing death as they are saved by the hero or heroine. The danger of machines and the fear they evoke is used in such dramas to create an audience that is 'thrilled rather than traumatized' by the threat of technology (Daly 2004: 32).

The railway crash and its repercussions, which Daly also considers, very usefully highlight the ambivalences around technology in the late nineteenth century. It is well known that Dickens survived a fatal train crash on 9 June 1865 during which he helped wounded and dying passengers, and that the after-effects, including a terror of train travel, remained until his death five years later. The danger of railway technology was a widespread concern, far exceeding the actual dangers of rail travel. There were terrible accidents, such as the Abergele accident on 20 August 1868 in which thirty-two people died after a collision between trains,[2] but the actual efficiency and reliability of the railways laid the foundations for a fundamental reconfiguration of cultural and geographical space. Train travel transformed the social, cultural and physical landscapes of Britain and America, leading to standardized time, the rapid availability of fresh produce in cities, the speeded-up delivery of mail and the possibility of cheaper leisure excursions, among many other effects. But, as many critics have pointed out, it also brought entire populations into contact with a very visible modernity. The uncertainty of the modern world that railway technology embodied is what appears to lie behind the ambivalence it evoked. The *Saturday Review*, for example, commented after the Abergele disaster: 'We are, in the matter of railway travelling, always treading the unknown . . . All that we know of the future is that it is full of dangers; but what these dangers are we cannot conjecture or anticipate' (29 August 1868: 281).

The shock of train travel inspired a range of cultural and literary responses, from the railway melodramas to novels and poetry of the period. In Tennyson's poem 'Charity' (1892), a young bride experiences a terrible accident:

> Two trains clash'd; then and there he was crush'd in a moment and died,
> But the new-wedded wife was unharm'd, tho' sitting close at his side:

In Amy Levy's poem 'Ballade of a Special Edition' (1889), the sensational newspaper hawked round the streets of London sells its stories of 'murder, death and suicide' through such 'Shocking Accidents' as occur when 'misdirected trains collide'. Levy's poem goes further than the melodrama of Tennyson, connecting the shocking sensations of railway technology and its potential consequences with the emergent media technologies of the time that were harnessed to great effect in 'yellow journalism' (the forerunner of tabloid journalism). Dickens himself used his experiences in the story 'The Signal-Man', in which a railway worker has premonitions of his own death in an accident. Dickens's post-traumatic suffering links him to a new illness produced by modern technology: 'Railway Spine'. This term was coined in the 1860s by medical practitioners to describe the physical disorders of seemingly unharmed train-crash survivors, such as the tremors experienced by Dickens. Debates about the exact causes, nature and legal responsibility for 'Railway Spine' continued through later decades, with the foremost expert, John E. Erichsen, first locating the cause in an internal compression of the spinal column, then later seeing the condition as more of a psychological nervous disruption.[3] 'Railway Spine' demonstrated how technology could disturb the proper functioning of the human body long after its immediate impact was felt, and that the impact was greatest in the unseen or invisible dangers that technology posed.

The railway carriage itself, with its different class of compartments, may have maintained social distinctions, but the train crash was a social leveller, bringing everyone equally under the destructive power of this technology. As Ralph Harrington describes, the train crash 'crystallised in a single traumatic event the helplessness of human beings in the hands of the technologies which they had created, but seemed unable to control; it was a highly public event which erupted directly into the rhythms and routines of daily life; it was no respecter of class or status; it was arbitrary, sudden, inhuman, and violent' (Harrington 2003: n.p.). In the train crash, and in 'Railway Spine', the victim is not just vulnerable to technology, but invaded by it – a technology that brought great benefits but, in its destructive effects, actually blurred the boundaries between classes and positions, between the inner and outer, between the physical and mental, demonstrating that the effects of technology were often invisible to the naked eye.

The visual technologies of the late nineteenth century, technologies that changed what was visible or changed how things appeared, are also an important element in the technological imaginary of the Victorians. Photography was well established by the end of the century, with advances such as smaller, portable cameras, shorter exposure times and easier-to-use photographic plates making it possible for amateurs to take it up as a pastime. Rather than capturing formal or ceremonial moments only, therefore, the photograph of the 1890s could also capture an unwary moment, a passer-by or a street scene. As Lynda Nead explores, the hand camera evolved into secretive forms of the 'detective camera' that could be hidden or disguised on the body of the photographer (2007: 112–22). This illustrates how the photographic 'revolution in visual representation was thus two-fold . . . it created a new aesthetic and a new way of looking and . . . it expanded the range of possible subjects that could be turned into an image (112). Late nineteenth-century photography, and the moving images of cinema film that emerged after the premiere of the Lumières' Cinématographe in 1895, are a development from previous optical experiments and devices: the Daguerreotype had been unveiled in 1839 and the nineteenth century abounds with stereoscopes, dioramas, magic lantern shows, mutoscopes, zoetropes and peepshows. And the emergence of a visual technological culture in the late nineteenth century is apparent in a range of cultural forms, including sensation theatre with its special effects, department-store windows and *tableaux vivants* and wax museums. The new ways of looking, animating and interpreting the visual world were well served by photographic techonologies which could capture previously unseen aspects of human and animal motion, as documented in Eadweard Muybridge's studies in the 1880s, or could attempt to engage fully with the physical, intellectual and emotional experiences of audiences: many early Cinématographe films, for example, deployed 'phantom rides', filmed from a moving train. Photography and film thus gave access to a previously unexperienced world, offering scientific knowledge and popular entertainment, while also transgressing the proper, decorous boundaries of the individual who could, by the beginning of the twentieth century, be easily captured on film. In a foreshadowing of the late twentieth-century culture of surveillance, this could happen without permission, as in one form of 'actualities', the term used by producers for their films of everyday life: Nead describes how Lumière Cinématographe operators made and showed real-time films of London street scenes in the 1890s (2007: 124). The individual could also be psychologically and physically transported by visual technology. The spectator caught up in the sensation of a phantom ride, or unexpectedly caught on camera, could thus be interpreted as a victim of these new technologies, in much the same way that she could suffer the effects of train transportation. This highlights the fundamental ambiguity of late Victorian technology: an essential part of modern life that brought both big advantages and grave dangers.

UNCANNY TECHNOLOGY

That technology may have been understood as an ambiguous vehicle of progress by the late Victorians is hardly surprising, but what comes to prominence during this period is not only the ambiguity, but the magical aspect of technology, its potential affinities with the vibrant world of spiritualism and telepathy which had gained great popularity across the nineteenth century. The strangeness of electrical technology and the uncanny transformations worked by the inventions of Thomas Edison and his peers, in particular, brought the realm of technological advance into proximity with the ineffable realm of the spirit. The work of Edison who, in a 1920 *American Magazine* article, is attributed with creating a spirit telephone that could communicate with the dead, exemplifies how inexorably the supposed science of technology was imbued with strange and magical powers: Edison earned the nickname 'the Wizard of Menlo Park'. The magical powers of the entrepeneur-inventor clearly had a dark side: the link between electricity and death, for example, was forcefully asserted by Edison, as is discussed in chapter 4 below, in his attempt to prove the dangers of the alternating current (AC) system invented by Nikola Tesla and used by the Edison Company's rival, Westinghouse Electric Company. Edison's activities demonstrate his own partiality and showmanship, but his energies were directed into many outlets. His invention of the phonograph in 1877, the kinetoscope (to rival the Lumières' Cinématographe), the Kinetophone (aiming to synchronize a phonograph cylinder recording with motion pictures) and the fluroscope (for taking X-ray pictures), together with his improvements to the telegraph, telephone and so on, were the type of enterprises which made Edison the embodiment, in the public imagination, of the amazing wonders and potential of technological innovation. Edison appeared as a character in literature both during and after his life: he is fictionalized as the inspired inventor of a fantastical android in Villiers de L'Isle-Adam's *L'Eve Future* in 1886, is the model for the boy inventor Tom Edison Jr. in Philip Reade's sequence of dime novels (1891–2), stars in Garrett P. Serviss's *Edison's Conquest of Mars* (1947), and represents the triumph of American invention and mass production in John Dos Passos's *U.S.A.* trilogy (1938).[4]

Electricity, electrical science and electrical engineering transformed Victorian culture and it was electric light that epitomized this transforming power. Edison invented the incandescent electric light bulb in 1879; he patented it the following year and from 1882 onwards, spreading with remarkable rapidity, generating stations brought electric lighting to city dwellers across America and Western Europe. The coming of electric light is a transformation of culture at a fundamental level; it marks the coming of what Marshall McLuhan, in *Understanding Media*, calls the 'electric age'. 'The

electric light is pure information . . . a medium without a message,' writes
McLuhan (1964a: 8); it is a pure communication, all the more so because it
has no 'content', and in this purity it ushers in the modern world where
instant communication connects us in a web of interaction. But contained
within the modernity of electricity is also an inherent strangeness. From early
in the nineteenth century, the relationship between electricity and life itself
had become a topic of speculation (and motivated the creation of the creature
in Mary Shelley's *Frankenstein* of 1818). At the end of the century the scientific account of electrical phenomena remained arcane and obtuse to the
non–expert, and even experts themselves failed to achieve a universal understanding of electricity. Electricity took on an increasingly visible role in the
world, while remaining invisible and mysterious in its effects and powers.
As Jeffrey Sconce describes, 'electrical science [was] the quantum physics of
its day, a frontier of inquiry bordering science and the spirit that raised more
questions than it answered' (2000: 35).

The mysterious and even magical effects of electricity were exploited by
scientists and engineers in an attempt to engage with the public and with
potential users of this technological force. Carolyn Marvin describes how
many scientific electricians presented 'lectures with striking and wonderful
"effects"' (1988: 57): Edison Company representatives, for example, con-
cluded an 1887 electrical lecture in Boston with what appeared to be a
seance. As the *Electrical Review* of 19 March 1887 reported: 'Bells rung, drums
beat, noises natural and unnatural were heard, a cabinet revolved and flashed
fire, and a row of departed skulls came into view, and varied coloured lights
flashed from their eyes' (5). But it was Nikola Tesla, the Croatian-born
inventor and electrical engineer, who was one of the most spectacular electrical showmen. He contributed to the conception and invention of radio,
robotics, radar, remote control, computer science and ballistics, but his stage
performances with electricity were what earned him contemporary recognition. He held glass tubes in his hands that glowed without any direct electrical
connection and, using the special induction coil he had invented (the Tesla
coil), passed hundreds of thousands of volts through his body while electrical
streams flamed from his head and limbs. For the *New York Sun* in 1893, 'The
mere description of Tesla's actual experiments reads like an impossible fairy
tale' (cited Marvin 1988: 137).

Tesla and Edison's inventions, and the media and communication technologies of others, introduced a magical aspect into everyday lives where
voices of absent people could be heard, invisible aspects of the body revealed
and exotic or strange experiences viewed. These inventions enabled what
Marvin aptly describes as 'communication in real time without real presence'
(5); they 'relieved the drudgery of everyday life and transformed routine into
something new and strange' (Dadley 1996: 84). The new and strange in
electrical communication technology had already been expressed in literature
in the mid-nineteenth-century science-fiction stories of Edgar Allan Poe,
most notably in 'The Facts in the Case of M. Valdemar' (1845). This story

is the supposed first-person account of a mesmeric communication and connection with an old man called Valdemar, which delays his death for seven months, after which the body of Valdemar putrefies almost instantly. As Valdemar lies unmoving and unconscious, it is his vibrating tongue that enables him to communicate in his liminal state between death and life. Poe's emphasis on this 'swollen and blackened tongue' which protrudes from Valdemar's distended mouth and produces speech in a 'harsh, broken and hollow' sound as if 'from a vast distance' (Poe 1976: 200) does seem, as Adam Frank argues, to recall the communication at a distance of a telegraphic transmission, in which a message (or voice) is translated into the tappings of Morse code and electromagnetic vibrations (Frank 2005). Poe's 'Valdemar' thus connects telegraphic communication (Poe's story was published one year after the first corporate telegraph system was established between Washington and Baltimore) with the realm of mesmerism and spirit communication. But there is a clear rationale for such connections, particularly in the role that ideas of electromagnetism played in speculations about mesmerism and later hypnosis. The telegraphic-telepathic articulation was to resonate through the rest of the nineteenth century, and reveals how the transgression of boundaries and the production of uncanny effects are a persistent feature of technology. As discussed in chapter 5, Bram Stoker's *Dracula* (1897) connects typewriting technology to the uncanny vampiric force that Count Dracula embodies. In Poe's story and Stoker's novel, the uncanny effect comes from the liminal state that technology seems to delineate, between human and non-human, life and death.

The possibility of communicating beyond death, already associated by Poe with communication technology, became almost an obsession in the latter half of the nineteenth century with the fascination for spiritualism and spirit communication. Photographic technology was exploited to capture images of so-called spirit manifestations or extrusions and a range of devices were employed to try to establish the nature of physical-psychic phenomena (Noakes 2002). But it was more the success of remote communication via telegraph, telephone and radio (Tesla himself demonstrated the feasibility of wireless communications in 1893) that fed the psychic imagination of the Victorians. 'Telepathy', as Pamela Thurschwell notes, was newly coined in 1882 by F. W. H. Myers and was 'connected to other forms of tele-technology' and often imagined as functioning in the same way as these other technologies do, with the same popular 'scientific explanations or lack of them' (2001: 14). The Society for Psychical Research (SPR), founded in 1882, experimented with the possibilities of thought transference, thereby imagining the crossing of boundaries between subjects and states of being. Some writers considered the possibility of boundary-crossing communication in electrical and psychic forms, notably Mark Twain. In an 1891 article in *Harper's Magazine*, 'Mental Telegraphy', Twain considers his personal experiences of the coincidences of 'crossed letters' and mental communication over great distances. Twain, in his conclusion, links tele-technology and electricity with psychic-mental phenomena, writing that 'doubtless the something which conveys our thoughts through the air from brain to brain is a finer and subtler form of electricity, and all we need to do is find out how to capture it' (1891: 101). Twain had written to the Society for Psychical Research some years earlier in support of their work, declaiming 'telephones, telegraphs and words are too slow for this age; we must get something that is faster' (1884: 164). This interest in telepathy was matched by Twain's interest in new communication technologies: he had a telephone line installed in his Hartford home (one of the first installed in a private home) and was the first writer to submit a typed manuscript to a publisher.

The idea of 'mental telegraphy', influenced by or connected to tele-communication, features in Rudyard Kipling's story 'Wireless' (1902). This short story presents an experiment in wireless signalling to a station in Poole from an apothecary's shop, which is articulated with the simultaneous 'channelling' by the apothecary's assistant of Keats's 'The Eve of St Agnes'. The assistant has no pre-knowledge of Keats but reproduces sections of the poem, while in a semi-wakeful state, through some sort of mental and physical affinity with the original poet. At the same time, the apothecary's son tries unsuccessfully to catch a signal with his antennae, musing over the partial fragments of signals he receives: 'Have you ever seen a spiritualistic séance? It reminds me of that sometimes' (Kipling 1904: 199). Kipling is clearly presenting a potential kinship between seance and tele-technology, coupling the transmission of Morse code across the ether to the unconscious communication between dying men (the assistant and Keats) across a century; Kipling told Rider Haggard: 'We are only telephone wires' (cited Kipling 1904: 26).

An earlier novella by Henry James, *In the Cage* (1898), can be related to Kipling's 'Wireless': in James's story, telegraphy and telepathy become examples of a hyper-modern phenomenon of instantaneous communication. James's protagonist, a telegraph operator in a Mayfair Post Office, experiences an affinity with the wealthy, leisured people who submit their telegraphs to her for transmission, supposing an intense connection with a particular gentleman engaged in an illicit affair. The telegraphist is 'caged' behind wire, and wired into the telegraph network, but finds her emotional and intellectual life through her imagined connections with Captain Everad and his lover, and her relaying and processing of their messages. The telegraph, in this story, signals not a high Victorian optimism about perfect, instantaneous and universal communication, but a very new disturbance of space and human interaction. Richard Menke reads *In The Cage* as a modernist text about uncertainty and mediation, where instant (telegraphic) communication leads to a 'collapsing [of] distance into a proximity that was discursive, technologically mediated, and strangely invisible' (2000: 987). James's telegraphist is finally disillusioned of her romantic hopes, and accepts marriage to a grocer with a move to a less glamorous Chalk Farm office, but her work with tele-technology has connected her into an uncertain world of proximities and networks that exceed the barriers of her cage. Like the other accounts of telegraphy and telepathy, the disturbing broaching of boundaries in this text pre-empts the unsettling virtual communication dreams of the late twentieth century. As Thurschwell writes, 'at the end of the nineteenth century science is severing the links between materiality, visibility and transmission, allowing for a sort of telepathic imaginary' (2001: 29). Even Edison saw a possibility of new technology crossing boundaries: he proposed a potential use of the phonograph for recording the voices of the dying just one year after its invention, as a kind of 'spirit catcher', capturing the final communications of life leaving the body.

VICTORIAN SCIENCE FICTION

The nineteenth century does not merely bequeath an uncanny sense of technology to the inhabitants of the twentieth century: what emerges at the end of the nineteenth and the beginning of the twentieth centuries is a particular genre that, at its heart, engages with the effect of technological advance on human society and the human individual. Science Fiction (SF) does have its origins long before the 1880s, and historians of SF sometimes cite the ancient Sumerian *Epic of Gilgamesh* (*c*.2000 BCE), which involves a journey to the Moon (using the wings of a vulture and an eagle), as the first SF text. However, many would agree with Peter Nicholls that it is the 'cognitive, scientific way of looking at the world' which actually underpins 'SF proper', a way of looking at the world which 'did not emerge until the 17th century and did not percolate into society at large until . . . the 19th' (Clute and Nicholls 1999: 568). Thus, texts such as *Frankenstein* are taken as the earliest manifestation of a particular textual engagement with a newly formulated world of scientific and technological potential. It may not be just nineteenth-century science and technology that enables SF to flower as a literary and cultural genre – Adam Roberts contends that 'science' as a 'non-theological mode of understanding the natural world' far pre-dates the 1800s (2006: 4) – but the Industrial Revolution and the extraordinary technological advances and inventions of this century did have an impact on what fictions could be conceived by the Victorian and early twentieth-century writer. For one of the most influential SF critics, Darko Suvin, the main formal device of the SF text is the 'novum' (or 'nova'), the fictional apparatus, artefact or premise that underpins the world of the text and differentiates it from the world of the reader (Suvin 1979). The great discoveries and inventions of the Victorian era, which enabled people to travel at speed across continents and oceans, communicate across distances, illuminate cities, record voices, write mechanically and capture images of themselves and the world inspired many writers to imagine new technological nova and transformed and fantastical worlds.

The concerns of late nineteenth-century SF were shared across national boundaries and the stories written fall into a few main categories: fantastic journeys, future visions and utopias/dystopias, and invasion fantasies. The two biggest figures in the nascent genre of SF were Jules Verne and H. G. Wells, but there were many other SF writers. Verne was an influential writer of fantastic journeys, with his first book in the *Voyages Extraordinares* series, *Cinq semaines en ballon* (*Five Weeks in a Balloon*), published in 1863. In fantastic journey stories the protagonists embark on expeditions around the globe, into the centre of the earth, under the sea or to other planets, usually enabled by futuristic technology. Verne's 1865 *De la terre à la lune* (*From the Earth to the Moon*) has astronauts in a shell fired to the moon from a giant cannon; a later text by the Englishman John Munro, *A Trip to Venus* (1897), draws on his knowledge as a Professor of Mechanical Engineering to propose a more feasible form of interplanetary travel with a liquid-fuelled rocket. Verne's Captain Nemo and his submarine the *Nautilus*, which feature in two texts, *Vingts mille lieues sous les mers* (*Twenty Thousand Leagues Under the Sea*, 1870) and *L'Île Mysterious* (*The Mysterious Island*, 1874), are an impressive feat of technological imagining, with the luxurious *Nautilus* powered by electricity and containing every comfort its passengers might need, including a fully equipped library. With such iconic inventions, Verne's work, which was translated widely beyond the francophone world, 'consolidated a particular sort of technology fiction as being core to SF as a genre' (Roberts 2006: 129).

Verne wrote other texts besides the *Voyages Extraordinaires*, including the dystopic *Paris en XXᵉ siècle* (written in 1863, published posthumously in 1994) that imagines a grimly mechanized and electrical future that places no value on literature and the arts. This text makes a range of technological predictions, including gasoline-fuelled cars, electric chairs, calculators and a worldwide telegraphic communications network. The future visions and utopias imagined by other writers also involved advanced technology, for example, Edward Bellamy's (1888) *Looking Backward 2000–1887*, set in a collectivized utopian America of 2000 where everyone works in the 'industrial army' until the age of forty-five. In this future America there is no cash; Bellamy predicts instead payment through credit cards, homes are supplied with musical entertainment through a programmable 'musical telephone', continuous waterproof coverings are extended over the pavements when it rains, war has been outlawed and criminals are given medical treatment not prison sentences. The invasion fantasy, popular from the publication of George Tomkyns Chesney's *The Battle of Dorking* (1871) until the outbreak of the First World War in 1914, was also usually predicated on technological development: in Chesney's book, the unprepared English are overcome by the military might of an efficient German army. Robert W. Cole's (1900) *The Struggle for Empire: A Story of the Year 2236* imagines interstellar spaceships and intergalactic imperial struggle but, as Edward James points out, 'it may only be a future war story writ large, with the British and German fleets being rewritten as the fleets of Earth and Sirius' (James 1995: 43).

Science and technology feature differently in SF that offers mystical and spiritual transformations and powers rather than purely mechanical nova. Marie Corelli's *A Romance of Two Worlds* (1886) epitomizes this alternate strain. In this novel (Corelli's first) the protagonist, a depressed pianist, is cured and then, through a powerful electric force, experiences amazing new realms, including interplanetary travel and conversations with angels. The occult essence of electricity that Corelli imagines here enables her to combine Christianity, spiritualism, Theosophy and weird science. But it is not just in the reaches of Corelli's SF that such occult elements exist: what is observable in these late nineteenth-century texts is not just an interest in technological possibilities, but what Roberts describes as the 'blend of scientific-technical and mystic idioms ... characteristic of nineteenth-century SF' (Roberts 2006: 108). Indeed, SF was the genre best placed to explore uncanny technology given its contemporary emergence alongside Gothic, as in *Frankenstein*, for example, the modern genre most closely concerned with the uncanny in its historical and psychological manifestations. Brian Aldiss points out that 'Science fiction was born from the Gothic mode, is hardly free of it now. Nor is the distance between the two modes great' (Aldiss 1986: 18).

H. G. Wells is often, and probably justifiably, cited as the most influential father of SF and some of his writings do have a Gothic strain: both *The Island of Dr Moreau* (1896) and *The Invisible Man* (1897) feature a megalomaniac scientist who uses his knowledge and technology to create monstrous man-beasts (*Dr Moreau*), and produce an invisibility which will enable him to terrorize the nation (*Invisible Man*). Wells's influence is so great, though, because of what Adam Roberts describes as his 'lucid sense of the symbolic possibilities of the imaginative novum' (2000: 61). Thus, the time machine Wells imagines in his first novel *The Time Machine* (1896) enables him to create a future world of AD 802,701, in which technology lies defunct in the abandoned museums of the world of the beautiful, leisured Eloi, while below the earth the savage Morlocks tend dark machines and venture out at night to eat the Eloi. *The War of the Worlds* (1898) is a powerful invasion fantasy, with an invasion from Mars by tentacled Martians encased in tripod fighting-machines, who decimate southern England until they are overcome by terrestrial bacteria. In *The First Men in the Moon* (1901), contact with the inhabitants of the Moon (Selenites) is established after two men arrive there by using an anti-gravity material that powers their spherical spaceship: after one of the men escapes back to Earth, communication is maintained for a while via radio transmissions until the ruler of the Moon decides to cut off contact with the Earth. All of these texts offer a comment, not just on social concerns of the time (Darwinism, degeneration, class, imperialism, national security), but on what technology could achieve, and the moral and ethical issues and questions that would be raised. Wells's novels raised questions and posed ethical dilemmas, but they also appeared at a time when mass-market SF was really taking off, when dime novels and pulp publications were offering accessible accounts of the heroic escapades, romantic entanglements and daring possibilities that technology could enable. In such mass forms, driven by story and character and using exotic locations and simplified moral codes, the extensive cultural engagement with popular 'technology fiction' was set for the remainder of the twentieth century.

TECHNOLOGY IN THE TWENTIETH CENTURY

A diversity of texts, forms and movements engage with and explore technology across the twentieth century, often considering the moral, ethical or social aspects of the technological imperative. Different writers take up the challenge posed by mechanical innovations, but the indirect influence of technology is apparent in texts that seem to have no direct investment in the topic. As it transforms culture, manifestly in new forms of communication, production or transport and implicitly by altering the human relationship to the material world, the effects of technology and its uncanny resonances profoundly alter literature.

The impact of technology is in evidence from the earliest modernist movements of the twentieth century, right through to the formal experiments of late postmodernism at the century's end. It is impossible to dispute the centrality of technoculture to postmodernism and the literature of the late twentieth century, but there is a tendency, in generalizations about early twentieth-century literature, to identify the modernist movement in literature and the arts as an attempted escape from, or transcendence of, technological modernity. There are early twentieth-century writers and theorists – D. H. Lawrence, Virginia Woolf, Walter Benjamin, Theodor Adorno – who are acutely conscious of the effects of technology on art and aesthetics, and many modernists resisted the encroachment of technology and rejected the machinic zeitgeist that seems to characterize the early twentieth century. But, for Jonathon Crary, 'modernism, rather than being a reaction against or transcendence of processes of scientific and economic rationalization, is inseparable from them' (1990: 85). Thus, modernism, as a future-orientated movement, is bound up with the same forces of rational progress that drove new models of the workforce and workplace, even when explicitly rejecting the machinic organizational concepts of such models. Beyond this, technology is part of the cultural vocabulary that modernist innovation drew on for its renewing power, with many writers and artists taking terminology, ideas and scientistic models from the technological realm to elucidate their particular visions of aesthetic recreation. Hart Crane's poem *The Bridge*, for example, celebrates the engineering feat of the Brooklyn Bridge; the beauty it maintains in the tensions of its technological achievement becomes a mystical synthesis of American culture, history and potential. Crane is not alone in recognizing the symbolic power of technology: it features in the work of his contemporaries William Carlos Williams, John Dos Passos and Theodore Dreiser; it informs T. S. Eliot's vision of Europe in *The Waste Land* and permeates the Dublin of James Joyce's *Ulysses*. In attempting to give expression to the modern world, it seems inevitable that literature was articulated through the technologized perspective of the present.

If the dime novels and pulp magazines of the turn of the century offered SF fictions that revelled in the futuristic possibilities of potential technological innovation and imagined strong heroes battling forces of evil across the universe, the growing presence of technology in the world of the present had an immediate impact on conceptions of the body, space and human interrelations. In the area of manufacturing, the efforts of Frederick Taylor (*The Principles of Scientific Management*, 1911) and Henry Ford (assembly lines for automobile production were introduced in his factories in 1913) were fundamental in transforming the techno-economic paradigms of America, and of other Western nations. Taylor's scientific management engineered a workplace of repetitive, standardized tasks and regulated breaks, inserting the worker into an efficient machine of capitalist production. What emerges from such systems is the conception of the productive control of man and his regulation in effective production. In Amelia Jones's words, Taylorism and Fordism channel 'human labor into the most efficient, machinic production of parts and, ultimately, of machines that can be sold for a reasonable price but at a great profit' (2004: 14). Technology here functions as the framework within which the human operates: the machine becomes paradigmatic. Even the physical health of the human individual was seen, in the health reform systems proposed by Horace Fletcher and J. H. Kellogg and the turn-of-the-century physical culture movements, as a mechanism that could be regulated and improved through regime and diet. The control of the bodily mechanism continued to obsess, with amphetamines prescribed as diet pills in the 1950s, then the fitness craze of the 1970s and 1980s introducing aerobics, Jazzercise and home gyms. By the 1990s, people were employing a panoply of methods – diet regimes, exercise, injections, pills, surgery – in attempts to manufacture their ideal physical form.

The twentieth century sees many versions of the mechanical body and different engagements with the increasing proximity of human and machine. The fears expressed in Karel Čapek's *R.U.R.* (1921) and Kurt Vonnegut's *Player Piano* (1952), about the dangers posed to humankind by robots and automation, stand in stark contrast to the cyborgs celebrated in the cyberpunk fiction of William Gibson and the theory of Donna Haraway in the 1980s and 1990s. In the early century, the artists and writers of New York Dada used mechanomorphic portraits, representing the human as the machine, to comment ironically on the industrial and sexual politics of the time, and the sexual-political questions connected to the robot and cyborg persist through subsequent decades. There is a sexual taboo on the replicants in Philip K. Dick's *Do Androids Dream of Electric Sheep?* (1968), while Haraway's cyborg is a feminist figuration that serves to break down distinctions between human, animal and machine. In contrast, the posthuman celebration of the technological transformation of the human, inspired by the cyborgs of texts such as Gibson's *Neuromancer* (1984), suggests the possibility of transcending the gendered body altogether, leaving behind materiality and its awkward questions.

Technology may be persistently present in literature across the century, but what technology actually represented, enabled or undermined is not a constant for writers. At the beginning of the century, as Hal Foster argues, there were two primary 'positions on technology pro- and con- [which] can be schematically mapped according to the double logic of the prosthesis' as either the 'extension' or transcendence of the body, or the regressive break-down of the body (1997: 8). In a similar vein, Jeffrey T. Schnapp makes the useful suggestion that the early twentieth century sees two distinct modes of conceptualizing and interacting with the machines of modernity:

One, grounded in Enlightenment ideals, thinks of men and machines as *machines à reprise* (as duplication machines) and . . . it identifies modernity with the return of sameness: standardization, reliability, predictability, the leveling of differences. The other, anti-Enlightenment in spirit, thinks of men and machines as *machines à surprise* (as surprise machines) and . . . identifies modernity instead with non-recursive modes of repetition: with novelty, danger, unpredictability, the multiplication of differences. (Schnapp 1999: 34)

It is in Italian Futurism, and most clearly in the work of Filippo Tommaso Marinetti, that the 'surprise machines' of the modern world are embraced as metaphors and vehicles of a new cultural and literary movement. In key founding texts of Futurism, Marinetti foregrounds the automobile and the aeroplane as experiential models for describing new artistic forms. At the core of Marinetti's Futurism is an investment in a mechanical muse (figured as specific contemporary technological innovations) that counteracts both the redundant *passéist* elements of Western culture and the passivity of modern man. Marinetti imagines a powerful fusion of man and machine, often sexualized in an explicitly heterosexual way (but also undeniably homosocial) that armours the heroic individual and powers a forceful modern aesthetic.

In 'The Founding and Manifesto of Futurism' (published in Paris in 1909), Marinetti describes himself and his group of friends and their 'electric hearts' propelled from an 'atavistic ennui' of decadence into a modern world of steamships, locomotives and trams (Flint 1972: 39). Marinetti is then fully invigorated by a fast drive in his car, a 'snorting beast' that both threatens and inspires his masculine self, crashing into a ditch only to be revived for him to continue his drive. It is this drive and the crash that preface the 'Manifesto of Futurism' that presents a celebration of speed, force, aggression and technological power. The manifesto claims to 'hymn the man at the wheel' and celebrates the beauty of 'a racing car whose hood is adorned with great pipes' (Flint 1972: 41). The manifesto explicitly rejects museums, librar-ies and academies; they are dead and defunct. Marinetti instead points to the technological potential of the twentieth century, a potential which had hardly reached Italy at his time of writing, taking the techno-industrial landscapes of factories, trains and cars as the image and inspiration for a new form of defiant, revolutionary culture. Elsewhere, in 'Multiplied Man and the Reign of the Machine', Marinetti imagines a 'Future man' who could externalize his will, manifest prosthetic mechanical adaptations and become 'an omnipresent velocity' (Flint 1972: 91, 92).

It is not just Futurism at the beginning of the century that responds to the machine as a powerful image and the technological as a way of expressing the essence of the modern world: the technological imaginary is at work in a range of early twentieth-century movements in literature and the arts. The machine in whatever form was the central icon of Constructivism, an important movement in post-revolutionary Russia, but Vladimir Tatlin had already initiated the movement with his constructions made from industrial materials in 1913–14. In Constructivism, the artist was understood as an engineer and art was defined as a useful object in the new society, a technological rather than aesthetic achievement. The principles of Constructivism had a place outside Russia, notably in the pedagogic programme taught at the Bauhaus school in Germany between 1923 and 1928 by Hungarian László Moholy-Nagy. The influential industrial design that emerged from Bauhaus, and the stress on functionality and the mass production of design, reveal the undeniable influence of the technological on the possibilities and conceptions of art and design in the twentieth century: offices, homes, interiors and equipment were not only manufactured by, but conceptualized through, technology. It was the shaping force of the human-inhabited spaces of the twentieth century but, more than this, there was no space in human existence that was not reconfigured through emergent and developing technologies: as this study highlights and discusses, technology served to shape work, leisure, selfhood, communication, textuality and even death. Thus, the political and social realities of technology, and its power to delineate the vectors of human existence, prove to be its most enduring effects in the twentieth century.

The speed, force, aggression and power of technology that the Futurist Marinetti celebrated came to a culmination in the application of technology in war: from the First World War to the terrorist anxieties of the century's end, technology was bound up with death, destruction and human conflict. The death-dealing power of technology was reflected on by war poets who directly experienced the vulnerability of the human form when faced by increasingly sophisticated war machines, and a generation of people was mobilized in resistance to the apocalyptic potential of nuclear weapons. But, as the deadlocked confrontation of the Cold War in mid-century revealed, the technologies that counted most in war were technologies of information processing and control rather than the visible weapons of destruction. Spying, propaganda and their technological manifestations thus feature in the literature of the 1950s, and inform subsequent postmodern fiction where the symptoms of paranoia, the implosion of meaning and the individual absorption in a technological mediascape have their origins in the Cold War and its intelligent machines. The increasing dominance of visual technologies in modern warfare, a tendency that is theorized by Paul Virilio, also has its apotheosis in postmodernity where media and military technology converge, on the one hand in the first Gulf War, and on the other in video gaming.

In his 'Technical Manifesto of Futurist Literature' (1912), Marinetti is inspired by a military technology, in this case an aeroplane, to imagine a new form of writing, liberating words from 'their prison in the Latin period' (Flint 1972: 84). Marinetti is 'told' by the 'whirling propellor' of the need for '*words-in-freedom*' and '*the imagination without strings [l'immaginazione senza fili]*' (89). Thus, at the heart of the new literature that Marinetti proposes, and attempts in pieces such as *Battle of Tripoli* (1914) and *Zang Tumb Tumb* (1912), is a language of immediacy and compression. The aeroplane is of great importance to Marinetti and propellers, aeroplanes and the perspective and experience they enable inspire a range of Futurist aeropoems and aero-paintings through to the late 1930s. However, the resonances of Marinetti's poet-pilot and his propellor dictation extend beyond the simple use of the aeroplane as technological icon. Schnapp connects Marinetti's 'Propellor Talk' to 'a network binding aviation to contemporary literary forms, to the news media, to industrial typography and image technologies, and to new technologically inflected redefinitions of both heroism and everyday life' (1994: 158). For Timothy Campbell, though, it is Marinetti's response to the velocity of experience and sense impressions, marked by the irruption of technology into experience in the 'Technical Manifesto', that requires the closest attention. Translating the *fili* (*l'immaginazione senza fili*) as 'wires' as well as threads or strings, Campbell demonstrates how the 'Technical Manifesto' functions 'as a site in which writing, sound experiments, and the wireless meet' (2006: 79). The electrical communications of the day – and Marinetti often refers to electrical power – give rise to a new aesthetic that Marinetti registers as an imagination without wires. In his 'wireless writing', therefore, Marinetti attempts to record the visual, acoustic and bodily data of a modern technoscape in an immediate and unmediated way. It is in the modern theatre of war where this immediacy is manifest most obviously and responded to in Marinetti's own writings, but also in the intense develop-ment of wireless technologies that could record, transmit, assess and com-municate this war most effectively.

Other writers in the twentieth century were also profoundly affected by new technologies for writing and communication. The impact of the type-writer on literature, in terms of both narrative content and formal experi-mentation, was wide reaching. Various critics (notably Friedrich Kittler) argue for a radical shift in culture in the face of post-Edisonian inscription technologies; the first half of the twentieth century sees a shift from the Symbolic transcriptions of culture, to cultural transcriptions that simulate the Real (sound recording), create the Imaginary (as cinema does) or 'invert the material basis of literature' (using the typewriter) (Kittler 1999: 183). Typewriting brought literature into the realm of machine standardization and separated it from the metaphysics of presence implied by the writing hand. Typewriting machines also produced a new, modern figure, the type-writer girl perfectly attuned to the writing mechanism, who became the subject of fictional and erotic speculation. The typewriter also inspired the literary experiments of poets such as William Carlos Williams, e e cummings and Charles Olson, and was central to Jack Kerouac's composition of *On The Road* (1951). With the advent of digital computing, new forms of machine literature became possible, forms such as cyberpoetry and hypertext fiction that utilize the interactive potential of the computer and seem to fulfil the post-structuralist idea of the non-linear, interconnected, playful text. Printed texts also explored the impact of new digital writing technologies on the status and nature of the literary, illustrating, as Marinetti's 'wireless writing' experiments had done decades earlier, how literature is transformed by the modern technoscape.

The modernist Ezra Pound expressed great disdain for Marinetti and his 'automobilism', but in his own writing Pound himself drew on the technolo-gies and sciences of his age, including physics, engineering and mathematics, making repeated use of ideas and forms of electricity and radiation. For Pound, the 'current hidden in the air or in wire' was the basis of what he called 'the electric world' of today and, with his fellow Vorticist Wyndham Lewis, he imagined the symbol of the vortex as a kind of supercharged electromagnetic dynamo, 'great hollow cones of steel . . . charged with a force like electricity' (Pound 1954: 155; 1912). Technology in Pound's writing, as central as it is to his attempt to describe the method and abilities of the modern 'serious artist', is also a matter of a transformed world that the artist works in and a transformed art and consciousness in this new world. Pound was, however, ambivalent about the new media technologies of the early twentieth century. He might have written that 'the cinema is the pho-nograph of appearance' (Pound 1980: 79), but in *Hugh Selwyn Mauberley* (1917) the 'prose kinema' and 'pianola' represent a debasement of culture. Pound was a frequent cinema goer, particularly enjoying Tarzan, Mickey Mouse and Fred Astaire, and composed letters and poems on a Corona typewriter (Campbell 2006: 99), but he also hated using the telephone and only got a radio set in 1940, as a gift from Natalie Barney (Tiffany 1995: 245, 247). Beyond *Hugh Selwyn Mauberley*, media technology features as a degenerative force in Canto 29, where the 'wail of the phonograph' becomes 'The wail of the pornograph', part of the feminized, soft and degenerate culture which must be forcefully shaped by the male principle. Radio too is problematic: in Canto 38, Marconi and his radio waves – 'electric shakes through the a'mosphere' – seem to take the place of the Pope in a world of armament brokers, war and corruption. However, Pound did, from January 1941 to July 1943, deliver his infamous broadcasts over Roma Radio, actively deploying the power of this media, and also wrote two BBC radio operas in the early 1930s, *The Testament of François Villon* and *Cavalcanti*.[5] Pound's poetry rejects but also mirrors the age of radio, cinema, advertising and telegraphy in his formal deployment of montage, collage, the single 'image', the rupturing of subject and syntax, non-linearity, simultaneity, and the free use of citation. The intensification of the technological world has a very real impact on his work – it both provides recognizable analogies (electric switchboards, telegraph wires, antennae) for describing the power and function of the artist and creates a new mode of communication. It invades the fabric of his art and his consciousness alike: 'We have several new media, whatever they are worth in themselves,' Pound wrote in 1928, 'they have an effect on consciousness' (108).

Where telegraphy and early radio transmissions had presented magical possibilities in the everyday, in the Western world by the 1920s the cinema and the radio were commonplace entertainments and communication across a distance featured in most people's lives. Thus, many of Pound's contemporaries, including Virginia Woolf and James Joyce, also registered the effects of new media, reconceiving the nature of their literary enterprise in the light of the revelations of cinematic seeing, for example. Some writers engaged directly in the cinema or wrote glowingly about the artistic potential of the silent film in the 1920s, while a decade later theorists such as Adorno and Max Horkheimer bemoaned the mindless homogeneity emerging from the machines of Hollywood. The Auden generation was also deeply suspicious of the politics of technology, particularly the propagandist power of broadcast media, but writers such as Louis MacNeice and George Orwell also patriotically produced radio material that was a counterforce to the fascist use of radio propaganda in the Second World War. Radio was not just a propaganda tool in the early century, though, and drama on radio in Britain and America explored the new aural spaces enabled by this technology. Radio was the first wireless broadcast medium but its place in the private home was eventually supplanted by television. Although cinema had introduced a spectacular visual technology that by 1935 included sound and Technicolor, it was the quotidian presence of the television screen that assimilated the technological image into mass culture. Guy Debord's diagnosis of a 'Society of the Spectacle' in which 'everything that was directly lived has moved away into a representation' and everything is 'mediated by images' (1967: 7), is one response to the ubiquity of technological images in the second half of the twentieth century.

By the end of the twentieth century both work and leisure were dominated by screens (computer, TV, mobile phone, camcorder, cinema, CCTV, LED advertising and digital signage screens) and by the technologically produced and mediated image. This shift in culture is exemplified in Will Self's *Dorian: An Imitation* (2002), a reworking of Oscar Wilde's *The Picture of Dorian Gray* (1891), set in the 1980s gay scene and the Princess Diana hysteria of the 1990s. In Self's *Dorian* the handpainted portrait in the attic becomes *Cathode Narcissus*, a video installation piece by the artist Baz Hallward, and it is the multiple screen images of *Cathode Narcissus* who suffer the degenerative effects of depravity and AIDS. Dorian is thus bound, not to the authenticity, aura and materiality of the art object, but to the simulacra of a screen image. The novel therefore presents the human subject enmeshed in and infinitely reproducible through the electronic and virtual zones of screen life: it is no accident that, in the metafictional 'Epilogue' of *Dorian*, *Cathode Narcissus* is launched on to a website with the slogan 'Download Some Perfection Today' (270).

The virtual Dorian that substitutes for the authentic art object in Self's novel articulates a cultural shift resulting from technological advance, but it poses questions about technology that pre-date the World Wide Web, questions about the relationship of humans to their technologies and about what those technologies do to the world as we experience it. The uncanny connection between Dorian and the recorded Dorian on the video echoes the uncanny connection between Kipling's radio operator and the wireless signal, disturbing an easy division between discrete human subjects and inert material world. And, as at the end of Self's *Dorian* the novel collapses realist novel and virtual techno-realm, so does technology, as an idea and a tangible object, bind us inevitably into the substantial connections of the social and material world. The transformation of human subjectivity that *Dorian* explores does pose the question of whether human agents are the passive products of technology, or whether technological effects are driven by cultural and human forces: does technology determine us or do we determine it? This question is fundamentally a theoretical and philosophical one, and it highlights the fact that the interrelations between literature, culture and technology cannot be fully considered without an attendant comprehension and analysis of the theoretical perspectives on technology that also emerge in, and shape, the twentieth-century technological imaginary.

2 Writing Technology: Literature and Theory

As this present discussion of technology has so far proceeded without a detailed consideration of the actual definition of 'technology', it seems apposite to ask at this point: what then is technology? Is 'technology' simply the term used to designate the advanced tools used by modern man? Is it instead a set of rules, a method of mechanizing that rationalizes the world and governs the production and implementation of technological objects? Or is it more than this – does it tend towards the technologizing of everything from the objects of production to the nature of social interaction and communication? Other questions arise, particularly ones pertaining to the status of technology as either subject to human control, or an autonomous system that imposes itself on humans. The emergence of the modern technosphere in the early twentieth century, in which technology pervades all aspects of work, leisure and human interaction, poses these questions most acutely, questions that many philosophers and critical theorists across the century sought to address. In turn, their theoretical perspectives have influenced the interpretations and actual production of the cultures they attend to, changing the way technology is read and deployed. This chapter surveys and considers some of the theoretical explorations and constructions of technology that came to currency in the twentieth century, placing these historical theories alongside a range of twentieth-century texts and exploring how they can be read in the light of different writings on technology. The chapter concludes with a consideration of the more contemporary theorists of technology who have informed the ideas and analyses across this study as a whole.

As the first chapter has shown, technology does not erupt into the twentieth century, marking a radical break from the previous centuries. The Victorians were technological creatures, not just in the traditionally accepted sense as the heirs of the Industrial Revolution, but as the first to experience a new type of high-speed, wireless world and to experience a world made strange by electrical technology. That the uncanny and supernatural elements of electrical and communication technology persist into the twentieth century is clearly shown by Jeffrey Sconce in his *Haunted Media* (2000). Sconce explores how the resonances of the nineteenth-century 'spiritual telegraph' persisted into the twentieth-century interest in radio 'DX fishing' (that is, scanning the ether in search of globally distant transmissions), in radio contact with extraterrestrials, and in concerns about the limbo state of television taking over its audience and the paranormal breaching of the boundaries between self and film/television screen. If the twentieth century inherits an ambiguous sense of what technology is and what it can and does do, the century provides no definitive or singular response to this ambiguity. Thus, even the simplest definition of technology as the tool of humanity is radically reframed in the light of the increasing technologization of human life. Lewis Mumford, for example, distinguished between the tools that the user directly manipulates, and machines that are independent of the skill of the user. For Mumford, the rise of megamachines (the first of which was, for Mumford, the mass organization of labour in ancient empires), and of 'megatechnics', will ultimately reduce humans to a passive role in a depersonalized collective machine culture (1967). Max Weber, approaching technology much more as a set of rules, rather than objects, arrives at similar conclusions, characterizing the rise of the West as the rise of 'rationalization', the rise of rule-governed systems in science, law, economics and bureaucracy, in which needs are 'expressed in numerical, calculable terms' (1947: 185). In the late twentieth century it is the philosopher Jacques Ellul who most forcefully argues for the all-encompassing nature of the 'technological demand', in the service of which is put all our scientific, political, economic and intellectual powers.

S. J. Kline, in his article 'What Is Technology?' (1985), does posit a useful merging of the two positions of technology as objects and technology as rules. His argument is that technology is a system that encompasses both hardware (tools) and software (rules of manufacture, technique and utilization). But this useful overview does not resolve the problem of the nature of technology itself, the question of whether it has an essence and whether that essence is essentially helpful or harmful for human autonomy and liberty. Such problems and questions, along with detailed considerations of the exact effect of technology on human culture, occupied a range of important thinkers in the twentieth century, among them Walter Benjamin, Theodor Adorno, Martin Heidegger, Herbert Marcuse, Marshall McLuhan, Fredric Jameson, Jean Baudrillard, Gilles Deleuze and Félix Guattari. That some of them may have shared common ground, or responded to the same historical events or technological developments, does not mean that their responses are necessarily similar: what emerges from an examination of their ideas is not a solution to, but rather a deeper understanding of, the complex debates about technology in the twentieth century.

MECHANICAL REPRODUCTION

The advent of cinema and after it TV technology had an enormous immediate bearing on the culture of the twentieth century: the impact of the new media technologies on the literature of modernism has been explored by a number of critics and it is discussed in detail in the following chapter. In terms of theoretical writings, though, it is the work of the German critical theorist Walter Benjamin and particularly his 1936 essay, 'The Work of Art in the Age of Mechanical Reproduction' (Benjamin 1999), that has, since its composition, consistently been used to assess the aesthetic and political effects of technological media. In this essay, Benjamin explores the cultural effects of media technology and attempts to base a Marxist aesthetic on his analysis. The core idea of Benjamin's analysis is the 'decay of the aura' of the art object in the modern age of mechanical reproduction (1999: 216). Benjamin argues that the intangible power, or aura, of art stems from its original cult value in ritualistic purposes, an aura that persisted through the bourgeois era in the elevation of art above everyday experience.

For Benjamin, with the advent of such innovations as photography and particularly film, art becomes formally embedded in social practice and politics: he argues 'when the age of mechanical reproduction separated art from its basis in cult, the semblance of its autonomy disappeared forever' (220). What emerges as a result of mechanical reproduction is an equality of access to art and the exposure of previously unseen parts of the world. Citing particularly the use of the close-up, 'focusing on hidden details of familiar objects' (229), and slow motion in which 'movement is extended' (230), Benjamin argues that the 'dynamite of the tenth of a second' of the film frame radically restructures the world. For him, 'a different nature opens itself to the camera than to the naked eye – if only because an unconsciously penetrated space is substituted for a space consciously explored by man . . . The camera introduces us to unconscious optics as does psychoanalysis to unconscious impulses' (230).

The narrative focus of twentieth-century naturalist fiction can perhaps be compared to the 'unconscious optics' that Benjamin poses in his essay and, further, the perspectival focus and movement of such modernist writers as James Joyce and Virginia Woolf seem to rely on just such a new way of viewing the world. The new, technological, forms of art are different, for Benjamin, because, instead of the 'natural distance from reality' maintained by a painter and his creation which produces a 'total' picture, the cameraman penetrates into reality, assembling 'multiple fragments'. By virtue of the very technology that enables them, the camera's fragments produce 'an aspect of reality which is free of all equipment', not framed from a distance like a painting (1999: 227). The reception of film is also radically different: film is watched in a 'state of distraction' rather than 'contemplation' and thus points to the 'profound changes in apperception' in the age of mechanical reproduction (232).[1] Benjamin is cautious in some respects, though, and he does point out how Hollywood studios and their films 'respond to the shrivelling of the aura with the artificial build-up of the "personality" outside the studio' (224), and how a key effect of the politicizing of art through mechanical reproduction is the aestheticizing of politics: fascism.

Some of what Benjamin argues about the formal effect of technology on art can be deployed in a consideration of the work of the modernist poet Williams Carlos Williams. Williams is well known for making the association between poetry and machines in the introduction to his 1944 volume *The Wedge*:

There's nothing sentimental about a machine, . . . A poem is a small (or large) machine made out of words. When I say there's nothing sentimental about a poem, I mean that there can be no part that is redundant.

   Prose may carry a load of ill-defined matter like a ship. But poetry is a machine which drives it, pruned to a perfect economy. As in all machines, its movement is intrinsic, undulant, a physical more than a literary character. (Williams 1969: 256)

Here Williams highlights precision, movement and physicality ('no ideas but in things' as he puts it in 'A Sort of Song', 1944), key facets of all his poetry and reflected throughout his oeuvre in his focus on the commonplace and the precision of his verbal compositions. The kineticism of language and of modern life, a speed and movement enabled by technology, is also prevalent in Williams's work as is his response to the impact of radio and newspapers on language. His development of the variable poetic foot can be seen as a way to embody and express the technologically inflected American idiom, and from very early in his career Williams was clear about his response to the modern world: in the face of the 'great towers of Manhattan' in the early poem 'The Wanderer' (first version 1914), he declares: 'How shall I be a mirror to this modernity?' (Williams 2000: 28). The technology of life, and the life of technology, can be seen from poems such as 'Overture to a Dance of Locomotives' (1921) to 'Perpetuum Mobile: The City' (*Adam & Eve in the City*, 1936), while pieces such as 'The Attic Which Is Desire' (1930) formally include the electric technology of the twentieth century in the form of the neon advertising sign. Williams does not just deal with technology thematically or celebrate the technological achievements of the modern age. As Eleanor Berry (1988) points out, he creates a machinic aesthetic, one that enables the clarity of pieces such as 'Poem (As the cat)' (1930):

> As the cat
> climbed over
> the top of
>
> the jamcloset
> first the right
> forefoot (Williams 2000: 352)

The precision of movement of the observed cat, and the precision of the mechanical cuts of the line breaks in the poem, create a pattern and a movement that is perfectly economical. There is no auratic presence or painterly frame, simply the multiple fragments of movement that constitute the reality of this moment. Williams's machinic aesthetic (which is very distinct from the technophilia of the Italian Futurists, for example) is as applicable to natural subject matter as it is to cityscapes. Essentially, there is no futile affiliation to an organic or natural sense of 'voice', the enjambment in 'Poem (As a cat') severs the intonational expression of the single sentence, producing instead an object, a poem, out of fragments that work together in a kinetic way. The mechanical production of this poem, sliced into tercets functioning with three syllables, does not aspire to arcane or hermetic art status: its beauty comes from its precision and accessibility.

Williams's work, as a doctor and poet, required a penetration into reality that suggests he shared much common ground with the cameraman that Benjamin describes. In the poem 'Simplex Sigilum Veri' (1929), Williams offers detailed description of the mass-produced objects on his desk – 'bottles | words printed on the backs of ‖ two telephone directories | The Advertising Biographical | Calendar of Medicine' – without abstracting them into an artificial whole (Williams 2000: 321–2). But it is two specific technological objects that are crucial for understanding Williams's work: the typewriter and the car. In *A Novelette and Other Prose*, Williams writes of the importance of both moving between patients' houses in his car which meant that he would 'Write going', and of his typewriter: 'This is the alphabet qwertyuiopae[sic]dfghjklzxcvbnm' (1969: 278, 282). Roy Miki suggests a connection between Williams's use of the car and the improvisational technique of his experimental prose (Miki 1983) and Williams's poems are fundamentally impacted by his mechanical manipulation of his compositions on his typewriter to get the layout correct. The writing technologies of the twentieth century had an enormous influence on the creation and production of literature, and Williams shares with many other modernists, such as Ezra Pound and e e cummings, or later poets such as Charles Olson, an interest in using the mechanisms of the typewriter for producing poetry. For Williams's writing, the use of the typewriter manufactures the exactness and moving segments of his poetry, a movement derived from precision engineering that is also manifest in the car. And the use of technology enables a connection, a refusal of artistic aloofness and an erasure of the aura of the fetishized 'voice', that brings his work closer to the positive technological effects that Benjamin identifies in 'The Work of Art in the Age of Mechanical Reproduction'. This points to the empowering facet of Benjamin's theories, offering an art that is released from elitism by the power of technology, a democratizing force in culture and one that makes the quotidian, as revealed through mechanical devices, its worthy subject.

Williams was aware, though, of the totalizing potential of technology and the technological object (whether machine or poem), writing that 'As soon as we make it we must at once plan to escape – and escape . . . To stop before any machine is to make of it a fetish', warning that 'knowledge itself is just such a machine' (Williams 1974: 62–3). In contrast, although

Benjamin was very conscious of the aestheticization of politics in fascism that was related to the politicization of art in the age of mechanical reproduction, he was more hopeful about the consequences of the 'simultaneous collective experience' (Benjamin 1999: 228) that a film audience would have. Williams's assertion of the need for continual movement, for escape from our creations, brings him closer to the ideas of Theodor Adorno on technology.

The writings of Theodor Adorno, a German critical theorist and member of the Frankfurt School, along with Walter Benjamin, Max Horkheimer and Herbert Marcuse, are highly critical of the 'technological rationality' of the twentieth century. Adorno's major works, written after the Second World War, respond to the unprecedented technologized slaughter of the war and the Nazi genocide. Adorno is not alone in this; the interest of many twentieth-century philosophers and sociologists, such as Ellul, Mumford, Hannah Arendt, Heidegger and Marcuse, was initiated by the traumas of the mass slaughter of the war. Adorno's own enterprise, characterized by his notion of the 'negative dialectic', was focused on negating what he saw as the false emancipation of technology and the totalitarianism it produced. In *Dialectic of Enlightenment* (1947), with Max Horkheimer, Adorno identifies the key error of the modern age: the reduction of knowledge to power and ultimately to technology.

For Horkheimer and Adorno, technology is a mode of thinking; it is 'technological rationality' (1947: 121), and technological rationality is, at base, a way of distancing, grasping, manipulating and getting power over. This process has disastrous effects on the freedom of thought and knowledge as 'Thinking reifies itself into a self-running, automatic process striving to be like the machine which it itself produces so that ultimately the machine can replace it' (25). The effects of technological rationality and its imposition of a singular perspective, mode of operating and goal, can, Horkheimer and Adorno argue, be clearly seen in the Culture Industry of film, radio and magazines, which they describe as a 'mass deception' in which 'culture wraps up everything with similarity, making everything 'univocal' (40). The technological mediation of every aspect of life makes everything ontologically similar; the world can only be seen, they argue, through this technology as it covers the entire spectrum of daily reality and makes it seem only accessible to and at the disposal of technological mastery. What emerges here is a 'fetishism of technology' (41) in which the inhumanity and privilege of the bourgeois era is replaced by the barbarisms of an era of universality and uniformity.

Unlike Benjamin's celebration of the levelling, demystifying and liberatory effect of technological reproduction, Adorno sees the ultimate effect of such socio-epistemological levelling to be fascist totalitarianism. '[S]tandardization and serial production', for Horkheimer and Adorno, destroy what makes the 'logic of art different from that of the social system' (121) and thus destroy its ability to criticize society and technological rationality.

Everything is harmonious in technology: there is no discord or dissent, no distinction between the world of the cinema and the outside world, between the systematic routines of men and women at work and the fabricated, systematic amusement they enjoy in their leisure time. Even individuality, so apparently important to the late capitalism of the West, is a 'pseudo-individuality' (155), a rational and technological production of the supposedly extravagant, extraordinary or spontaneous. The manipulation of human life in support and development of technology is the crucial condition for fascist totalization and this is what Adorno fundamentally points to. Adorno's interrogation of modern technology, in *Dialectic of Enlightenment*, *Negative Dialectics* and elsewhere, is concerned primarily with the fate of the freedom and integrity of the individual person. However, Adorno's theories make it difficult to conceive of an individuality that is not already co-opted to or produced by the Culture Industry. Moreover, unlike Benjamin's celebration of the usurpation of the elite power of art by technology, Adorno retains an idea of art that remains impervious to mass or general comprehension. What Adorno fails to acknowledge, above all, is that technology is never total or universal in its uniform effects, that new machines or unexpected malfunctions produce shocks and disturbances to the smooth functioning of the system and that the uncanny effect of technology, its ability to disturb complacencies, lies at the heart of its fascination for humankind.

Virginia Woolf's perspective on technology may seem, at first glance, to share much with Adorno, particularly his fears about the fascistic tendencies of technological rationality. Woolf is consistently critical of the monologic of rationality. Her writing – both non-fiction, such as *A Room of One's Own* (1929) and *Three Guineas* (1938), and her novels – criticizes a masculine scientistic rationality that dominates and destroys the ambivalent and ambiguous: this is the rationality associated with Mr Ramsey and William Banks in *To The Lighthouse* (1927), and with Sir William Bradshaw in *Mrs Dalloway* (1925). But Lily Briscoe's reconciliation with William Banks (and implicitly with Mr Ramsey) in *To The Lighthouse* demonstrates that Woolf does not simply reject what they embody: she does not demonize rationality and the technological advances of her age.

In a 1926 essay, 'The Cinema', Woolf identifies the formal possibilities which this mechanical mode could enable, highlighting cinematic transitionality as a potential liberation from the organic form of the novel, and pointing out the new language of cinema which suggests 'thought could be conveyed by shape more effectively than by words' (56) and so presenting something 'real with a different reality' (55). Such comments draw Woolf closer to Benjamin's celebration of the 'unconscious optics' of cinema, and many critics have sought to propose analogies between Woolf's writing and the cinema. Resisting a simplistic causality between cinematic form and the modernist novel, it is possible to see a consciousness that could be termed filmic in scenes such as the following:

the great doors stood open. A shaft of light like a yellow banner sloped from roof to floor. Festoons of paper roses, left over from the Coronation, drooped from the rafters. A long table, on which stood urn, plates and cups, cakes and bread and butter, stretched across one end. The barn was empty. Mice slid in and out of holes or stood upright, nibbling, Swallows were busy with straw in pockets of earth in the rafters. Countless beetles and insects of various sorts burrowed in the dry wood. A stray botch had made a dark corner where the stacks stood a lying-in ground for her puppies. All these eyes, expanding and narrowing, some adapted to light, others to darkness, looked from different angles and edges. (Woolf 1941: 76)

This incredibly visual passage uses perspectives, angles and close-ups that could be associated with a camera eye, even staging the contrasts of light and dark so crucial for the filmic image and narrative. It comes in the middle of Woolf's final novel, *Between the Acts*, written during the early years of the Second World War, but similar passages could be found in *Mrs Dalloway* and *To The Lighthouse*. What *Between the Acts* also offers, though, is a very careful examination of the impact of modern technology on art and on the ideal of English communal life. Technology is a pervasive feature of the life of Pointz Hall and the neighbouring villages of *Between the Acts*: from the telephone that Isa Oliver uses to order fish for lunch, to the cars that carry the audience home and the gramophone that marks the passage of the pageant, drawing the audience together and holding them (however impermanently) in one place. Technology can control and contain – the ping-ping bell of the phone in the office, or the bell in the shop that is an 'infernal, agelong and eternal order issued from on high' (1941: 89) – but it is also enabling. Technology is not something that necessarily wraps everything up in univocality and mass deception, as Adorno would have it, and so would destroy the artistic endeavour of Miss La Trobe's pageant: it can, as Benjamin might suggest, contribute to the making of the pageant as a democratic and inclusive art.

The gramophone is very important in *Between the Acts*; it marks a mechanical passing of time, and timing of the silence in the pageant as it 'chuff chuffs' away 'accurately, insistently' (110) while the audience sit and wait, but it also brings the audience together. It gives the audience a way of partaking of the past, through the records of the calls of street sellers that are played, and of experiencing music communally, as all strata of the rural community engage together as audience and actors. Moreover, the technology as epitomized by the gramophone in *Between the Acts* is not seamless and faultless. In contrast to the smooth standardization that characterizes Adorno's account of technology, the gramophone is not a streamlined, ideal, dehumanized technology but one that, in its very disfunctioning, reveals the gaps, fragments and blanks that are also part of the 'meaning' and experience of art. Technology in the form of the gramophone and of the loudspeaker, 'megaphontic, anonymous' (135), that speaks at the end of the pageant is a democratizing force and one that takes power and control away from a singular, controlling hand or voice, creating instead a disembodied language that does not 'belong' but simply communicates. The gramophone is ultimately the final disembodied voice that announces the oppositions and contradictions that have been momentarily conjoined by the pageant '*Unity – Dispersity*. It gurgled *Un . . . dis . . .* And ceased' (146).

But there is another technology that frames and disturbs the text of *Between the Acts* (and the pageant that is put on): the aeroplane. Near the beginning of the novel Isa recalls seeing an aeroplane propellor at Croydon aerodrome, and later we find out that an 'aerodrome' has been built in the neighbourhood. More spectacularly, at the end of the pageant:

the word was cut in two. A zoom severed it. Twelve aeroplanes in perfect formation like a flight of wild duck came overhead. *That* was the music. The audience gaped; the audience gazed. Then the zoom became drone. The planes had passed. (140)

This interspersing of the 'music' of military technology into the artistic world of the text/pageant, offers a more foreboding vision of technology. The aeroplane stands in stark contrast to the plane that appears in *Mrs Dalloway*, skywriting an advertisement for Kreemo Toffee and bringing together the diverse peoples of London in a communal but multivocal interpretation of the meaning of the aeroplane's writing and manoeuvres. The aeroplane in *Mrs Dalloway* liberates the people from their subservience to the mysterious black car that embodies the hierarchies of British society, but the aeroplane in *Between the Acts* tears the audience from their communal experience and manufactures the possibility of death and loss. This is technological power in the service of death, the transformation of technical possibility into technological domination and destruction. Woolf refers therefore to the mechanical slaughter of the Second World War, which was beginning as she wrote *Between the Acts*, and which was to inform Adorno's response to technology.

At the end of the pageant the Rev. G. W. Streatfield stands up and speaks in an attempt to interpret and close off the pageant (to give it an absolute ending). It is this embodiment of patriarchal power and tradition that is cut off by the aeroplanes passing overhead, pointing again to the ambivalence of technology in the novel. Here it destroys the Reverend's attempts to control meaning, but also, as a shadow of modern war, threatens the integrity of the whole community. What the mechanical objects and technological modes of *Between the Acts* pose, if they have any coherent function at all, is a resistance to, rather than imposition of, a single, coherent meaning. The heteroglossia of the text, which includes technological voices and noises, stands perhaps as the text's ultimate resistance to the monologic of fascism and Stalinism, the totalitarianism that plunged Europe into the horror of the Second World War.

THE QUESTION CONCERNING TECHNOLOGY

Benjamin's and Adorno's explorations of the effects of technology point to the system or world view that technology emerges from, but do not necessarily identify a technological essence. Martin Heidegger is the key philosopher of the twentieth century who is interested in uncovering technology 'in its essence', for example, in his essay 'The Question Concerning Technology' (1955: 6). The twentieth-century context in which Heidegger writes is one where the overshadowing threat of nuclear destruction and the rise to dominance of mechanical technologies of extraction have brought the dangers of technology to the fore. But for Heidegger the danger of modern technology lies not in technological things (the threat of atomic weapons or environmental contamination), it lies in the human enslavement to the way of technological revealing. The apparently dominant power of technology threatens human autonomy as it presents the false freedom of technological imposition, domination and overpowering:

The threat to man does not come in the first instance from the potentially lethal machines and apparatus of technology. The actual threat has already affected man in his essence. The rule of Enframing threatens man with the possibility that it could be denied to him to enter into a more original revealing and hence to experience the call of a more primal truth. (1955: 28)

Heidegger points out that the etymological origins of 'technology' stems from the Greek *technikon*, that is, that which belongs to *techne*. He therefore argues that '*techne* is the name not only for the activities and skills of the craftsman, but also for the arts of the mind and the fine arts. *Techne* belongs to bringing-forth, to *poiesis*; it is something poietic' (13; *sic*). For Heidegger, therefore, the basis of technology is 'bringing-forth'; technology in essence is not a technological thing or things, but the way these things disclose or reveal themselves. What modern technology has done is to take this essential 'bringing-forth' and extend it to a challenging of all nature. Modern technology looks at things as disposable and seeks to make them even more disposable, subjecting all of nature to humanly chosen ends. Thus, modern technology is an all-encompassing imposition; it is disrespectful and blind to nature, and self-blind to its own essence as technology (as revealing, disclosing, bringing forth) rather than its function in satisfying human ends.

So, instead of revelation or disclosure, what happens in modern technology is the transformation of anything, any potential or energy, into an ordered system, so that it can become a 'standing reserve' ('*Bestand*') (17). What Heidegger terms 'Enframing' ('*Ge-Stell*') is the essence of modern technology as he sees it, gathering together everything, including mankind itself, into a certain and single way of revealing or bringing-forth, turning everything and ordering everything into a standing-reserve, immediately at hand to be used. Heidegger sees salvation in a power above the realm of modern technology, in a recollection of a time when technology as *techne* was a poetic 'bringing-forth', a revealing that was not utilitarian:

Because the essence of technology is nothing technological, essential reflection upon technology and decisive confrontation with it must happen in a realm that is, on the one hand, akin to the essence of technology and, on the other, fundamentally different from it.

Such a realm is art. (1955: 35)

Heidegger sees art and technology as kindred and both in essence ontological (that is, concerned with what it means to be). But where art presents things for contemplation, pointing us to Being, to mystery and the impalpable, technology presents things transformed into something useful, functional in the world of man. His essay calls for an attention to the meaning of technological things, not in order to reject them, but so that the relentless and insidious claims of technology on our attention can be resisted. In a later discussion on technology, Heidegger makes explicit his attitude towards technological things:

> For all of us, for some to a greater and some to a lesser extent, the contrivances, apparatuses, and machines of the technological world are indispensable. It would be silly to rail blindly against technology. It would be shortsighted to condemn the technological world as the work of the devil. We depend on technological objects; they even challenge us to ever greater improvements. Nevertheless, we may unwittingly become so firmly shackled to technological objects that we end up their slaves. (1959: 53–4)

It is difficult to read Heidegger's philosophy without also acknowledging the shadow cast by his Nazi affiliations and silence on the Holocaust after the Second World War. Nevertheless, his writings on technology offer a practical response to the challenges of living in a modern techno-age and highlight the danger of enthralment to gadgets, appliances and machines. They also suggest, in a very contemporary way, that the domination of nature destroys human freedom as it destroys the natural world.

Of modern novelists, D. H. Lawrence is the one most concerned with the transformation of the organic and natural world into a set of resources at the service of a mechanical imperative. But it is important to acknowledge that Lawrence does not display a simple and absolute antipathy to technology and industrialization; there is Paul Morel's excitement about railways and his final turn towards the electric lights of the town at the end of *Sons and Lovers* (1913), or the crucial role of the car in Birkin and Ursula's 'honeymoon night' in Sherwood Forest in *Women in Love* (1920). It is impossible to ignore, though, the fact that Lawrence condemns a mechanization of life and nature and a destruction of the environment that is fundamentally at odds with the vitalism he celebrates. In the same vein as Heidegger's analysis of the essence of technology, Lawrence identifies the effect of the technological enframing of the world on the individual. In *The Rainbow* (1915), it is Tom Bragwen and Winifred Inger who wholeheartedly succumb to the transformation of mankind into a standing-reserve in the productive service of mechanization, and this is what makes them eminently suited to each other. Tom is described in his 'only happy moments' as 'serving the machine' and Winifred is 'in service of the machine' (350). With Winifred's comment,

'What is he at home, a man? He is a meaningless lump – a standing machine, a machine out of work' (349), it becomes clear that the enframing of man goes hand in hand with the emasculation that Winifred (as lesbian lover of Ursula) also represents. In *Women in Love*, Gerald Crich's commitment to the mechanistic impulse recalls both Adorno's sense of the dangerous standardization of technological rationality and Heidegger's diagnosis of the perversion of *techne* solely into technology:

Perfect instruments in perfect organisation, a mechanism so subtle and harmonious in its workings that it represents the single mind of man, and by its relentless repetition of given movement will accomplish a purpose irresistibly, inhumanly. (Lawrence 1920: 256)

In *Lady Chatterley's Lover* (1928), Lawrence presents his most sustained attack on technologization. As in his other novels, it is mining, the destruction of the English landscape and the penetration of man's 'solitude' by 'industrial noises' and 'wicked, electric lights' that Lawrence decries (124). In Mellors, the gamekeeper, he presents the authentic individual beset by the horrors of the modern world; 'the world of the mechanical greedy, greedy mechanism and mechanized greed, sparkling with lights and gushing hot metal and roaring with traffic . . . ready to destroy whatever did not conform' (124). For Mellors, the technological achievements of modern consumer society – 'Motor-cars and cinemas and aeroplanes' (226) – have destroyed the being of man, have 'kill[ed] off the human reality' and produced instead 'little twiddling machines' (226). The vision of Tevershall that Connie gets on her trip through the town is a similar one of the enframing of the natural and human world in the service of mechanical necessity, in which 'The new England blots out the old England. And the continuity is not organic, but mechanical' (163). Connie's husband Clifford's close association with prosthetic technology – his wheelchair, the radio he listens to avidly, even his fashionable novel writing – mark him as more than physically unmanned; they designate the ontological unmanning that technology perpetrates on modern man.

It is possible to draw contiguities between the critique of technologization in *Lady Chatterley's Lover* and Heidegger's identification of the transformation of natural and human energy into an ordered and controlled system, but, as with Lawrence's other novels, there are also strong parallels with Adorno's critiques of technological media. Lawrence condemns popular culture more widely, identifying the cinema and jazz music as mass deceptions that capture their audiences like a 'drug' (1928: 270) and manifest what Lawrence describes in other terms as the 'utter negation of natural beauty, the utter negation of the gladness of life . . . the utter death of the human intuitive faculty' (158).

The essence of technology, as Lawrence represents it, is not just its function in the mass deception of working men, its destruction of the English countryside, and its emasculation of Man but that, by transforming the world into a ordered system of mechanical relations, any other type of relation or knowledge becomes impossible to consummate. Just as Heidegger calls on an organic sense of humanity and its poetic abilities to retrieve the possibility of other types of knowledge and Being, so Lawrence, through the muscular prose and vivid sensuality of his writing, attempts to recall us to a pre-industrial vitalism and communion with the world.

THE MEDIUM IS THE MESSAGE

In 1964 the Canadian cultural and media theorist Marshall McLuhan authored a book which offered a vision of individual communion with the world, but it was diametrically different from Lawrence's organicist vitalism. In McLuhan's interpretation, the twentieth-century technological age heralds a new era of global community, instantaneous relations and the decentralization of power. McLuhan does have aspects in common with more techno-phobic diagnoses in his description of the mechanical age of the nineteenth and early twentieth century centuries. For McLuhan, the age of the machine has its necessary corollary in print culture. The mechanical age is one of explosion, of the separation and serialization of functions, of discrete operations in an order. In this, it reflects the legacy of literacy and print culture which produced a fragmented, visual, private experience of the world, one composed of repeatable, mechanical Gutenberg technology, or 'smooth uniform lines of type and organization' (McLuhan 1964a: 305).[2]

What McLuhan identifies in his present, and in the future, is the advent of the electric age. In McLuhan's analysis, machines are essentially an 'outering of a process' (165) and what the electric age brings is a technological extension of the central nervous system: 'we have put our central nervous systems outside us in electric technology' (57). As a result, the world is reconfigured, it becomes 'audile-tactile' (159) rather than solely visual, it experiences implosion and decentralization or the 'flexibility of multiple small centres' (78). The electric age is configured around 'instant, organic interrelations of electricity' (268), 'electric information movement' which is a 'mosaic . . . of simultaneous touch and interplay' (202). The mosaic is 'discontinuous, skew, nonlineal' (365) and 'the simultaneity of electric communication . . . makes each of us present and accessible to every other person in the world' (270). What emerges, for McLuhan, is a 'global village' (101) in which humans return to a tribal, rather than a mechanical, mode of functioning. People are now, according to McLuhan, 'returned psychically and socially to the nomad state . . . it is called information-gathering and data-processing' (375). The idealism of McLuhan's claims are difficult to ignore; his sense of a global village, for example, elides the very real, differential access to technology across the globe, which is only exacerbated with every new innovation or upgrade which makes existing appliances obsolete. Nevertheless, McLuhan is an influential and insightful theorist who turns attention to the altered parameters of body, subjectivity and community.

The best-known ideas to emerge from *Understanding Media*, a text often celebrated as particularly prescient, include McLuhan's vision of a global village, the concept of 'remediation', that is, that the '"content" of any medium is always another medium' (8), and his dictum that the 'medium is the message', that is, that the content of any specific media is not its message; its message is how the medium 'shapes and controls the scale and form of human association and action' (9). McLuhan also envisaged an electric 'global network' (380) five years before the ARPANET Internet prototype was launched. He emphasized the central role of information in the technological economy long before it became a commonplace of the late twentieth century, and speculated on the next stage of 'transfer[ing] our consciousness to the computer world' (67).

Understanding Media is, as its title indicates, especially concerned with analysing the new forms of technological media emergent in the twentieth century. In doing so, McLuhan identifies what he sees as two distinct types of media, hot and cold, and argues that 'if the medium is of high definition [hot], participation is low. If the medium is of low intensity [cool], the participation is high' (1964a: 348). For McLuhan, film is a hot, high-definition media that requires a passive audience, while TV is cool because its 'mosaic image demands social completion and dialogue' (319), and he goes further, claiming that with TV 'the viewer is the screen' (341). In McLuhan's analysis, the 'effects of technology' are not to transfer ideas or rational speculation, but inevitably and fundamentally to transform our apperception of the world: 'the effects of technology do not occur at the level of opinions or concepts, but alter sense ratios or patterns of perception steadily and without any resistance' (19). Technology does not stimulate an epistemic shift, in McLuhan's formulation, but effects an inevitable physical evolution of the human being. In opposition to a Heideggerian sense of the dangers and potentials of technology as ontology, the physicalism of *Understanding Media* inserts our selves as electric bodies into a field of techno-phenomena.

McLuhan's ideas certainly resonate with the cyber-enthusiasts of the late twentieth century and with the imaginative, virtual worlds created by cyber-punk writers from William Gibson to Pat Cadigan. His vision of the effect of electric technology as an extension of the human nervous system and of a global village/network of information nomads seems to predict the World Wide Web and various digital experiments in connectivity and virtuality. However, McLuhan's ideas about technology are not simply relevant to those writers and those cultural manifestations that explicitly embrace the electronic age. Looking at the contemporary Australian poet Les Murray, whose work seems apparently inimical to an electric cybernetic era, it is possible to consider a more nuanced extrapolation of McLuhan's ideas.

Les Murray's work evinces an obvious concern with national consciousness and identity, a commitment to the Australian land and landscape, and a calculatedly provocative stance, rejecting cultural snobbery and instead writing of ordinary people. Murray has often been characterized as a Romantic, anti-Enlightenment poet (Almon 1997), possibly even a 'bush poet', but it would do Murray a disservice to limit him to such characterizations, as Peter Porter points out in a review of his *New Collected Poems*: 'Murray has never been just a bush poet . . . I cannot think of any poet more at home with technology' (Porter 2003). It is not solely that Murray does acknowledge the technologization of life in many poems, especially ones that explore the horrors of war; his commitment to multiplicity and a nomadic sensibility brings him closer to the mosaic and the 'global village' that McLuhan prophesizes.

In Murray's work, there is a clear acknowledgement of the intensity of the modern technological world. In 'The Fire Autumn', he writes that 'Since mankind went critical, time is a fiery screen | on which all the scenes we may call the world play at once' (1998: 34). The contemporary world that Murray depicts is one fundamentally transformed by machines and technology, a world where older identities and certainties are eroded, for Murray an ambivalent process that involves both the neglect of metaphysical speculation and the release from traditional hierarchies. In poems such as 'Machine Portraits with Pendant Spacemen' (1983), we see both the mechanical 'slapstick flow | of fast work in the Chaplin Age' and the 'bursts of algorithim' and 'liquid Cool' of the electric, information, space-shuttle age. In the comparable sequence, 'The Sydney Highrise Variations', we are offered what Steven Matthews describes as a 'surprisingly flexible view of modern architectural and technological advances (2001: 98). Matthews notes that Murray also 'celebrates those aspects of technology and speed which appeal to him' (16). The speaker of the poem 'The Powerline Incarnation' is plugged in (literally) to the electric network and experiences, simultaneously, the extremes and oppositions of life: 'Mozart | and Johnny Cash' records, electric food mixers and life support machines, mountains and towns. The speaker undergoes what McLuhan might describe as the 'instant, organic interrelations of electricity', but there is an obvious ambivalence in this poem in which the body electric brings both 'happiness' and 'burn', both knowledge and madness, indicating Murray's awareness of the costs or losses that the electric age brings. In a later poem, it is clear that, unlike McLuhan's celebration of the return of tribal man in the new 'global village' of instant communication, what Murray imagines is the transformation of the interior of Uluru (Ayers Rock) into a tourist's mall with 'Outback shop fronts', 'fluorescent lights' and a 'children's playworld' ('Inside Ayers Rock'; Murray 1998: 435).

Perhaps McLuhan's electric age of instantaneous communication and simultaneity is more obviously evoked in the work of Lavinia Greenlaw, a British poet who consistently engages with science and the impact of modern technology. The title poem from her 1997 collection, 'A World Where News Travelled Slowly', carries clear resonances with McLuhan's description of the advent of the electric age of interconnection. In her 1993 collection, *Night Photograph*, the modern world Greenlaw depicts is one infused with technology and through this obtains the imminent potential for communication, movement and the transformation of perspective. Greenlaw's 'Electricity' holds the promise of 'no edge, no end and no beginning' between lovers (1993: 27), and other poems imagine a world transformed into a tactile, supra-visible scene inscribed in the viewer ('Night Photograph', 'From Scattered Blue'). Ambivalence is here also, with Greenlaw framing an exploration of the dangers of a technological world of interpenetration and contamination through the radium-painted clock-faces and X-rays that poison and kill in 'The Innocence of Radium' and 'A Letter from Marie Curie' (Greenlaw 1993). She also clearly locates, in poems such as 'The Cost of Getting Lost in Space', the potential for loss, lost communication and being lost in a speeded up, technological world. In neither Les Murray nor Lavinia Greenlaw do we see an uncomplicated celebration of technology, but in both poets what modern technology (in McLuhan's electric age) does effect is a fundamental disintegration of the boundaries between self and world.

TECHNOLOGY AND POSTMODERNISM

McLuhan's ideas, and the world they describe, mark a clear shift away from the mechanical focus of philosophies of technology in the first part of the twentieth century towards what could be termed more postmodern approaches to the question of the nature and effect of technology. Jean Baudrillard is indicative of this shift and he theorizes a postmodern world in which new technologies and technological forms of media and information have radically transformed social and cultural experience, and indeed the status of reality itself. The 'hyperreality', 'cyberblitz' and predominance of 'simulacra' that Baudrillard identifies as the essence of the late twentieth century all arise, as he describes it, from the effects of technology, particularly media technologies. In an interview, which is titled as a direct response to Benjamin's statement on mechanical reproduction and art, 'The Work of Art in the Electronic Age' (1988), Baudrillard expresses his ideas through reference to McLuhan, arguing that: 'the means of communication, the medium, is becoming a determinant element in exchange and quite often dominates its function, even technologically – as McLuhan has it – dominates the content, the message, the subject communicated, the very substance of communication' (1988: 145). Baudrillard also expands McLuhan's description of TV, wherein 'the viewer is the screen' (McLuhan 1964a: 341), to describe a postmodern world in which 'not only are there screens and terminals in technical terms, but we ourselves, the listeners, the TV spectators, become the terminals of all this communications network' (Badrillard 1988: 146). This connects clearly to the central ideas of Baudrillard's 1983 essay, 'The Ecstasy of Communication', in which he posits the 'screen and network' as the contemporary replacements of the 'scene and mirror' (1983: 126). For

Baudrillard, information and media technologies have caused the implosion of meaning into pure effect and, in this world of cybernetic noise, bodies and the world become merely 'a control screen' (127). The image that Baudrillard uses to describe the subject in such a situation is 'the exact position of an astronaut in his capsule, in a state of weightlessness that necessitates a perpetual orbital flight and a speed sufficient to keep him from crashing back to his planet of origin' (128).

Drawing further on McLuhan, Baudrillard distinguishes between a 'hot', visceral obscenity and promiscuity (of commodities, messages, wars) of the modern machine age and the 'cold and communicational, contractual and motivational obscenity of today' (1983: 131). In this contemporary technological world, where the optical fibre cable connects you with everything, there is no privacy, merely a 'delirium of communication' (132) and, as Baudrillard argues in other texts (e.g. *On Seduction* 1979), the media takes 'hot' events (sports, wars, catastrophes) and converts them into 'cool' media events. Baudrillard does not simply celebrate the hyperreality of the technological world, but he has been criticized, particularly in his response to the first Gulf War, for a disabling capitulation to the effects he describes. However, as is discussed further in chapter 4, Baudrillard articulates a real concern about the politics of Western techno-power and its consequences for human subjects across the world.

Other theorists present critical views of the late twentieth-century world and its information and media technologies. In the work of Fredric Jameson, with his Marxist analysis of postmodernism, technology is associated with what Jameson terms the 'postmodern sublime'. For Jameson, late capitalism presents 'the moment of a radical eclipse of Nature itself' (Jameson 1991: 34) and thus 'the *other* of our society is . . . no longer nature at all, as it was in precapitalist societies, but something else which we must identify' (35). This *other* is not simply technology, in Jameson's argument, but technology stands 'as adequate shorthand to designate' it (35). The postmodern sublime is technological, argues Jameson, as we are now in the 'Third Machine Age' (36) in which, epitomized by the smooth surface of the TV or computer, the 'technology of our own moment no longer possesses . . . capacity for representation' (37). Advanced technology becomes the sublime, not simply because it escapes direct representation but because through it, and the awesome conversion of humanity it proposes, it becomes possible to grasp the real issue; 'to think the impossible totality of the contemporary world system. It is in terms of that enormous and threatening, yet only dimly perceivable, other reality of economic and social institutions that . . . the postmodern sublime can alone be adequately theorized' (38). Crucially for Jameson's idea of the postmodern technological sublime, our machines are 'machines of reproduction rather than of production' (37), and in discussing the aesthetic possibilities of video art he even postulates that 'the deepest "subject" of all video art, and even of all postmodernism, is very precisely reproductive technology itself' (95). Reproductive technology has, for Jameson, replaced the productive machine, and has transformed the experience of social and cultural relations, and even consumption itself, the 'technological bonus of pleasure afforded by the new machinery' giving rise to 'another type of consumption: consumption of the very process of consumption itself' (276). Fundamentally, what Jameson terms 'advanced technology' (38), the technology of information, eludes physical representation and in its sublimity affords us a way of grasping the inconceivability of the social order and power structures of late capitalism. Jameson offers a useful way of thinking about how the technology that can seem to overwhelm the human can actually provide an insight into the social and political position of the human subject in the late twentieth century.

For Jameson, it is in 'a new type of science fiction, called *cyberpunk*' that the 'impossible totality of the contemporary world system' figured in/by technology crystallizes into narrative (38). He describes, particularly, William Gibson's 'exceptional literary realization' (38) of the postmodern sublime, and in doing so points to the key perspective in Gibson's work, what Dani Cavallaro describes as 'fundamentally economic' (38), that can be obscured by the sheer novelty of the world he imagines in his writing. It is Gibson, after all, who is credited with the invention of cyberspace, first described in his 1982 story 'Burning Chrome' as 'the simulation matrix, the electronic consensus-hallucination that facilitates the handling and exchange of massive quantities of data' (Gibson 1995: 197) and developed further in the groundbreaking novel *Neuromancer* (1984):

Cyberspace. A consensual hallucination experienced daily by billions of legitimate operators, in every nation, by children being taught mathematical concepts . . . A graphic representation of data abstracted from the banks of every computer in the human system. Unthinkable complexity. Lines of light ranged in the nonspace of the mind, clusters and constellations of data. Like city lights, receding . . . (67)

This 'non-space' of cyberspace delineates a terrain that has no physical dimension or location but nevertheless exists and can be inhabited by individuals whose subjectivities are fundamentally transformed. Cyberspace, in Gibson's conception, is populated by subjects who are hyperreal, artificial intelligences (Wintermute and Neuromancer in *Neuromancer*), digital reproductions of the dead (Dix McCoy the 'Flatline' in *Neuromancer*), and even the humans who 'jack-in' and become data constructs themselves (particularly Case, the protagonist of *Neuromancer*). But the distinction between 'real' and 'virtual' are fundamentally transgressed in Gibson's novel, with real characters (Armitage/Corto) revealed to be programmed by computers, whole dynasties created out of clones (the Tessier-Ashpools), Case experiencing through Molly's body and consciousness via a simstim link, and Molly using cerebral implants while working as a prostitute to erase her work experiences. The real is not a useful referent in *Neuromancer*, there is only the hyperreal, simulacra and communicational delirium that Baudrillard describes in his writing.

Gibson's writing is extraordinarily prescient about the impact of techno-logically produced virtual spaces on notions of identity and reality coming, as *Neuromancer* and the early stories and novels do, before the spread of computing technology and the inauguration of the World Wide Web. It is only subsequently that Gibson's cyberspace has become synonymous with the electrical-digital zone in which much of the world's commerce, com-munication, information and leisure is conducted. The questioning of iden-tity that is central to Gibson's work can be equated with the questioning that Baudrillard raises with his assertion of the 'screen and network' as the crucial sites of postmodern identity. This is what Scott Bukatman describes as 'terminal identity', the interface with the screen at which and through which traditional conceptions of identity are disrupted and reconfigured. All identity in Gibson's cyberpunk writing is constructed through technology, the technological medium of communication and commerce determines identity and, as Baudrillard puts it, 'being is convertible into infinite forms, and values of identity are constituted primarily through the manipulation of technology' (1988: 145).

There are different ways of thinking about the determining power of technology that lie outside the boundaries of science-fiction writing. The novels of Angela Carter are fantastical, but not SF in any direct way. However, in *Passion of New Eve* (1977), identity is constructed through technology, here the technologies of the cinema and futuristic surgical science, which produce the gendered feminine subjects of Tristessa and Eve out of male bodies. This technological transformation of the body is also shared by Gibson's cyberpunk, as Cavallaro notices: 'in Gibson, cosmetic surgery is used . . . as a leitmotif designed to emphasize the body's constant construction by the social and economic structures of cyberculture' (2000: 110). Such constructions of bodies through technology are a pervasive feature of postmodernism, but as Cavallaro's point makes clear, they also reveal the economics that lie behind the technologization of culture.

It is possible, as other critics have done, to connect the cyberspace of Gibson's novel with McLuhan's ideas about the extension of our central nervous system through technology, but what is most immediate and obvious about the technological postmodern space that Gibson imagines is its unrep-resentability, its 'unthinkable complexity', and the fact that it approaches the 'technological sublime' as Jameson describes. By both describing and admit-ting the limits of description, Gibson hints at the space and structures that exceed individual human comprehension. When his characters become part of the matrix they become part of a totality that contains and transforms them without their being able to conceptualize this totality. Presenting cyberspace as sublime is the key feature of Gibson's fiction, which indicates that it does, as Jameson suggests, figure the 'impossible totality of the con-temporary world system'. Ultimately, then, it may be possible to conclude, with Tony Myers, that in 'the technologies of the matrix . . . subjectivity is reduced to a function of the system in a manner reminiscent of the most pessimistic critiques of capitalism' (2001: 905).

DESIRING MACHINES

If the work of a writer such as Gibson appears to inscribe a quintessentially postmodern approach to the technological, then the late twentieth-century philosophers Gilles Deleuze and Félix Guattari offer a more complete radicalization of the distinctions between human-organic and machine-constructed. It would be inappropriate and incorrect to ascribe a systematic 'idea' of technology to Deleuze and Guattari as their work is itself an attempt to deterritorialize thought, to escape the systems and order of Western philosophy. But the 'machinic' figures extensively in their diagnoses and descriptions of the human organism and its function/place in the world. In their alternative philosophical lexis, which describes a materialism without subjectivity, Deleuze and Guattari foreground desire as primary, as a productive and connective force and, crucially, as Deleuze states, desire 'only exists when assembled or machined' (1987: 96). A body, a human body, a collectivity, even an idea, is defined by the relation of its parts, and by its actions and reactions, not by any idea of organic unity. Indeed, Deleuze and Guattari's understanding of the world is one not of organic or natural unities at all: the construction of the organism and the assertion of natural dualities are, for Deleuze and Guattari, stratifying effects which restrict, code and order productive, heterogeneous flows and affects. These writers posit instead a 'mechanosphere' of assembled, fabricated, machined proximities, meanings and affects (1988: 514). Thus, they write in *Anti-Oedipus*: 'Everywhere *it* is machines – real ones, not figurative ones: machines driving other machines, machines being driven by other machines, with all the necessary couplings and connections' (1984: 1). In the flows of this mechanosphere, 'the subject [is] produced as a residuum alongside the machine, as an appendix or as a spare part adjacent to the machine' (21). This undermines the centrality of the human subject and removes any distinction between human and machine. Technology does not sit in any kind of opposition to human existence, thought or desire; indeed, for any kind of tool or technological object to exist and have meaning it must be part of an assemblage, a social 'machine' that connects it to structures, objects, humans, purposes and so on. Deleuze writes that 'the machine is social in its primary sense' and that 'the history of technology shows that a tool is nothing without the variable machine assemblage which gives it a certain relationship of vicinity with man, animals and things:' (1987: 105, 104). Further, in Deleuze and Guattari's writing, the work of art is itself a 'desiring machine' (1984: 34) and thus, in terms of literature, 'A book itself is a little machine' and we need to ask 'what is the relation (also measurable) of this literary machine to a war machine, love machine, revolutionary machine etc. – and an abstract machine that sweeps them along' (1988: 4). Deleuze and Guattari's radical explorations of the machine make it impossible to think of the human relationship to technology in any abstract sense as all is manufactured and assembled; there is no set essence that defines 'human' or 'machine' – just a succession of interconnected relations and affects. They place literature within these interconnections and challenge us to see the literary text and the act of reading and interpretation as itself a machine process, a productive association of assembled parts: '[t]here is no longer a tripartation between a field of reality, the world, a field of representation, the book, and a field of subjectivity, the author. But an arrangement places in connection certain multiplicities taken from each of these orders' (1988: 23).

What this might actually mean in terms of the literary depiction of the technological nexus of humans, machines and desires can be seen in the work of contemporary writers such as Kathy Acker and Don DeLillo. DeLillo's writing shows a persistent interest in the effect of media technologies, particularly in the transformation of real event into virtual representation. Many of his characters struggle to come to terms with a complex, technological world that institutes systems that de-individualize or alienate them, a version of a mechanosphere that harnesses and organizes desires and meanings. In DeLillo's 2003 novel, *Cosmopolis*, the mechanosphere is the city of New York, a zone of proximities, flows and forces that produce human subjectivities. As Eric Packer crosses the city in one day in his bulletproof white limousine, specific events and encounters structure his identity – meals with his wife, an anti-capitalist riot, a medical examination, a funeral, a rave, a haircut. As he ends his journey on the West Side Highway, Eric also ends his life in a confrontation with an unravelling social outcast. Eric is constantly surrounded by machines, screens that continually monitor his heart rate, a spycam permanently on, telescreens throughout his limo, a handorganizer, an electron camera in his watch. But this is not just ambient technology; Eric, a multimillionaire currency trader, has an acute sense of the machinic structure of capitalism, of 'the interaction between technology and capital' (2003: 23) that governs the Western world. He perceives himself moving into a 'touchless' realm of technological interaction, transcending 'hand-held space' (13) and the antiquated structures of 'skyscraper', 'ATM' and 'computer'. There is no meaning to/for Eric outside the technology–capital interaction, and even the anti-capitalist rioters are inside this market-machine: 'They don't exist outside the market . . . There is no outside' (90). The human subject adjacent to the forces and flows of the technological city will eventually 'be absorbed in streams of information' (104). In his ending, Eric slips into the machinic assemblage which has, throughout the novel, produced him, seeing his own death in his watch-face camera before he has experienced it in his physical body: 'O shit I'm dead. . . . He'd always wanted to become quantum dust' (206).

Acker's *Empire of the Senseless* (1988) inverts Eric Packer's vision of 'mythical . . . cyber-capital' (DeLillo 2003: 207) and presents the couplings and connections of the mechanosphere as productive of a liberated, inorganic mode of subjectivity. *Empire of the Senseless* displays Acker's indicative concerns with undermining the closure of narrative and the determinacy of patriarchy, and expressing a transgressive bodily realm (in this novel figured through the trope of pirates and tattooing). *Empire of the Senseless* engages with US imperial powers and effects and writes across two important inter-texts: Twain's *The Adventures of Huckleberry Finn* (1884) and Gibson's *Neuromancer* (1984). What the male protagonists in these texts share with Acker's Thivai is a desire to escape from a system which actually privileges them over racial and sexual others. In engaging with *Neuromancer*, Acker shows how dreams of an escape from the 'meat' realm into cyberspace are gendered (Thivai escaping from the 'half-robot' Abhor) and ultimately impossible. Escape or transcendence is an illusion: all objects, people, animals, environments are adjacent and so connected; meaning is fabricated from proximity; nothing is outside the assemblage and nothing is essential or organic; everything is marked and made. Acker presents a social 'machine' which must be acknowledged, even as the importance of attacking the stratifying and restricting forces and codes of particular assemblages is asserted. What a novel like *Empire of the Senseless* reveals is the possibility of thinking through a completely inorganic mode of being that refuses the transcendent dreams of cyberspace.

MEDIA TECHNOLOGIES, THEORY AND THE HUMAN

In exploring the interaction of literature and technology, and in unearthing the impact of specific technologies on the form, content and conception of the literary text in the twentieth century, my study draws much of its theo-retical substance from contemporary work on technological media, from what Nicholas Gane usefully terms 'media materialism' which 'privi-leges . . . analysis of material structures of technology over the meanings of these structures and the messages they circulate' (2005: 25). This approach to media and technology disputes the causalities usually in play in the humanities and in the study of literature: the work of Friedrich Kittler, particularly, challenges traditional literary history with an alternate account that foregrounds media technology, technological invention and the dis-courses they give rise to. 'Media determine our situation,' Kittler states in the Preface to *Gramophone, Film, Typewriter* (1999: xxxix), and in his exami-nation of phonography, cinematography, the mechanization of writing, and computing and digital technologies, it is the media technology itself, rather than its social interpretations, which is pre-eminent. Kittler's work is influ-enced by the information theory of Claude Shannon, which provides him with the structures through which to explore the technical components of a communication system over its semantic content.

Kittler's concern is with a wide range of materialities of communication, which includes media technologies, bodily regimes and institutional appara-tus, and alongside information theory he draws on post-structuralist analyses of power and discourse (Foucault), psychoanalysis (Lacan) and the media theory of McLuhan. Kittler takes McLuhan's concept of remediation to an extreme where, he argues, in the era of digital technology and optical fibre networks 'the general digitisation of channels [of communication] and information erases the differences among individual media' so 'any medium can be translated into any other' (1999: 1, 2). The end point of this process will be, Kittler posits, the elimination of the human factor in the production of any knowledge: 'Instead of wiring people and technologies, absolute knowledge will run as an endless loop' (2). Rather than McLuhan's theory, which offers media technologies as extensions of man, Kittler takes technology rather than the human as *a priori*. Technological forms are his primary object of study and precede and inform any questions of meaning; he relegates the human as merely an affect of technology.

Kittler could be subject to the accusation that he argues a form of techno-determinism which negates any human agency, but what he actually proposes is a very complex interaction between substantive technological change, humanity and autonomy that forces a recognition of the active, productive, material effect of technology. Kittler shares with Paul Virilio an interest particularly in the power and effect of military technology and he ascribes a form of agency to this technology. In Kittler's formulation, the essence of the military-industrial complex and technological advance in war is not a matter of 'free human agents fighting against each other' but of the struggle for dominance between technologies; 'military and media technologies especially really do overtake each other' (Armitage and Kittler 2006: 28).

Kittler certainly seems, as John Durham Peters argues, to have 'no use for the category of "the human" or "experience"', and to offer 'a media studies without people' (in Kittler 2010: 5), but this extreme position requires us to attend closely to the actual constitution, form and history of media technology and to avoid anthropomorphizing technology. The translators of Kittler's *Gramophone, Film, Typewriter*, in their introduction, describe Kittler as 'focusing on the intrinsic technological logic, the changing links between body and medium, the procedures for data processing, rather than evaluat[ing] them from the point of view of their social usage' (in Kittler 1999: xiv). Kittler himself bemoans the vagaries of 'many of today's media theorists [who] write lengthy books on computing or the Internet without any concrete experience of how these things actually work' (Armitage and Kittler 2006: 26).

The importance of Kittler's media materialism for an examination of literature and technology is twofold. First, he offers a perspective that, without seeing any particular technology as inevitable, enables us to recognize the impossibility of standing outside the reconfiguration of culture, communication and textuality that specific technologies produce; 'all of us are thrown into the age of typewriting', he claims, 'whether we like it or not' (Armitage and Kittler 2006: 29), and the same is true of the contemporary digital age. Second, it embeds literature as always and only a material and technological process; there is 'no such thing as thoughts . . . only words', so 'Literature is not an island but stands in relation to the external field of technical media' (Armitage and Kittler 2006: 23). For a media historian such as Lisa Gitelman, who takes Kittler's media materialism seriously while resisting the 'lingering determinism' and 'historicity rather than history' of his work (Gitelman 1999: 233 n.1), the import for literature lies at a fundamental level. By looking at specific media technologies in the context of their historical emergence, Gitelman highlights how 'technology is enmeshed within textuality' (8) and how inscriptive technologies (the phonograph, typewriter, digital networks) embody 'historically and culturally contingent experiences of textuality' (19). This forces a questioning of ideas about how meaning is authored and conveyed. Where Gitelman differs most obviously from Kittler's position is in her focus on the social meanings of technology and, though challenging traditional humanities disciplines, she does not give up the idea of people or 'publics', 'users' and 'bodies' (see Gitelman 2006).

Drawing on Kittler, Gitelman and Virilio in this study, I explore technology as a generative force in culture, often tied in closely to the military, paying attention to the materiality of technology and not just to its interpretation or representation. But I am also concerned with the social meanings and politics of technology and its impact on literature. Technology shows us a literature that is only, ever, a material practice embedded in technology and meaningful only through the external processes and channels that constitute it. The materiality of technology also points to a further concern in my study, and that is the place of the human body in the techno-sphere of the twentieth century and beyond. Crucial for the ways in which machines are considered here is a sense of their intimacy with human beings and an awareness of the possible collapse of the distinction between the human body and technology. A critical exploration of technology and the human–machine relationship needs to highlight the dangers of theoretically erasing the human. What must remain in any theory of technology is the possibility for a politics of agency and embodiment, and an awareness of their bearing on crucial questions about inequity and oppression: what Kittler's theories are unable to offer is any framework for thinking about gender, race or class in relationship to technology.

One of the most useful figurations of the human–machine interaction that continues to resonate is Donna Haraway's conception of the cyborg. Her essay 'Manifesto for Cyborgs' (1985) offers a fundamentally non-anthropocentric epistemology that is very much the product of Reagan-era American culture but that continues to be significant for understanding technology. Instead of a presentation of the human as always and only an effect of technology, or an opposition or fundamental difference between humanity and technology, Haraway describes a contemporary merging of them in figurations of the cyborg as 'creatures simultaneously animal and machine' (1985: 149) who refuse myths of wholeness but are 'needy for connection' (151). As discussed further in chapter 6, Haraway's 'Manifesto for Cyborgs' has had an important impact on the conceptualization and critical examination of cyberculture, but it forms part of her wider study of what she terms 'naturecultures'. Haraway's term 'naturecultures' describes a recognition of the inextricability of the natural and the cultural, of the fact that 'nature' is itself 'one of culture's most startling and non-innocent products' (1991: 109), while culture, as the product of biological organisms, is also natural. This leads to Haraway's project to rethink humanness and to challenge the notion of the differentiated independent human subject. Haraway provides a way of thinking about technology as both natural and cultural and of reimagining what we understand the human to be. Haraway also introduces questions of gender and race, and feminist and postcolonial politics, into the theorization of technology.

Developing further the potential of the human–machine relationship, Rosi Braidotti argues that the 'link between the flesh and the machine is symbiotic and therefore can best be described as a bond of mutual dependence' (Braidotti 2002: 223). In opposition to the ontological divide between human and technology, which for Heidegger serves to constitute human subjectivity, she argues that it has become 'historically, scientifically and culturally impossible to distinguish bodies from their technologically mediated extensions' (228). Thus, drawing on a Deleuzian notion of the machinic and machine-like becomings that situate a dynamic, unfolding subjectivity outside the frame of anthropocentrism, Braidotti describes a techno-human subject turned outwards and merging into their environment. The technologies that pervade our everyday life and suffuse our perceptions, social interactions and material practices effect a fundamental reconfiguration of the notion of the self. Crucially, for Braidotti, this poses the opportunity for a different conceptualization of sexual difference and bodily materialism.

Materiality is also a key concern for N. Katherine Hayles in her examinations of science, technology and culture. In her study *How We Became Posthuman* (1999) Hayles explores the tendency to erase embodiment in twentieth-century technological advances in cybernetics, artificial intelligence and artificial life, and argues for the importance of retrieving embodiment and recognizing it as fundamental to the contemporary position of human–machine interactions. Hayles's analysis of the consequences of the erasure of embodiment and emphasis on the specific material properties of media and information technologies is particularly useful in thinking about late twentieth-century literature and culture.

Hayles is also very interested in the contemporary media ecology and what she sees as the dynamic interrelations of this ecology. Here too materiality features strongly, but in a specific sense as 'a selective focus on certain physical aspects of an instantiated text that are foregrounded by a work's construction, operation, and content' (Gitelman and Hayles 2002: np). Literature and social relations exist increasingly in an electronic realm, but for Hayles this provides an opportunity to fully acknowledge the physical and material aspects of textuality and meaning-making. The computer screen produces what she terms a 'flickering signifier', that is, not the flat and static mark of the semiotic signifier but a lively and multilevel signifier produced by a scanning electron beam and activated by the layered computer code used to create the screen text-image. The multiplicity of language thereby becomes a material effect of an instantiated text, of bodies engaging with bodies. Hayles shows how texts have bodies just as readers/users have bodies, and argues that it is not a case of an abstract, intellectual connection with disembodied verbal constructs but of a reader's physical, active, proprioceptive engagement with an instantiated text. What Hayles, Haraway and Braidotti present, then, is a return to the body, a body conflicted, reconfigured and far from being the organic repository of a unqiue, differentiated consciousnes, but a body nonetheless which has, in the presence of technology, a meaningful role and a politics that must be recognized. Their analyses highlight that, however important a proper focus on the technical components of communication and information systems are, it is vital to reconfigure rather than negate the nature of the human and human autonomy in our theorizations of technology.

3 Media Technologies and Modern Culture

Well before Marshall McLuhan's 1964 vision of an electric age of 'pure information', the electrical technologies of the early twentieth century were beginning to transform not just the spaces of work and engineering, but the spaces of leisure and media. Examining the cultural terrain of the 1900s and 1910s, it is possible to see the importance of electricity to the newly developing leisure industries – industries that were responding to the demand for cheap entertainment by the growing, urban working classes of the period. Electricity was fundamental to the visions of progress offered at the various World's Fairs at the turn of the twentieth century, many of which had pavilions devoted to electricity (the 1904 Louisiana Purchase Exposition had a 'Palace of Electricity', for example). But these impressive monuments to progress were also intended to amuse and divert, and the thousands of light bulbs illuminating the World's Fairs in Europe and America were part of a continuum of displays that included many electric-powered pleasure rides. Beyond the World's Fairs, the new amusement parks of the twentieth century revealed the extent to which electrical technology was producing new possibilities of play, as well as production. The bodies inserted into these processes of play were introduced to novel perspectives and the innovative world of technological leisure, and the media modes and machines that delineated it informed the innovations of modernist literature on both formal and thematic grounds. What emerged were new kinds of texts that took the perspectives deriving from media forms as inspiration for their experiments in perspective, narrative and structure. The new electrical technologies of entertainment and leisure were not devoid of political impact and this led, in turn, to literary explorations of the power and politics of specific technological forms.

The rise of electric leisure is encapsulated by Coney Island, on the southernmost point of Brooklyn, New York. The resort reflected both the refined and less salubrious forms of leisure open to the late nineteenth-century American, with piers, hotels, bathing-houses, restaurants, booths, hawkers and the odd freak show. The first railroad had reached the middle of the island in 1865 and in 1876 a 300-foot tower, the centrepiece of the Centennial Celebration in Philadelphia, was assembled in the middle of Coney Island, the first of many pieces of technological flotsam from World's Fairs and Exhibitions to end up there. With the completion of the Brooklyn Bridge in 1883, it was easier for the working people of Manhattan to travel out to Coney Island for their leisure. In 1890, the introduction of electricity meant that lights were placed along the beachfront to enable night-time 'Electric Bathing'. With this coming of electricity, Coney Island functioned as a transformation of nature into spectacular leisure, embedded in the techno-logical innovations of the modern age.

With the establishment of huge amusement parks – Steeplechase Park (opened 1897), Luna Park (opened 1903) and Dreamland (opened 1904, destroyed by fire in 1911) – Coney Island attracted tens of thousands of visi-tors daily, with an estimated 20 million visitors in the 1909 season. Coney Island's attractions were subject to continuous innovation, with new roller coasters, toboggan rides, water chutes and scenic railways added every season alongside the freak shows, nickelodeons, cycloramas, beer gardens and dancing pavilions. Technological spectaculars, re-enacting naval battles, floods, tenement fires, and even Heaven and Hell, were a key feature of the amusement parks, as were other technological oddities, such as the Ajeeb 'Turk' chess-playing automaton.[1] Luna Park itself, a spectacle of decorative, oriental turrets and facades, was illuminated by 250,000 light bulbs at night. This was technology as amusement and diversion, play and pleasure, rather than efficient function and production, what Rem Koolhaas calls 'Fantastic Technology' (Koolhaas 1994).

The interactions between Coney Island and Manhattan, between the leisure space of fantastic technology and the supposed rational space of prag-matic technology, are complex and reveal the central place of electric leisure in the new metropolises of the twentieth century. Coney Island is not the controlled overflow of the productive machines of Manhattan, but rather the testing ground for ideas of modernity and the urban as an artificial zone of production and consumption. As Koolhaas writes, 'The paraphernalia of illusion that have . . . subverted Coney Island's nature into an artificial para-dise – electricity, air-conditioning, tubes, telegraphs, tracks and elevators – reappear in Manhattan as paraphernalia of efficiency to convert raw space into office suites' (87).

The electric leisure that is illustrated by the rides, attractions and spectacles of Coney Island reveals the centrality of a carnivalesque element to the technologies of the early twentieth century. This electric leisure also enabled a reconfiguration of gender and class behaviour. As Ellen Wiley Todd describes, young immigrant women found in 'new forms of commercialized leisure' ways of expanding 'the traditional boundaries of permissible hetero-sexual interaction':

Brightly lit dance halls, amusement parks, nickelodeons and later movie houses opened them up to a stimulating, often erotic, world of pleasure. New dances demanded sensuous bodily movement or physical closeness. Darkened theaters encouraged kissing and petting. Mechanized rides at Coney Island flung couples together or exposed women's bodies to eager male bystanders. (1993: 3)[2]

Electric leisure thus posed the possibility of transforming the (gendered) individual and her relationships with others. The transformation of leisure and of the relationship between peoples was not confined to a space of popular or mass culture, however, and many modernist writers and artists were profoundly interested in electricity and new machines. Moreover, what the innovative media technologies of the first decades of the twentieth century – cinema and radio – offered were new ways of perceiving the world and a new terrain for the literary to inhabit.

MODERNISM AND THE CINEMA EYE

The link between technology, leisure and movement is a profound one at the beginning of the twentieth century. The naming of films as 'moving-pictures' highlights what critics have identified in the birth of cinema: a close parallel to the new modes of perception that had already been produced by the technologies of railway travel (as explored by both Wolfgang Schivelbusch and Lynne Kirby). It is hardly an accident that, when cinema was publicly premiered by the Lumière brothers on 28 December 1895, in Paris with their new Cinématographe, it involved a showing of *Arrival of a Train at La Ciotat Station*. The (probably apocryphal) story of the first audiences fleeing in fear highlights nonetheless the connections between train travel, speed, visibility and technological anxiety that were made at the time and which continue to resonate.

While the Lumières and others were working in Europe, Edison in American was also developing his own moving-picture device, the Kinetoscope, then adapted as the Vitascope, and over the next ten years films were made and projected across the Western world by a variety of entrepreneurs and companies. These early films were not concerned with narrative: the main draw of early film was its sheer visibility – being able to see real things and people moving in front of you on the screen was the thrill for the first audiences. Tom Gunning's useful phrase for this period in film is the 'cinema of attractions' (see Gunning 1986, 1989b). Combined with this was the experience, of many early film audiences, of seeing themselves or people they recognized, or places and events they knew, in the so-called 'actualities' – the cinematograph was, of course, a camera as well as a projector, and screenings usually involved the showing of films shot earlier that day or week in the location of the screening.

The 'magical' element of early film must also be recognized, with many early film-makers (Georges Méliès most prominently) moving from stage magic to film-making – using film to create fantastical transformations and imagine futuristic journeys. The early genre of chase films (from *Stop Thief!* by James Williamson, 1901 onwards) became popular and these were enhanced by the use of multishot filming, pioneered in pieces such as Edwin Porter's *The Life of an American Fireman* (1903). Thus, in later chase films, the innovative idea of jump-cut editing increased the narrative tension of the story. The centrality of narrative to film-making emerged slowly, and by the 1910s mainstream cinema had become enthralled to narrative conventions and film production protocols. D. W. Griffith is usually seen as an important figure in the move towards narrative cinema: his *The Birth of a Nation* from 1915 is acknowledged as the first feature-length film at more than three hours' running time. The dominance of narrative continuity and intelligibility in films, from about 1908 onwards, coincides with an interest in film versions of the classics like Dickens and Shakespeare, but avant-garde cinema, especially in the 1920s, continued to experiment with non-narrative cinema. Soviet cinema of the same period, dominated by Sergei Eisenstein, led the cinematic world in the use of innovative techniques such as montage editing.

Cinema in its early years was part of the fledgling leisure industry geared towards the growing urban classes. Although the early audiences for the Lumière showings, for example, were distinctly middle class, by the 1900s cinema was widely perceived as a proletarian entertainment, with vaudeville theatres and music halls putting on film shows as part of their entertainment bills. The first Nickelodeon (a building converted especially for showing films) was opened in Pittsburgh in 1905, and in Britain film theatres began to open from 1907 onwards (see Christie 1994: 52–5). By 1912, with the opening of the first Picture Palace (the Gaumont Palace in Paris), cinema had been established as its own distinct form of spectacular mass entertainment.

Along with the growth of the cinema came the growth of cinema literature, both the popular film magazines which, from 1911 onwards, contributed to the cultivation of cinema celebrity (see Shail 2006), and the various forms of film criticism and theory that took over from the oral 'lecture' that accompanied many early film shows (see Marcus 2007: chapter 4). Writers such as H. G. Wells were deeply engaged with the new medium and not just in terms of the early attempts to screen his stories and his own writing for the screen, but through the 'sheer ingenuity and range of optical speculations' in his work and 'their refraction of the manifold political, social and cultural implications of the cinema' (Williams 2007: 179). Cinema has an impact on many modernists; Ezra Pound was a regular cinema-goer and shared this enthusiasm with many of his contemporaries. Gertrude Stein was a fan of Charlie Chaplin, writing of her meeting with him in America in *Everybody's Autobiography* (1937) and, according to Susan McCabe, associating her poetry with his 'bodily semiotics' (2005: 58), while Hart Crane's poem 'Chaplinesque' (1921) celebrates the vagabondage of Chaplin's comic persona. Katherine Mansfield and Dorothy Richardson write of cinemagoing in their fiction, with Richardson making a regular contribution to the film journal *Close-Up*, edited by Kenneth MacPherson, Bryher and H.D.

from 1927 to 1933. James Joyce, famously, was centrally involved in a doomed enterprise to set up the first cinema in Dublin, the Volta, in 1909 (which failed after six months) and met with Sergei Eisenstein in Paris in 1929 (Joyce felt Eisenstein was one of the few directors who could film *Ulysses*). Samuel Beckett planned to study screen writing with Eisenstein, and there is a whole range of American writers who wrote (successfully or otherwise) for Hollywood (F. Scott Fitzgerald, William Faulkner, John Steinbeck). On the other side, D. H. Lawrence deplored the cinema (along with Jazz and Flapper fashions), and Aldous Huxley imagined a dystopian society doped by a multisensory version of Hollywood films ('Feelies') in *Brave New World* (1932). T. S. Eliot was a fan of the music hall, but not so keen on cinema – there is a real sense that his savage critique of the homogenization of the urban lower middle classes in *The Waste Land* (especially in the 'Fire Sermon' section) is coloured by a sense of the passivity and mechanical response elicited by popular cinema (and a 'sweating' rabble that 'sees on the screen' appears in the manuscript of the poem (see Trotter 2007: 146)). The cinema, as subject matter, features in literature almost from the moment of its emergence, but seems always to provoke questions about the status of the subject in, or as a viewer of, this technological media.

In 1904, Rudyard Kipling published a collection of stories, *Traffics and Discoveries*, that included tales of imperial exploits, some set during the Boer War, and tales that consider the most significant new technologies of the time – electric power, the car and the radio. *Traffics and Discoveries* also reflects on the cinema. In 'Mrs Bathurst', Kipling writes of a naval warrant officer called Vickery who, while on leave in Cape Town, goes to see a cinematograph show 'Home and Friends for a Tickey [threepence]'. In the 'actualities', he recognizes a woman from his past (the 'Mrs Bathurst' of the title) and compulsively returns to the film show again and again. We are told of his later disappearance and that his body, and that of a companion, have been found up country, burnt black by lightning. This is not the first story to reflect on the power of the new cinematograph films, which had by its publication been around for nearly a decade, but it is a story that captures some of the uncanny aspects of cinema and as such has captured the imagination of many recent commentators. In a range of studies (Christie 1994; Daly 2004; Trotter 2007; Marcus 2007), 'Mrs Bathurst' stands as an exemplary exploration of many of the dynamics of, and questions raised by, early cinema. Vickery's obsession with the cinema image of Mrs Bathurst walking out of the frame suggests something of the uncanny power of this media to suspend the agency of the viewer and to bind them to the absent-presence of the image. Mrs Bathurst functions as a metonym for the compulsive attraction of the cinema itself and the blank, unseeing eye of the cinema screen. The 'blindish way she had o' lookin' (Kipling 1904: 276) precedes her manifestation on screen: 'she looked out straight at us with that blindish look which Pritch alluded to. She walked on and on till she melted out of the Picture' (279), and she is compulsively repeated every evening at the same time in the film showing. Mrs Bathurst's repetitive 'blindish' looking offers us the blank, indiscriminateness and infinite repeatability of camera technology, while Vickery is presented as artificial and automatic, a product and a victim of the technological, from his ceaselessly clicking false teeth (his nickname is 'Click': 273), to his immersion in the image, to the electricity that destroys him. The questions about the power of the cinema raised by Kipling's story, its transformation of the cinematic subject (on the screen or in the audience) to a compulsive automaton and the indiscriminate 'blind' eye of the camera resonate though texts written in the first decades of cinema.

What can be seen in Kipling's story, and in the wider responses to cinema in the literature of the early twentieth century, is that this new visual technology instigated a series of questions that impacted on both the form and the themes of literature. A disrupted sense of a coherent bodily self, an experience of discontinuity, fragmentation, movement and rupture, a sense of mechanical transformation or mechanical enslavement, and an uneasy awareness of the interplay of absence and presence were among the effects of cinema. For the writers of twentieth-century modernism, these effects were embedded in the somatic experience of early twentieth-century life and provoked many writers to reconsider the status of their literary undertakings.

In 1926, while writing *To The Lighthouse*, Virginia Woolf formulated her own impressions of cinema in the article 'The Cinema'. In this article, published in the New York magazine *Arts* in June 1926, and the *Nation and Athenauem* in July, Woolf comments on documentary and actuality film, mainstream narrative film and avant-garde film. Woolf is less than complimentary about cinema in its current state, but she reflects on the curious absent-presence of cinema – the effect of seeing things 'as they are when we are not there' (1926: 55) – on the prospect of cinematic representation as a condensed language of images, and on the possibility of cinema representing the chaos of the modern world which, for Woolf, is embodied in the city street. This essay, one of Woolf's few published writings that discuss cinema, is deeply interesting for what it resists and for what it predicts for cinema. 'The Cinema' opens with an image of savagery, of 'bright-eyed, naked men who knocked two bars of iron together', and highlights the chaos of the contemporary world that cinema captures: 'a cauldron in which fragments of all shapes and savours seem to simmer' (54). Woolf goes on to identify a 'simple' art of the cinema – the direct reproduction of events – which requires no effort from the viewer. However, she also points to the 'difficulties' that cinema poses to the 'eye' – the effect of cinema in offering, in the presentation of 'real life', 'a different reality from that we perceive in daily life'. In this, for Woolf, 'We see life as it is when we have no part in it', a 'beauty' that 'will continue . . . whether we behold it or not' (55). This distance of spectator from cinematic reality is key to the potential that Woolf sees in cinema, a questioning of the nature of perception and the relationship between the perceiving consciousness and the external world.

In 'The Cinema', Woolf is keen to reject narrative cinema, particularly the filmic adaptation of the classics which, for her, translate literary complexity into symbolic shorthand: 'A kiss is love. A broken cup jealousy' (56). Where Woolf sees the symbolic potential for cinema is in the accidental, the momentary 'unintentional' effect. The example she gives, of a 'shadow shaped like a tadpole' that appears in the corner of the screen, in a showing of the 1920 German Expressionist film *The Cabinet of Dr Caligari*, and 'quivered, bulged, and sank back again into nonentity', suggests the possibility that 'the cinema has within its grasp innumerable symbols for emotions that have so far failed to find expression' (56, 57). This protoplasmic entity, an accident in the screening, poses the nascency of an alternate realm of signification. The future for cinema, Woolf argues, might contain within it 'violent changes of emotion', 'collision', 'fantastic contrasts', 'speed', that at the moment are only realized in the dream workings of the unconscious mind (58). It is the city, for Woolf, that both embodies and suggests what the potential for cinema is, 'the chaos of the streets . . . when some momentary assembly of colour, sound, movement suggests that here is a scene waiting a new art to be transfixed' (58).

The connection between cinema and the city is not confined to Woolf; it runs across modernist literature and is an important aspect of Joyce's work as well: Laura Marcus points out that urban modernity is the structuring principle of the different 'city symphony' films of the period (Paul Strand and Charles Scheeler's *Manhatta*, 1920, Walter Ruttmann's *Berlin: Symphony of a Great City*, 1927, Dziga Vertov's *Man with a Movie Camera*, 1929). This highlights what Walter Benjamin also identifies in his 1939 essay, 'On Some Motifs in Baudelaire', as the continuity of the experience of the modern city with cinematic form. Benjamin points to the 'shocks' of the modern metropolis and modern technology, which have become the norm for the modern poet. He argues that the city and 'technology has subjected the human sensorium to a complex kind of training', while in film 'perception in the form of shocks was established as a formal principle' (1999: 171).

The correlation between the technologized urban space – such a central concern for modernist literature – and cinematic form indicates how it is possible to think about the parallel between literature and cinema during this period. In modernist literature, the fragment and the fragmentary have an important role: many would suggest that this is a reflection of the contemporary world. This modernist world is one no longer shored up by grand narratives and certainties, but one speeded up by the various new communication and travel technologies, a world epitomized by the experience of the city – discontinuous, anonymous, dynamic. But it is also one way of thinking about what cinema can do, and did do, in the work of Eisenstein and others (and the 'jump-cut' is not just a feature of avant-garde film but of popular film such as the chase sequence, and the form of montage used by D. W. Griffith). Thus, if modernist literature is dynamic and discontinuous, if it rejects temporal continuity or spatial continuity, if it works with the associational structure of mental processes rather than a Victorian idea of realism, if it presents a dissonance (within which emerge new unities), if it offers a truth composed of fragments – then it is working with the new formal possibilities suggested by cinema.

Contemporary commentators on both Joyce and Woolf identified a cinematographic aspect to their writing, and in Woolf's work this goes far beyond the evocation of a dynamic and multiple visual perspective on the modern city (as is experienced in the skywriting scene in *Mrs Dalloway*). Elaine Showalter describes this whole novel as 'very cinematic', pointing to Woolf's use of 'such devices as montage, close-ups, flashbacks, tracking shots, and rapid cuts in constructing a three-dimensional story' (Introduction, in Woolf 1925: xxi). Whether such an argument of analogy is valid (can Woolf's technique really be simplified as 'very cinematic'?), the idea that a different way of seeing related to a new idea of perception itself is certainly something that cinema offered to its early twentieth-century audiences. An emphasis on the scopic is prevalent in modernist literature, and particularly a sense of the precision of vision, enacted in the neutral camera eye and matched in modernist writing. What can also be seen, particularly in Woolf's writing, is an understanding of the links between the workings of cinema and dreamwork as exposed in the discourses of psychoanalysis. This is manifest as an attention to the gestural and incidental as potentially meaningful, and a cinematic sense of the trace of memory, always there in a filmic projection, which necessarily shows as real and present that which has passed in the moment of filming. Thus, in the 'Time Passes' section of *To The Lighthouse*, the empty house is precisely described as it decays with no human inhabitant or observer, and the lighthouse beam enters the house to project a shadow image of the dead Mrs Ramsey on the wall. In a contrasting section in *Orlando*, just after the protagonist has mused 'Time has passed over me' (1928: 190), she drives her car out of London. The city streets moving before and beside her, the 'real' in constant movement and flux, cannot be 'seen whole or read from start to finish'. This fluxional visual field is represented as the full and indiscriminate screen of the cinema and, instead of producing a trace of Orlando's self, creates an absolute depersonalization – 'a person entirely disassembled' until the continuous 'green screens' of the countryside mean she 'regained the illusion' of self-possession (192).

Reading recent analyses of the cinematic in Woolf, it is possible to see how criticism on cinema and modernism has moved on from the idea of simple formal correspondence, for example, from Alan Spiegel's ideas about the 'camera eye' in modernist fiction from Flaubert to Joyce (1976). Recent work on film, cinema and modernist literature has explored more detailed and nuanced ways of thinking about the formal and aesthetic contiguities between these two modes. Susan McCabe identifies 'cinematic possibilities for enacting new forms of embodiment' that are explored in a range of American modernist literature (2005: 17), taking 'Eisenstein's highly soma-tized theories of montage' (21) as a useful starting point for considering how cinema impacted on lived and inscripted bodies. Explorations of cinematic bodies and cinematic phenomenology can thus be unearthed in the work of H.D., Marianne Moore, Gertrude Stein and William Carlos Williams, all of whom acknowledged an interest in cinema. But, as McCabe also points out, there is an anxiety about (male) hysteria and fractured corporeality underlying the way that cinematic montage features in the work of Eliot and Pound. Their reaction to cinema – the 'dissociated male hysteric' – that McCabe reads in 'The Love Song of J. Alfred Prufrock', *The Waste Land* and 'Hugh Selwyn Mauberley' (15) – might also usefully be applied to John Rodker's *Adolphe 1920*. Rodker's sense of the cinema, in his poem 'London Night', is part of the fragmented, visceral speed of the modern city, which disrupts the agency of the individual: the 'clicking of the reel . . . | Flicker of light . . .' invades the watching audience who 'thrill to the rush and the clatter . . . and spatter | The night with our souls' (Rodker 1996: 19). In *Adolphe*, Rodker presents a concentrated stream-of-consciousness narration of one day in the life of the protagonist, Dick. Dick visits a carnival, fairground, bars and jazz cafes, and visual technologies are part of the intense, modern, mechanical world that invades his boundaries in a text that negates any distinction between interiority and the exterior world. As Andrew Crozier describes, the protagonist's 'identity is realised as if projected on a screen of liminal events' (in Rodker 1996: xx), where his viewing of mutoscopes (peepshows) and a film projected in a fairground booth produces a complete disorienta-tion of self and a 'sickly' 'wave of nausea' (Rodker 1996: 138).

In contrast to an hysterical disorientation of the body, David Trotter postulates a 'will-to-automatism' (2007: 10) provoked by the example of cinema which gave rise to modernist explorations of the 'neutrality of litera-ture . . . as a medium' (9). The 'impersonality' celebrated by writers as diverse as Joyce, Eliot and Katherine Mansfield could be linked to such a sense of the possibility, exemplified by film, to record existence in itself, the 'myriad impressions' of Woolf's 'Modern Fiction', making mimesis itself a theme, rather than merely an aim, of literature. Stewart Garrett (2000) points to the 'affiliations' between cinema and modernistic writing through what he terms the 'textual flicker' effect of modernism: that is, that the photogrammatic unit, whose presence is felt in early cinema and in avant-garde cinema, is aligned to the textuality of modernist writing, with its 'intervallic play' and 'detached mechanism' of style. This serves to highlight how the mechanism of cinema (the whirring projector) intrudes into the representation of the 'real' that it offers. This effect is reflected on even by Kipling's character Pyecroft, in 'Mrs Bathurst': 'You 'eard a little dynamo like buzzin', but the pictures were the real thing – alive an' movin' (1904: 276). Thus, the rep-resentational machine of cinema made certain writers more aware of the mechanisms of their own art, how the 'real thing – alive an' movin' that they were interested in writing about similarly depended on the dynamic processes of a linguistic machine.

Thinking further about the body-effects of cinema, Tim Armstrong's study (1998) describes how the technologization of the body in film parallels its technologization in other areas of culture, while Sarah Danius considers the internalization of technologies of cinema in modernist fiction, pointing to a 'closer relation between the sensuous and the technological' and to the 'new perceptual and epistemic realms' of modernist literature influenced by visual and aural technologies (2002: 2, 3). Danius points particularly to Thomas Mann, Marcel Proust and Joyce, but the idea of 'new perceptual domains' and the 'sensuous and technological' merging to produce new knowledges can be clearly seen in the work of less canonical, women modernists such as Mina Loy and H.D. H.D., who wrote eleven articles for the journal *Close Up*, acted in three films directed by Kenneth Macpherson and edited one of them with Bryher: the film *Borderline*, which featured Paul Robeson in the lead role. The connection between H.D.'s Imagist poetic and what she later celebrated as the classicism of (German and Russian) cinema can be located in what Laura Marcus describes as 'the interplay between an aesthetics of formal restraint and one of emotional spiritual or "psychic" transcendence' (Donald et al. 1998: 97). For H.D., it was cinematic 'vision', potentially both artistic and spiritual, that interested her, a vision that is mirrored in her own psychic experiences of 'the series of shadow – or of light-pictures . . . projected on the wall of a hotel bedroom in the Ionian Island of Corfu, at the end of April 1920' (H.D. 1974: 41). This 'writing on the wall' episode, as H.D. described it, appears to parallel the unobserved vision of Mrs Ramsey etched by light in *To The Lighthouse*, but for H.D. what was crucial about the cinema image was its potential to project the artist's mind in a kind of psychic mechanism of externalizing the inner subconscious. The porous borders between the psyche, the material body and the external world are what H.D. located in the technological disruptions of cinema. The subjectivity and play of the ambiguous (silent) image, the figuration of a desire in fragments of intense visual impression and sensuous experience, connect her idea of the beauty of cinema (very much associated with the pre-Hollywood Greta Garbo) with her poetry. In her 'Projector' poems (published in *Close Up* in 1927), the projector's light becomes Apollo in a new form, offering a revelation of illumination and a transformation and spiritual renewal:

> old forms dispersed
> take fresh
> shapes
> out of nothingness; ('Projector II', H.D. 1984: 355)[3]

The connection between cinema and psyche was crucial for H.D. and underpinned her sense of the hieroglyphics of silent cinema, a reworking of the Emersonian hieroglyph, which proffered the possibility of a universal language of symbol (in the way that Woolf suggests at the end of 'The Cinema'). Sergei Eisenstein explored the hieroglyphics of cinema and their correlation to Imagist poetics in his 1929 essay 'The Cinematographic Principle and the Ideogram'. For H.D., as for many of her modernist contemporaries, the advent of sound with the 'talkies' in 1927 spelt the end of the aesthetic possibilities of cinema.

Cinema precipitated widespread examinations of the status of human perception and sense data; its direct account of life exceeded the possibility of literary mimesis and thereby challenged the status of literature itself. The impact of the cinema on the work of Joyce has been an abiding concern in critical accounts. Alan Spiegel's early study on cinema and modernism focused on Joyce as exemplar of a modernist 'camera eye' in fiction for obvious reasons. Joyce's Cinema Volta enterprise and his 1929 meeting with Eisenstein are biographical proximities to the new form, but the term 'montage' has repeatedly been used to describe the disruptive form and scopic intensity of *Ulysses*. The rapid succession of visual impressions in *Ulysses*, read in terms of montage, sheds light on the way this text creates meaning, not through the imposition of a central perceiving consciousness, but through the juxtaposition and repetition of events, sense data and motifs. The potential formal analogies between *Ulysses* and cinema reveal how this text, along similar lines to Woolf's novels, explores the status of mechanical representation – the perception of the world without a self. What is often termed the 'polyvisual' aspects of Joyce's writing appear crucially informed by his cinema viewing (see Williams 2003: 96). Joyce's experience of a huge range of film forms – documentaries, slapstick comedy, biblical spectaculars, trickfilms – is evidenced by the films shown at his Cinema Volta in Dublin in 1909–10 (see Williams 2003: 97), and by his reference to a saucy 1897 coin-operated peephole show (a Mutoscope), 'Willie's Hat', in the 'Nausicaa' episode of *Ulysses* (see Marcus 2007: 95). The cinema for Joyce was interesting precisely because of its mass appeal, as well as for the questions it raised about language and perception.

Ulysses uses many techniques more usually found in early film (magical transformations, objects seeming alive, especially but not only, in the 'Circe' section) and other more general visual and formal strategies that parallel those in cinema. As well as montage, visual detail appears in extreme close-up with an atomized focus on individual elements: Karen Lawrence describes details in *Ulysses* 'documented with such precision that they are almost unrecognisable' (1981: 187). Joyce seems to parody the jump-cut techniques of the chase film in the 'Wandering Rocks' section, creating, as Andrew Shail suggests, a simultaneous present of twenty-nine different streams of action (2008). The ubiquitous presence of telephone, telegraph, photography, electric lighting, phonography, advertising, journalism, cartoons and music halls in *Ulysses*, and the text's deep concern with the place of this technology in the world and the experience of the early twentieth-century city, signals this text's immersion in the technological mass media of the early twentieth century. Donald Theall explains how 'communication technology, machines and the machine-like processes of old and new forms of everyday culture pervade the action [of *Ulysses*] . . . Joyce is producing the counter-epic of the new culture of time and space – those changed and changing relationships between space, time, speed, distance, control, and electro-mechanics – that emerged during the first decades of the twentieth century' (1997: 40). It is the very conception of the semiotic field in *Ulysses* that engages with media technology, participating in a 'new communicative cosmos' in which the kinetic and the gestural figure as central parts of the semiotic field (Theall 1997: 188). Meaning comes from everywhere and is centred nowhere: Joyce's later work, *Finnegans Wake*, was even more profoundly to encompass emerging mass media and popular culture. What the work of Joyce and his contemporaries demonstrate is how profoundly literature has been altered by media and entertainment technologies.

As the nation at the heart of the machine-age, and the site of the world's first parks of electric amusement and the corporatization of cinema in Hollywood, America offers a particularly intense experience of the effects of technological media and leisure on human perception. The work of Ernest Hemingway demonstrates the effect of electric communication on one form of American modernist writing. Hemingway's direct, abrupt style, matching the directness of the material it narrates, can be read as the product of his first journalistic experience on the *Kansas City Star*, where he was subject to the restrictions of telegraph communication as he wrote police and emergency-room reports.[4] In terms of cinema, however, it is the fiction of John Dos Passos that most obviously engages with the 'Camera Eye' – the name of one of the four types of sections that make up his trilogy *U.S.A.* (1938), alongside the fictional narrative, biographies of key Americans and the documentary-montage 'Newsreel' sections. Visuality is fundamentally important for Dos Passos – he studied art and continued to paint and draw through his writing career – but he is specifically attuned to the explosion of technological visual culture in America (including printed advertising, film, billboards, posters and neon signs). What Dos Passos perceives, and what he represents in texts from *Manhattan Transfer* onwards, is the 'newly industrialized and commercialized visuality' of modern culture (North 2004: 141), what he describes as Americans' shift 'from being a wordminded people [to] becoming an eyeminded people' (Dos Passos 1936: 105). That this shift is connected to both a liberation of perspective and a debasement of human relations can be seen at the beginning of two contrasting chapters of *Manhattan Transfer*. The prefatory paragraph of 'Five Statutory Questions' uses a Coney Island roller coaster as the vehicle for a mechanical montage of perspectives, while the opening of the 'Nickelodeon' presents an automated, commercial culture of sexuality that has its roots in the peepshow 'stereopticons' that pre-dated cinema.

His sense of 'eyemindedness' underpins Dos Passos's montage method in *Manhattan Transfer* and later texts: Dos Passos retrospectively attributes this method directly to cinematic influences, writing: 'Somewhere along the way I had been impressed by Eisenstein's motion pictures, by his version of old D. W. Griffith's technique: Montage was his key term' (1968). But an adoption of cinematic methods in his writing in the 1930s and 1940s does not mean Dos Passos was blind to the functioning of the Hollywood star system, so criticized by Horkheimer and Adorno, or to the central role that cinema took in interpellating an audience into the structures of capitalism and constructing them as a mass of consumers. The work of Dos Passos illustrates how writers who explored or embraced the revelations of cinematic seeing, and its dispersal of the centrality of the individual perceiving consciousness, could also fully acknowledge the political questions raised by this media technology. This acknowledgement, in turn, points out that such technologies are socially embedded: mechanical equipment cannot produce discrete singular consequences but is inevitably caught up in the networks of power and effect that constitute human society. In the narrative of the rise to fame of Margo Dowling, in the *The Big Money* volume of *U.S.A.*, Dos Passos's criticism of Hollywood is explicit: Margo's fame comes at the cost of her integrity and honesty, and epitomizes the fragmentation and alienation of modern consumer capitalism (see Juncker 1990). Dos Passos appears foremost in an American modernist utilization of the new knowledges and formal possibilities produced by the 'camera eye', while remaining critical of the politics of modern media. Like Joyce's, his texts cannot exist without the technological mass media of the early twentieth century but do not cede ethical or political authority to the mass, networked power of such media. The awareness of the political and ideological impact of media technology that is apparent in Dos Passos's writing became crucial for the writers who engaged with and explored the technology that would bring culture, commentary and world events into their own homes: radio.

TALKING ACROSS DISTANCES: RADIO MODERNISM

If cinema technology had the potential to abolish individuality and draw its audience into an undifferentiated, consuming mass, then the history of radio shows its potential to create a different sense of commonality between its audience who listened in from multiple geographic points. Like cinema, however, radio offered a new way of experiencing the world and reflecting on the nature of sense data and, as a result, it gave other opportunities for writers exploring the modern world through the technologies that characterized it. Nevertheless, the demagogic power of radio broadcast and the sweeping reach of the radio network concerned many writers of the early twentieth century and influenced how and why they wrote about radio.

Radio technology developed at the same time as cinema and film technology, but it was initially confined solely to functional communication between two points; its role as a mass, affordable, broadcast media only developed after the First World War when it quickly became ubiquitous. As the BBC's first Director of Talks, Hilda Matheson, wrote in 1933, 'the general public is rapidly becoming synonymous with the wireless public' (207). Guglielmo Marconi successfully sent and received the first radio signal in the same year that the Lumière brothers premiered their Cinématographe, then transmitted across the English Channel in 1899, sending the first trans-atlantic radio telegraph message in 1902.[5]

Radio's difference from cinema stems from the common ground they share: the production of a technologically mediated and reproduced reality. But if cinema reproduces a reality perceived visually, radio is fundamentally a blind and invisible medium, offering only the physical experience of mechanically produced vibrations; a sound whose origin lies outside the mechanism receiving it as electromagnetic waves and then transforming it into resonance. This is the uncanny talking across distances that Kipling explores in his story 'Wireless', a communication through the ether which, in Kipling's story certainly, implies the potential to traverse time as well as space, to affect the consciousness of the receiving subject and disrupt their boundaries. The perceptual psychologist and film theorist Rudolf Arnheim described this as 'the overlapping of frontiers, the conquest of spatial isola-tion' (1936: 13). To this ability to draw geographically disparate individuals together, crossing distances and borders, can be attributed both the popularity of and anxiety about radio. As Michele Hilmes puts it, in the early twentieth century, 'Utopian predictions for radio as a unifying and culturally uplifting medium collide with dystopian fears surrounding its unique ability to tran-scend traditional boundaries of time and space, and the social distinctions that these boundaries maintained' (1997: xvii).

Radio telephony was perfected during the 1914–18 war and its immediate aftermath. Alongside the continued official communication use of radio after 1918, increasing numbers of amateurs constructed and experimented with their own transmitters and receivers. Broadcast radio emerged from the incidental actions of these amateurs and engineers: most commentators offer Dr Frank Conrad, an engineer at the Westinghouse Pittsburgh plant, who began leaving a phonograph playing in front of the microphone while adjust-ing the transmitter in his garage in 1920, as the catalyst for radio as a new form of media. Radio-set owners who picked up his signal began writing in requests and, by November, a radio station, KDKA, in Pittsburgh had begun a regular transmission, opening with a broadcast of the 1920 presi-dential election results. It is clear, though, as Tim Crook points out, that 'radio services were being broadcast in other parts of America before the KDKA election results' and an American entrepreneur, Lee De Forest, had broadcast election returns in 1916 (1998: 59, 60). In the USA, twenty-five radio stations were licensed in 1921, and more than 600 just a year later, with radio stations based in radio and electrical manufacturers and dealers, newspapers and publishers, schools and colleges, department stores, and other commercial and retail businesses. Unlike the development of radio in Europe, the American constitutional commitment to free speech and the ruthlessly market-driven economy underpinned the rapid expansion of radio stations, services and networks in conjunction with commercial interests. As public broadcasters were sidelined and the new national networks of the National Broadcasting Company (NBC) and Colombia Broadcasting System (CBS) were established (in 1926 and 1928 respectively), the airwaves were filled predominantly with popular music and discussion, with comedy and dramatic narratives coming to prominence in the 1930s.

In Britain, entertainment radio had already been premiered in an experimental Marconi broadcast of the soprano Dame Nellie Melba in June 1920. In October 1922, the British Broadcasting Company was established and began broadcasting, under John Reith as General Manager, in November: it would become the British Broadcasting Corporation (severing links with radio manufacturing) in January 1927. The reach of the BBC service expanded over the early 1920s with new transmitters and relay transmitters, and, by 1924, 70 per cent of the British population could receive the signal, rising to 85 per cent in 1925 (Geddes and Bussey 1991: 14). By 1939, radio had reached near saturation in Britain and during the Second World War, as was the case across Europe and America, there was a great expansion of the radio industry for war purposes and a concerted effort to utilize the propaganda potential of this, almost universal, media.

The impact of radio technology on literature has not received the kind of intensive critical examination that has been practised on the interactions between literature and cinema. The 'wireless' technology of radio provoked a range of interesting speculations and innovations in writing by such diverse figures as Kipling, Henry James, F. T. Marinetti and Pound, but the extent to which modernism can be read through the effects of radio is only beginning to be unearthed (see Avery 2006; Cohen, Coyle and Lewty 2009). Radio functions to transform notions of spatiality; it enables sound to reach across and through diverse populations, carrying specific ideas about culture with it, what Rudolf Arnheim described in 1936 as 'the importation of culture on the waves of the ether . . . sound in silence' (14). As with cinema, radio suggested itself as a technological medium for existing forms of literature, and thus literary adaptations featured early on with the BBC broadcasting readings from Shakespeare in 1923. But, unlike cinema, as an aural medium it was also eminently suited to becoming the channel for what were otherwise diverse forms of media: news reports, music (popular and highbrow), discussion, sports commentary, variety, comedy and, in the later 1920s and 1930s, serials and soaps. Under Reith's directorship, the BBC cultivated a firmly middlebrow cultural content, assiduously avoiding what was seen as the vulgarizing effect of American popular culture (but still airing some US imports such as the incredibly successful 'minstrel' serial *Amos 'n' Andy*). Within the general radio milieu of voice and music, the development of radiogenic writing – a literary form to which radio technology was intrinsic – did not seem inevitable. The first British radiogenic production, that is, a drama written and performed specifically for the radio, was Richard Hughes's *A Comedy of Danger* (January 1924), set at the bottom of a coal mine. The opening line, 'The lights have gone out', explicitly articulates and make dramatic use of the basic feature of radio drama, its blindness, rather than trying to compensate for a missing optical world.

Subsequent writers for the BBC evolved their radio drama with the technology available to them. Lance Sieveking's experimental morality play, *The First Kaleidoscope* (September 1928), utilized a 'dramatic control panel' that could use sounds from different studios, fading them in and out. Sieveking was followed by Tyrone Guthrie with *The Squirrel's Cage* (1929) and *The Flowers Are Not For You to Pick* (1930), which explored what Guthrie described as the 'symphonic possibilities of the medium' (cited Crook 1999: 204). As John Drakakis indicates, both Sieveking and Guthrie expressed the techniques of radiogenic texts 'through analogies to cinematic superimposition, fluidity and cross-fading' (1981: 22). But this is not to assert that radio drama functioned solely as the poor alternative to visual media. Writing in 1936, Arnheim pointed out the unusual spatial properties of radio, not available to media optics:

Wireless, unlike the film, does not force what is simultaneous into the narrow, compulsory limits of the screen, but even the mere simultaneity brings about a close contact in the acoustic sphere, because there the individual things do not lie *beside* and separate from each other as in visual space, but *overlay* each other completely (121).

This highlights what John Drakakis regards as the fundamental feature of radio drama, its creation of a synthetic reality which can foreground the constructedness of the human apperception of the world:

A radio play, by its very nature, cannot present an analogue of experience in the same way that, for example, a photographic image can. Hence its imagery must be rhetorical rather than simply iconic. This means that just as the structure of a radio play is man-made, so it refers to other structures of experience outside itself which are also the products of the human mind. (Drakakis 1981: 29–30)

For theorists and historians, radio played a crucial role in the creation of communities, especially national communities, out of disparate and separated peoples and in disseminating a shared form of culture. In this, the technology of radio itself does not function to dehumanize or mechanize culture; indeed, radio is not necessarily seen as a machine itself. For Hilda Matheson, radio is not a technology so much as a global network:

Broadcasting is not strictly speaking another machine; it makes use of apparatus . . . but fundamentally it is a harnessing of elemental forces, a capturing of sounds and voice all over the world to which hitherto we have been deaf. It is a means of enlarging the frontiers of human interest and consciousness, of widening personal experience, of shrinking the earth's surface. (1933: 14)

Indeed, it seems obvious to take radio as the prime example of a universal techno-scientific network, drawing the world closer, only now being surpassed by the Internet. But, for Marshall McLuhan, the effect of radio is to fragment rather than consolidate. In his analysis of electric media, McLuhan identifies radio as a 'hot medium', 'one that extends a single sense in "high definition"' (1964a: 24). In his analysis this means, not that the radio audience is compelled to complete a missing visual picture, but that such 'hot' media 'do not leave so much to be filled in or completed by the audience' (25). The 'intensity' of radio (as hot media) means 'specialism and fragmentation', according to McLuhan (rather than participation and community), and necessitates a 'cooling off' in its audience (what McLuhan describes as a 'somnambulism') in order to cope with the shocks of the intense, hot, new media (25, 26). But the shock of radio may not be solely due to its intensification of a single sense; what is also shocking about radio is its promiscuity with signification and identity. The possibilities of passing and masquerading in radio were extensive as 'radio's ability to escape visual overdetermination had the potential to set off a virtual riot of social signifiers' (Hilmes 1997: 20). Radio translates all possible communication into one mode, thereby releasing a plenitude of potential signification that contributes to what Toby Miller describes as 'its promiscuous social tourism' (1992: np).

The centrality of radio to early twentieth-century British culture is illustrated by the range of literary and artistic figures appearing on the BBC as broadcasters and writers for radio, particularly figures associated with the Bloomsbury group. So Leonard and Virginia Woolf, E. M. Forster, Clive Bell, Harold Nicholson, Vita Sackville-West, Roger Fry and J. B. Priestley all appeared on the BBC through the 1920s and 1930s (see Whitehead 1990 and Avery 2006 for details). Kate Whitehead argues for the importance of the Bloomsbury radio appearances in consolidating the whole notion of the 'Bloomsbury group' as a cohesive social-artistic group and in generating a 'new radio genre', 'the radio chat show' (1990: 121). But it was more than conversation that the Bloomsbury group offered in their radio appearances; much of the broadcasting by Leonard Woolf, for example, took the form of radio essays on culture and politics, while E. M. Forster, who first broadcast in 1928, took radio as an occasion to realize his epigraph in *Howard's End* 'only connect' and 'saw radio as an excellent opportunity to speak his convictions about freedom' (Avery 2006: 61). Radio was not just a medium, therefore, but a way of understanding and creating an audience and an idea of culture and ethics: Todd Avery argues that it was through their 'negotiations of radio as the first modernist vernacular' that the ethical ideas of specific British writers emerged (9).

H. G. Wells and T. S. Eliot also came to be important radio figures, Wells more so for the radio adaptations of his texts. As Avery describes, Wells only appeared on radio eight times, but radio was crucial in the future worlds his science-fiction stories imagined (*The First Men on the Moon*, 1901, for example) and forty adaptations of his texts appeared on the BBC between

1926 and 1946 (Avery 2006: 84–92). Eliot's work also appeared on radio – D. G. Bridson produced a radio performance of *The Waste Land* in 1937 – but it was as radio broadcaster that Eliot's engagement with radio is most important. Eliot made eighty-one broadcasts (poetry readings and cultural talks) over a thirty-year period (for details, see Coyle 2001b), through which he developed and advanced his ideas about culture. His first radio broadcasts in 1929 were on seventeenth-century English literature, demonstrating how Eliot was working through this medium as he shaped a dramatic aesthetic fundamentally indebted to the Renaissance. For David Coyle, Eliot's radio broadcasts 'sought to appropriate the very voice of mass culture to speak against its most characteristic impulses' (2001a: 146): for Eliot, radio was 'an essentially *oral* medium, capable of phatic and even fatidic speech' (144). Eliot shared this idea with W. B. Yeats whose ten broadcasts on the BBC between 1931 and 1937 – reading poetry both unpublished and well known – were motivated by a sense that the new technology of the broadcast medium could rekindle the oral art of poetry. The radio could thus have a redemptive and restorative power; electric media could give a wider audience access to what might otherwise be elite cultural values. What Eliot's work with radio demonstrates is how far British modernism was culturally constructed through this new broadcast medium.

For many 1930s writers, mass media was an ambiguous factor in contemporary society: radio (and other forms such as popular cinema and journalism) was inextricable from the technological, capitalist society that had produced it. Such mass media had a dangerous homogenizing power, but also challenged many leftist writers and their aesthetic through its wide audience reach. Throughout the work of Auden, Christopher Isherwood, Louis MacNeice, George Orwell and Graham Greene, there is an anxiety about radio, what Keith Williams terms 'literary anxieties about wireless "monoglossia" and propagandism' (1996: 63), necessarily amplified by the central role of radio in American mass culture and in promulgating and reinforcing fascist hegemony in Italy and Germany. Radio broadcasting was born in Italy under the fascist regime of Mussolini, and in Germany the 'art of the radio' was applied to light entertainment as well as direct propaganda to bind the German people more firmly into a 'National Family' (see Bathrick 1997). But many of the 1930s writers anxious about radio also worked with mass media: Aldous Huxley, Isherwood and Greene were all involved with movie adaptations or script writing and Auden's famous verse commentary for the GPO Film Unit's *Night Mail* documentary (1936) engaged directly with the communications of a technological mass society. Auden's poetry explored the effects of technology and technologized media in a variety of ways, but his participation in radio broadcasting can be specifically noted. From 1936 until his death, Auden read his poems on BBC radio (both live and recorded), but while in Spain in 1937 he was recruited to make radio broadcasts in support of the Republican cause. The impact of his brief experience as a broadcaster on local Valencia radio can be read in his poem 'Spain 1937', which acknowledges, reluctantly, the place of propaganda in the Spanish Civil War: 'To-day the expending of powers | On the flat ephemeral pamphlet and the boring meeting' (Auden 1979: 54). George Orwell's involvement with radio propaganda was much more sustained than that of Auden: Orwell was employed by the BBC's Eastern Service from August 1941 to November 1943 as Talks Assistant, later Talks Producer, for the Indian Section. The Indian broadcasts of news, commentary, features and arts that Orwell coordinated were aimed at an Indian intellectual class with the purpose of reinforcing ties to the empire. Orwell thus found himself as a 'functionary of an ideological state apparatus dedicated to the survival of the British Empire in the East which he had been excoriating for more than a decade' (Kerr 2002: 474), interpreting, explaining and ameliorating the politics of Empire.

Orwell was responsible for writing the weekly 'newsletter' of news commentary, which reported world events from the perspective of London, reading them himself on the air from 1942. He produced over 240 newsletters for broadcast (half in English and the rest for translation) and openly described his own contributions in a 1943 edition of broadcast scripts, *Talking to India*, as 'Five Specimens of Propaganda' (Kerr 2002: 478, 479). The importance of this experience for Orwell's imagining of a technologized and deathly society, controlled by propaganda and self-censorship, in *Nineteen Eighty-Four* will be considered in the following chapter. What it reveals here is the power of radio language and the radio voice to impose a specific version of the world. This power of the radio voice was used by a range of propaganda broadcasters during the Second World War, such as William Joyce ('Lord Haw Haw'), Iva Ikuko Toguri ('Tokyo Rose'/'Orphan Ann') and Ezra Pound (in his Radio Rome broadcasts). It makes the link between politics and radio in the twentieth century undeniable.

The link between politics and radio is incontrovertible in the America of the 1930s. As Bruce Lenthall describes, there was for intellectuals on both the conservative right and Marxist left an opposition to radio, which seemed the essence and articulation of the increasingly homogeneous American mass culture. Nonetheless, radio's status as a mechanism through which to address the population at large appealed to a group of writers and directors in the 1930s – notably Archibald MacLeish, Norman Corwin and Arch Oboler – who sought to make their art relevant and socially committed. The Free Company formed by a group of writers, including MacLeish, Sherwood Anderson, Maxwell Anderson, Stephen Vincent Benét and Orson Welles, in 1940, created a set of radio dramas exploring what they saw as the fundamental freedoms and right of Americans: these dramas were aired on CBS in early 1941 (see Boyd). CBS's airing of these plays illustrates that the national radio networks in America were not opposed to quality 'sustaining programmes' (that is, ones without commercial sponsorship) and sometimes actively generated them: CBS had announced a new non-commercial drama series, the *Columbia Workshop*, in the winter of 1935–6, and over the

next decade the *Columbia Workshop* offered radio dramas and radio adaptations (of Shakespeare, Mark Twain, Oscar Wilde and Ernest Hemingway)
and original radio dramas by writers, including Arthur Miller (who wrote
fourteen radio dramas for the series in the 1940s).

Many of the *Columbia Workshop* broadcasts were formally innovative and
thematically challenging, with the second broadcast – Leopold Prosser's
Broadway Evening of 25 July 1936 – a soundscape of a walk through Manhattan,
with no focus on plot, character or key events. It was Archibald MacLeish's
Fall of the City, broadcast on the *Columbia Workshops* on 11 April 1937 to
critical acclaim, which really established the political and aesthetic possibilities
of this radiogenic form. MacLeish, who had founded his reputation as a poet
in the expatriate Paris of the 1920s, took the mass-media radio form as the
ideal stage for an artistic engagement with mass society, a way to make the
poet's voice relevant and to generate poetry as social force. For MacLeish,
'radio will reach an infinitely greater number of people and should be
capable . . . of shaping sections of that greater number into a living audience'
(1937: 10). *Fall of the City* presents the vanquishing of an ancient city by a
nameless conqueror who, it is revealed at the end, is just an empty suit of
armour. The citizenry of the city cannot perceive this, and it is left to the
radio announcer, who narrates much of the drama, to give voice to their
blindness which is also ours as radio *listeners* – 'They don't see' – and con-
clude 'Masterless Men | Must take a master', in a chilling foreshadowing of
Hitler's victories across Europe (MacLeish 1937: 37, 40).

The role of the radio announcer, read by Orson Welles in the broadcast,
is fundamental to MacLeish's use of the radiogenic form in *Fall of the City*.
As he explains in his introduction to the published script, the announcer,
unique to the radio form as it had developed, is 'an integral part of radio
technique' (1937: 9) who can function as a 'Greek Chorus' (8). Arnheim
had earlier pointed out the structural role of the announcer who, for him,
'is one of the purest of radio features achievable in words . . . nothing but a
voice, his corporeal existence is not included in the broadcast' (1936: 197).
For MacLeish, radio drama is the ideal media for a new form of poetry: he
writes that 'the American slate is still approximately clean' of verse plays
written for radio and, as these plays consist of 'sounds and nothing but
sounds', they excite 'only the word-excited imagination' (1937: 7). 'The ear
is already half poet,' argues MacLeish, 'It believes at once: creates and
believes' (7); thus, radio technology enables a new type of unmediated communication between a poet and a mass audience.

MacLeish uses the radio announcer in *Fall of the City* as part of a modernist
articulation of a world of plurality without fixed certainties – he is in the
position of narrator but cannot control or order the world, or ever directly
and fully know it. In the later play *Air Raid*, broadcast 27 October 1938,
the radio announcer also has a crucial role, articulating the horror of the air
raid on a Spanish town as a first-person witness to the attack. His report
emphasizes the aural experience of modern warfare, presenting the limited

perspective of the waiting villagers who only know of the imminent attack through sounds – the air-raid siren and the approaching planes: 'We can't see it: we hear it' | 'We hear them: we can't see them || We hear the shearing metal: We hear the tearing air' (1939: 28, 31). In this play, the technological transport of radio, taking listeners across the thousands of miles separating America from Europe, is explicitly a vehicle for bringing the reality of European war home:

> Ladies and gentlemen:
> You have only one thought tonight all of you.
>
> You who fish the fathoms of the night
> With poles on roof-tops and long loops of wire.
>
> Those of you who driving from some visit
> finger the button on the dashboard dial,
> until the metal trembles like a medium in a trance,
> and tell you what is happening in France
> or China or in Spain or some such country.
>
> You have one though tonight and only one: will there be war? (1939: 3)

The veracity of aural experience – hearing rather than being told – is what MacLeish emphasizes with language/word replaced by sound/word. Simultaneously, the 'transport' of radio is also explicitly presented as a faltering triumph of new technology, implicitly pointing to the ambivalence of technology which fails and kills and also brings the truth:

> But what your ears will hear within the hour
> no one living in this world would try to tell you.
> We take you there to wait it for yourselves.
>
> Stand by: we'll try to take you through. . . .
>
> *(The station cuts out: there is a moment's delay: it cuts in again)*
>
> [STUDIO DIRECTOR] One moment now: we'll try to take you. (1939: 4)

MacLeish's stark realization of modern, technological warfare, what his *Air Raid* announcer describes as 'perfect mechanical certainty' (33), which crossed the seeming divide between the American listeners safe in their homes and the suffering women and children of Europe, demonstrates how a social-democratic vision and critique found a space for articulation on American radio. There were limits to the liberal largesse of radio, though, and not all critical voices were heard: Langston Hughes wrote plays for radio in the 1930s but none were ever aired – the 'minstrel' show *Amos 'n' Andy* being the hegemonic representation of blackness on the American airwaves. This reinforced Hughes's critique that the 'medium fostered racial stereotypes and at the same time denied blacks a chance to combat those images' (Lenthall 2007: 43).

Perhaps the best-known radio drama event of 1930s America was Orson Welles's production of *War of the Worlds*, broadcast on 30 October 1938 (see Brown 1998). This production was part of his *Mercury Theatre of the Air* series that had premiered with an adaptation of *Dracula* in July 1938, but the unexpected response to *War of the Worlds* meant that Welles was, by the end of the 1938 run of *Mercury Theatre* broadcasts, a national radio celebrity. The stories of panicked listeners, who had taken *War of the Worlds* as a news broadcast and readied themselves for alien invasion, stand alongside the audience fleeing from the Lumière brothers' train in 1895 as an apocryphal account of credulous responses to new media technologies; but it did spark Hadley Cantril, a Princeton psychologist, to interview 135 listeners for a study of mass hysteria, published in 1940 as *The Invasion from Mars: A Study in the Psychology of Panic*. For Dorothy Thompson, writing in the *New York Herald Tribune* two days after the broadcast, *War of the Worlds* 'proved how easy it is to start a mass delusion'. Thompson saw, in its effect, a clear reflection of the power of radio as it was being used in fascist Germany to generate national unity and support:

The greatest organizers of mass hysteria and mass delusions today are states using the radio to excite terrors; incite hatreds, inflame masses, win mass support for policies, create idolatries, abolish reason and maintain themselves in power. (cited Brown 1998: 247)

It was the announcer in *War of the Worlds*, as a reliable voice of authority, that lay at the heart of the drama's impact on its listeners, with Welles later claiming a deliberate use of this device to caution his listeners against a too easy acceptance of the credibility of such authoritative voices. Welles's *Mercury Theatre* sponsorship was taken over after 1938, becoming the *Campbell Playhouse*, illustrating the commercial pressures that inevitably impacted upon radio drama in America. Although the Second World War meant the US airwaves were open to anti-fascist voices and MacLeish himself was employed doing propaganda work for the US government, the post-war environment of rampant anti-communism and commercial enterprise meant very little space for experimental or social-democratic radio drama.

On BBC radio, drama had, since the 1920s, been regularly commissioned for both the National and Regional Programme as part of their schedules of music and voice programming. However, the consolidation of BBC radio's role in defining and disseminating civilization and culture did not occur until the Third Programme was established in September 1946. Val Gielgud, Productions Director for the BBC's Drama Department from 1929 (he would become Head of Television Drama in 1946), played a key role in developing the radio medium as a form of 'national theatre'. However, some of his innovations, such as the 1937 'Experimental Hour', which broadcast MacLeish's *Fall of the City* but failed to find a mass audience, were short-lived. Writers from E .M. Forster to W. B. Yeats were involved in radio broadcasts, but even H. G. Wells, whose stories were adapted many times, never wrote literature specifically for radio. It was a later generation of writers, most notably Louis MacNeice, who were employed by and wrote for radio, exploring and adapting the formal features of this media technology in their work.

MacNeice expresses anxiety about the demagogic power of radio in his 1939 *Autumn Journal*, describing how 'Hitler yells on the wireless' and representing the propagandist atmosphere of the immediate pre-war period as 'taking order | Out of a square box from a mad voice − | Lies on the air endlessly repeated ' (30, 32). But from 1941 onwards, MacNeice was employed on Features productions by the BBC, filling 'the tall transmitters with hot news' as he puts it in *Autumn Sequel* (1954: 30). Features on the BBC, like the *March of Time* (launched on CBS in 1931) and its successors in America, involved the dramatization of news and events with actors, music and so on. Such a format attracted a much larger audience than straight drama, but the distinction between drama and Features was not absolute: MacNeice worked on both, developing his radio drama out of the experience of this Features format to become an 'air-borne bard', 'inventing sound | Precalculating microphone and knob' (1954: 28, 29). He was involved in the evening *War Report* series after the news and wrote the radio adaptation of the Eisenstein film *Alexandr Nevsky* (broadcast 2 December 1941). MacNeice's first full-length radio drama was the 1942 *Christopher Columbus* (with music by William Walton), broadcast simultaneously on both sides of the Atlantic to celebrate the 450th anniversary of Columbus's arrival in the New World. His introduction to the published text presents some key ideas about radio drama as MacNeice conceived it. For him, radio drama, a 'popular art-form which still is an art-form', is fundamentally concerned with words as physical sounds 'words-as-they-are-spoken' and 'words-as-they-are-heard' (1944: 7, 8, 9). For this reason, radio drama 'appeals to the emotions' functioning on a 'primitive plane', which is 'not *ipso facto* crude or false or childish' (10). Much like the American radio dramatists of the period, MacNeice is aware of the mass audience for radio drama, for radio drama as 'communication' and not self-expression (13). Similarly to MacLeish, he argues that the air waves are suited to poetry, particularly as the 'rhythmical pattern of words' is crucial to the 'wider and deeper pattern' of a radio drama (11), and cautions against 'writing . . . by the metronome' (17). He also celebrates the plastic possibilities of radio, which enable 'liberties with time and place' and scene length, allow the use of 'allegorical speakers or choruses' and (here influenced clearly by his Features work) he suggests that radio drama can 'get an effect . . . of up-to-the-minute actuality' (12). MacNeice slightly recast his remarks about the primitive plane of radio in his later 'General Introduction' to *The Dark Tower and Other Radio Scripts*, but continued to celebrate the aural nature of radio drama, writing here that 'sound alone is for most people more potent, more pregnant, more subtle, than pictures alone . . . its [radio's] narrow limits are also its virtue' (1947: 12).

Throughout his radio-drama work, MacNeice used the formal effects of Features – rapid cross-cutting between dramatizations with a narrative fragment, verse or song carrying the thread of the story. Also, as his critical comments in *Christopher Columbus* suggest, many of his radio dramas offer allegorical subjects, what MacNeice called 'moralities' or, in the case of *The Dark Tower*, a 'parable play', alongside radio dramas based on folk tales, translations and historical portraits (see Holme 1981: 48–9). But his popular work did exhibit a political consciousness: like MacLeish's *Fall of the City*, *Christopher Columbus* exposes the dangers of mass rhetoric in his Columbus, who is 'romantically dubious, demagogic' (Williams 1996: 200), part of what MacNeice described as his attempt to 'debunk the Columbus legend' (1944: 90). Like MacLeish, MacNeice recognized the importance of rejecting the objective mediation of a story, not least because of his interest in the materiality of 'words-as-they-are-spoken' and 'words-as-they-are-heard'. Like the announcer in MacNeice's radio dramas, the narrator in *The Dark Tower* is not an extradiegetic locus of control and order, but a character who plays the role of the Greek Chorus. This is a further demonstration of how radio writers, working in a hugely influential, potentially monologic form, used this form to present alternative perspectives instead of fixed points. As Arnheim pointed out, the announcer is a structural, non-corporeal function of radio 'in the loudspeaker' itself (1936: 197) and so cannot be endowed with the agency of an embodied and located voice/self.

In the 1940s, MacNeice worked alongside Dylan Thomas at the BBC, at a time when Thomas was working for Features and also making radio talks for the Welsh Home Service. His August 1945 *Quite Early One Morning* broadcast contained some of the characters, ideas and form that developed into perhaps the best-known radio drama, *Under Milk Wood*, first broadcast on 25 January 1954, two months after Thomas's death. Despite the fact that *Under Milk Wood* has been adapted many times for stage, television and cinema, Thomas was clear about the media specificity of his radio drama as a 'play for voices', writing that he 'wanted to make the town [of Llaregubb] alive through a new medium' (cited Drakakis 1981: 99, 101). The unity of this radio drama, with its seventy-four individual voices and chorus of children, depends fundamentally on the radio form and its ability to cross distances and establish relationships based on aural contiguity, rather than logical or physical connection. The fact that it was translated to a new wireless broadcast medium in a 1957 BBC television production says less about the supposed shortcomings of radio, the blind medium, and more about the 'television industry's deliberate cannibalizing of radio' (Hilmes 1997: 3).

The nascent television industry in Britain had been arrested in its development by the Second World War – John Logie Baird's 'Televisor' was first marketed in February 1930. Regular transmissions had begun in September 1929 from Baird's studio in Long Acre, under licence from the BBC, with the BBC taking over the running of the experimental service in 1932 (Geddes and Bussey 1991: 217). In America, a schedule of telecasting began in 1939, but in both nations transmissions and technological developments in TV were suspended until after 1945. TV broadcasts resumed after the Second World War and, in its development as a popular, mass medium on both sides of the Atlantic, it was the content format of radio that provided the key model for TV programming: this visual medium borrowed and adapted its format and programming (and artists and producers) from the supposedly blind medium of radio (comedy and variety shows, dramas and soaps) rather than reworking the narratives and visual conventions of cinema. The same approach to licensing and regulation (government control in Britain, a variety of commercial stations in America), that shaped the development of radio in these two nations, also shaped the new media technology of television.

By the end of the 1950s, TV had arrived as the dominant domestic media form in both Britain and America: by 1960, almost 90 per cent of American households owned a television set, while in Britain the number of TV licences reached 10 million. This medium was explicitly imagined, as one television director put it in 1955, as a 'window to the world' (cited Spigel 1992: 99). Thus, moving from the blind medium of radio, TV proffered a visible and audible reality in the individual, domestic space and opened this space out to an external world, thereby blurring the distinction between private and public. TV programming did tend to iterate a conformist and consumerist ideal of family life, but it was not solely a homogenizing and conservative force. There continued to be space for experimental and challenging writing, including the work of Paddy Chayefsky, Rod Sterling and Gore Vidal in America and Nigel Kneale, Ken Loach and Dennis Potter in Britain.

The lasting impact of television technology in the twentieth century lay in its blurring of the inside/outside boundary and its presentation of a personal electronic elsewhere: for Raymond Williams, this was a 'mobile privatization', a bridging of the disparate drives towards mobility and atomization in the modern world (see Williams 1974). The human individual who experienced this technology was one who could connect with the world and other people while potentially remaining immune from the actual effects of such connections. That 'the person or persons on the program seem to step into your living room and converse with you' was a possible televisual experience for Thomas Hutchinson in 1948; in 1950, the British television critic Kenneth Baily described how the television brings external events 'right into the home; they become inescapable' and indicates that there were programmes 'which thoroughly invade the mind' (Baily 1950:

113). Commentators in the 1950s stressed the 'immediacy', 'intimacy' and 'feel of reality' that TV offered (see Boddy 1990: ch. 5), a 'liveness' of the 'electronic presence' of TV, to use Jeffrey Sconce's terms, which made the TV screen offer something which appeared 'visibly and materially "real"' (2000: 126) but remained safely harnessed by the technological medium'. Thus, from the early days of TV, advertisements for television encouraged consumers to 'believe that the television set contained real life, that its illusions would materialize in their presence', what Lynn Spigel reads as 'a kind of *hyperrealism*' (1992: 1334, 1343). TV as a media technology heralds the advent of what could be termed postmodernism with its fragmentation of experience and alienation of the real. TV brings a version of the world to the individual and provides access to a much wider range of experience than that individual could otherwise achieve: in this, it prosthetically enhances the human subject. But it also reduces that human subject as human: the technologically mediated TV real has the potential to substitute the virtual relations of an atomized human subject for the complexity of embodied human relations. As a character in Don DeLillo's *White Noise* (1995) comments: 'For most people there are only two places in the world. Where they live and their TV set' (66).

BECKETT AND BROADCAST MEDIA

Richard Ellman's description of Samuel Becket as '*sui generis*' (1987: 91) is not an unusual one and reflects a tendency to characterize the uniqueness of Beckett's work. Nevertheless, the impact of broadcast media on the forms and ideas he develops in his writing for radio and TV is apparent. Beckett's radio dramas and TV pieces emerge from the questions posed by these technologies and explored by writers and critics in the 1930s and 1940s: an interest in medium specificity underpins Beckett's work with broadcast media. Beckett's first radio drama, *All That Fall*, was commissioned by the BBC and broadcast on the Third Programme on 13 January 1957, after *Waiting for Godot* had proved to be a success for Beckett. This marked Beckett's return to writing in English, and there may well be reasons why the space of radio technology created for him a new sense of the language. His subsequent radio works – *Embers* (1959), *Words and Music* (1962), *Rough for Radio I* (1961: English publication 1976), *Cascando* (1962: English broadcast 1964), *Rough for Radio II* (1960s: English broadcast 1976) – move from what could be heard as the realism of the Irish soundscape and setting of *All That Fall*, to the 'skullscape' of the later pieces and an explicit preoccupation with the stuff of radio. Both *Words and Music* and *Cascando* have words/voice and music as characters. Beckett's TV pieces – *Eh Joe* (televised 1966), *Ghost Trio* (televised 1977) and . . . *but the clouds* . . . (televised 1977) present voices fully disconnected from the protagonists on screen, conveying also a technological seeing that reworks the modernist interest in a constitutive absence in perception (see Zilliacus 1976 for full details of Beckett's radio and TV work).

The impact of technology on perception, and its disruption of the somatic location of experience that can be seen in other writers' engagement with cinema or radio, is a key formal and conceptual concern for Beckett's broadcast media work. *All That Fall* presents a recognizable location and characters – Maddy Rooney walking an Irish country road to the station to meet her blind husband, and their return home. But within this framework Beckett's radio drama reflects on the technology of radio itself and the formal implications of radio work. In this, he is working both from his predecessors and from a close contact with radio. Marjorie Perloff is correct to point out that the radio transmitter would have been crucial to the Resistance groups in Roussillon where Beckett spent the 1942–54 period (Perloff 1999), but the importance of radio media (Features, drama, comment) needs also to be considered. The structure of Features radio appears to influence the way motifs are presented in *All That Fall*: the musical motif, Schubert's quartet 'Death and the Maiden', draws the play together within the theme of death and loss, structuring it in the way that music and narration functioned in radio Features of the 1930s and 1940s. Dan Rooney's blindness in *All That Fall* obviously highlights the 'blind' status of radio and Beckett himself was concerned that the drama 'depends on the whole thing's *coming out of the dark*' (cited Zilliacus 1976: 3). *All That Fall* reminds the listener repeatedly of blindness in the tapping of Dan Rooney's stick, using sound itself to indicate that sound is all that radio offers. This is part of Beckett's denaturalization of sound in his radio dramas, which begins with the soundscape of *All That Fall* responding instantly to demands for apposite sound effects:

MRS ROONEY: Go, Mr Tyler, go on and leave me, listening to the cooing of the ringdoves [*Cooing*] (16)

MRS ROONEY: [*In anguish*] Mind the hen! [*Scream of brakes. Squawk of hen.*] (19)

MR ROONEY: I hear something behind us.
     [*Pause*]
MRS ROONEY: It looks like Jerry [*Pause*] It is Jerry.
     [*Sound of JERRY'S running steps approaching. He halts beside them panting.*]
(Beckett 1984: 38)

What Katherine Worth describes as the 'stylization' of sounds in *All That Fall*, which undermines their naturalistic relevance (Worth 1981: 199), is extended in *Embers* where Henry seems to order the soundscape, describing the sound effects: 'the sound you hear is the sea,' and summoning them into being; 'Hooves [*Pause. Louder*] Hooves! [*Sound of hooves walking on hard road . . .*] (Beckett 1984: 93). The soundscape exceeds Henry's control, though, failing to sound when he requires it, or offering unwanted sounds, finally leaving Henry to create his own sound effects; 'Thuds, I want thuds! Like this! [*He fumbles in the shingle, catches up two big stones and starts dashing them together.*] Stone! [*Clash*]' (100). This inability to order the sound world mirrors Henry's inability to control the voices and memories of the play. It is often argued that *Embers* takes place in Henry's consciousness (rather than any physical space) and the shifts in time and contiguity of temporally separate events would seem to suggest we are experiencing an old, lonely man's reminiscences by the sea. The ambiguity of the drama is central rather than incidental and down to its radio form: the key feature of radio, its crossing of boundaries and collapsing of geography and history, is the very stuff of this play, and nothing can be kept distinct. As Arnheim pointed out, in radio, things '*overlay* each other completely' (Arnheim 1936: 121). We never 'see' and so cannot fix who or what is speaking; the origin is the technology itself, a technology that, as in MacLeish's *Air Raid*, does not always function to transport us successfully and is not always in our control. In both *Words and Music* and *Cascando*, Croak and Opener respectively attempt to command communication and meaning from the sounds produced by the two other 'characters' of Word/Voice and Music. What *Rough for Radio I* shows is that the noise of radio (voice + music) 'goes on all the time' (Beckett 1984: 107), regardless of the listener who simply tunes in with 'two knobs' (108).

The status of sound (and silence) as signifiers in Beckett's radio dramas, which sound with uncanny pertinence, fail to sound when required by a controlling voice or continue perpetually without any listener as the destination of communication, serve to undermine the other signifiers out of which the dramas are constituted: words. Thus, the use of media broadcast technology as form serves to empty language of meaning, in a way impossible in a visual mode such as theatre drama, which will always have visible signs to supplement the slippages and failures of aural communication. This breakdown of communication is functionally and thematically connected to what Perloff describes as 'the dance of death that is [Beckett's radio drama's] subject' (1999: 264). Beckett's radio dramas consider the complex materiality of the radio, the tension between presence and absence in this media form, the tension of the protagonists, as Elissa Guralnick puts it, 'paralyzed by the desire to be and not to be, to speak and not to speak' (1996: 79). Arnheim points out: 'In a broadcast dialogue, only the person who is speaking exists acoustically' (Arnheim 1936: 158), and not to exist acoustically is not to exist at all in radio. Thus, Maddy Rooney worries about her presence, asking, 'Am I then invisible', 'Do not imagine, because I am silent, that I am not present, and alive, to all that is going on' (Beckett 1984: 22, 25). And, of course, she can never be seen by her husband, just as we can never see what the boy Jerry returns to him. For Henry, in *Embers,* the impossible presence of his lost wife, daughter and father is summoned in their voices and sounds (the sea for his father, hooves for his daughter and her riding lessons), only for the drama to end in absence 'Not a sound' (Beckett 1984: 104). In *Cascando*, the central figure, Woburn, is called up by the voicing of the drama (narration, description, musical invocation) but remains forever absent.

The possibility of absence is considered differently in Beckett's TV dramas which separate voice from body and present the limits of vision through the scopic technology of the camera. In *Eh Joe*, a character is trans-fixed by the camera moving in 'nine slight moves' towards a 'maximum closeup of face' (Beckett 1984: 201). He is also trapped by a haranguing female voice, the only (invisible) speaker in the piece. In *Ghost Trio*, a con-trolling voice that expresses its own artificiality – 'Mine is a faint voice. Kindly tune accordingly' – describes and directs the 'looking' of the piece: 'Now look closer [*Pause.*] Floor | *Cut to close-up of floor*' (248), but knowledge and understanding of exactly what we are looking at and why is never offered. This technologically mediated, objective, reality remains opaque to comprehension.

What Ulrike Maude suggests is that Beckett's radio and TV dramas dem-onstrate an interest in technology's ability to create 'virtual bodies' (2009: 127), just as Krapp creates a surrogate body in his recording machine in *Krapp's Last Tape*. Looking at the TV productions of Beckett's last play, *What Where* (1985 and 1987), with the indistinguishable heads of Bam, Bem, Bim, and Bom, Maude points to the repetitions and combinations of the play, 'the permutations . . . [that] bring to mind computer loops' (2009: 131). And it is here that we might begin to see the strong lines of continuity, and not rupture, between the electric media of the first half of the twentieth century and the cybernetic systems of information flows in all media that characterized the virtual worlds of computing at the close of the century. In both cases we, as humans, are connected in, up and through technology, with our very selves constructed out of those connections. Beckett's broad-cast media pieces explore the parameters of human subjectivity by consider-ing how technology can make and remake that subjectivity. His texts offer subjects who can neither curb nor escape the techno-systems that define them, and where the locus of meaning is always elsewhere, always deferred. Literature itself needs to be considered as part of these systems, hooked up to a network of signals and transmissions that exceed any individual control.

Zilliacus has argued that Beckett's radio drama signals a move towards interiority and non-corporeality, but his radiogenic writing can be read dif-ferently, and more politically. Like radio dramatists before him, he explores the material technology of radio and the physical impact of sound/voice and, as he does in stage plays like *Waiting for Godot* (1953), examines the function and effect of totalitarian oppression. The commanding power of two of Beckett's characters, Henry (*Embers*) and Opener (*Cascando*), aligns them to the figure of the announcer, so central to the radio drama aesthetic of the 1930s and 1940s, and to the anxiety (in MacLeish, MacNeice, Welles and so on) about the demagogic power of radio. In *Rough for Radio II*, Animator tortures Fox while the Stenographer takes notes of 'the words alone', waiting for the word that '*may be it*' (Beckett 1984: 115, 116). This enunciates an absolute power over language and thus its transformation into power alone;

the noise of totalitarianism. If the bleak landscape of *Waiting for Godot* is also recalled, a landscape that seems to have borne the annihilating force of the atomic bomb that ended the Second World War, Beckett's work in broadcast media can be seen to air a further concern that many other writers share: a concern with the power of technology to not only shape but to distort and even destroy the world.

4 Cold War Technologies

War has consistently been an impetus for technological advance, with new machines and methods generated in order to destroy rather than enhance human existence. But the technological advances in the wars of the twentieth century brought the deathly power of technology to its apotheosis in the invention of nuclear weapons. Such weaponry has an overwhelming power over material existence – the power of mass annihilation – but unlike the technologies used every day, nuclear weapons are only experienced as symbolic or imaginative artefacts. The enormous cultural impact of nuclear power and weapons, which cast a shadow over the whole of the second half of the twentieth century, bears no relation to a direct experience of this technology. It rests upon the ever-present threat to all life and all civilization, an uncertainty about the future of humanity in the face of a technology it has created.

From the outset the atomic bomb, first tested on 16 July 1945 and first used to bomb Hiroshima on 6 August 1945, was a deliberate and immediate symbolic spectacle.[1] For Brigadier General Thomas F. Farrell, one of the witnesses to the first atomic bomb test, it evinced a 'clarity and beauty' beyond language, 'that beauty the great poets dream about but describe most poorly and inadequately' (cited Brunner 2001: 183). The impact and effect of the bomb exceeded articulation: it was a technology that, as a psychiatrist writing on Hiroshima survivors described, had the 'power to make everything into nothing' (Lifton 1967: 278), and that transcended the capacity of verbal communication.

Earlier in the century, Walter Benjamin, writing in response to the development of modern warfare technology, focused on this issue of communication. In his 1936 essay, 'The Storyteller', Benjamin presents modern technological warfare as a key factor in the disruption of the possibility of narrative communication:

For never has experience been contradicted more thoroughly than strategic experience by tactical warfare, economic experience by inflation, bodily experience by mechanical warfare, moral experience by those in power. A generation that had gone to school on a horse-drawn streetcar now stood under the open sky in a countryside in which nothing remained unchanged but the clouds, and beneath these clouds, in a field of force of destructive torrents and explosion, was the fragile human body. (Benjamin 1999: 84)

As Benjamin goes on to argue, experiential storytelling has been replaced by information that 'lives only at that moment' (89) and is immediately expended. For Benjamin, it is as if industrial warfare makes the communication of experience impossible; rather than narrative coherence, it brings to pre-eminence information in and for itself. When set against the developments in information technology in warfare after 1918 and in the Second World War, it becomes clear that technologies of mass annihilation, and the self-inflicted uncertainty that derive from their existence, are necessarily accompanied by a drive for information gathering, the acquisition of a mass of transient data that might offer a knowledge to counteract the uncertainty and incomprehensibility of possible extinction. Alongside the crucial developments in weaponry (assault rifles, ballistic missiles), vehicles (amphibian landing craft, jet fighters, aircraft carriers, U-boats) and logistics, the Second World War initiated the invisible weapons systems that would come to characterize the military of the second half of the twentieth century. Radio, which had been perfected during and because of the First World War, was further enhanced and developed for military purposes, but new technologies of observation such as radar and sonar came into use after 1939 alongside an enormous development in photography and aerial surveillance. The Second World War is marked by its dependence on information and informatics systems, a new mode of warfare that moves further towards abstraction as the mass weaponry threatens even more devastating destruction. The importance of information to both the US and the British war effort led directly to the development of electronic computing and cybernetics: central technologies of the Cold War and generating forces for the digital revolution that redrew the cultural boundaries of the world in the late twentieth century.

ELECTRIC DEATH

Along with leisure, art and work, death was subject to comprehensive technologization during the twentieth century. From the cremation movement of the early century onwards, the destruction and disposal of human bodies has been transformed by technological processes. Professor Brunetti displayed his crematorium chamber at the 1873 Vienna Exposition, and supporters of this new technology were concerned with the sanitary issues of disposing of the dead. Cremation could abolish the 'repulsive offensiveness' resulting from graveyard pollution and was the best 'sanitary precaution against the propagation of disease among a population daily growing larger in relation to the area it occupied', as Sir Henry Thompson put it in his paper 'The Treatment of the Body After Death' in the *Contemporary Review* in January 1874. Thompson was Queen Victoria's surgeon and founded the Cremation

Society of England in 1874. Subsequently, the first cremations in purpose-built facilities, reducing human remains to their basic chemical compounds in an efficient, industrial process, began in the USA in Pennsylvania in 1876, and in 1885 at Woking in England. The body disposed of cleanly in cremation contrasts starkly to the gruesome, singed remains of the victim of electrocution: electricity was spectacularly demonstrated as a deathly technology at Coney Island at the turn of the century. Topsy the elephant, one of the entertainments at Luna Park, had killed her handler after mistreatment (she had already killed two others) but survived her planned execution by cyanide-laced carrots. On 4 January 1903, Topsy was electrocuted before an audience of 1,500, under the auspices of Thomas Edison's electrical company. The Edison Company film of the event, *Electrocuting the Elephant* (1903), shows Topsy collapsing dead just a few seconds after the 6,600 volt alternating current has been initiated; a very grim nexus of electrical and media technology and death on dramatic view.

The execution of Topsy at Coney Island was not just a ghastly stunt; it was the latest sally in Edison's publicity war against the alternating current (AC) of the Westinghouse Electric Company (which used Nikola Tesla's patents). Edison consistently attacked AC as dangerous in comparison to the direct current system used by the Edison Company. The 'battle of the currents' as it became known ran through the late 1880s and 1890s, during which Edison oversaw a number of animal electrocutions by AC current in his laboratories, using stray dogs and some larger animals. These demonstrations coincided with the movement in America to reform capital punishment, which ultimately culminated in the widespread abolition of hanging in favour of electrocution. Edison testified on the suitability of AC for state executions to the 1888 New York Gerry Commission into capital punishment, and in 1889 New York became the first state to bring an electrical execution Bill into law. Harold Brown, with Edison's secret support, was commissioned to build an execution device for three prisons, Auburn, Sing Sing and Clinton, devising an oak–chair apparatus with a head electrode that used a Westinghouse generator that he had needed to buy second hand (as George Westinghouse starkly resisted Edison's attempts to link his company with death by electricity). Despite the eventual dominance of the (ultimately safer) AC supply of electric current, Edison continued in his support of electrocution, making design adjustment suggestions for the chair at Sing Sing in 1892. In 1901, his motion picture company released a re-enactment of the electrocution of President McKinley's assassin, Leon Czolgosz: the fictionalized electrical execution, *Execution of Czolgosz*, has none of the burning, grimacing and struggling an actual victim would suffer. As Mark Essig points out, this hugely popular film 'brought alive the fantasy of the quick, clean death that supporters of the electric chair had long promoted' (2003: 262, 279). *Execution of Czolgosz* shows the common ground between the advocates of cremation and the exponents of electrical execution: technology offered the promise of transforming the process of dying and death into an orderly, modern process. As Edison told reporters in 1888: 'Touch a button, close the circuit, it is over' (cited Essig 2003: 291).

In the twentieth century, thousands of people underwent state execution by electricity (the number in the US is estimated at more than 4,300) and, on 12 January 1928, Ruth Snyder was one of these. Snyder, the first woman to be executed in the electric chair since 1899, was electrocuted at Sing Sing prison for the murder of her husband; her lover accomplice was executed a few minutes later. Tom Howard had been hired by the *New York Daily News* (one of the twenty chosen from 1,500 applications to witness the execution) and captured a graphic image of Ruth Snyder's death in the electric chair, using a secret camera. Howard's photograph was published the following morning under the front-page headline 'DEAD!', to great outrage and threats of state prosecution. As the caption describes, 'The picture is the first Sing Sing execution picture and first of a woman's execution,' and, in presenting a female body strapped to and killed by an anonymous electrical machine, offers a disturbing image of the deadly power of technology. The iconicity of the electric chair would inspire Andy Warhol to utilize it in his *Electric Chair* series of paintings and prints begun in 1963, the year that the Sing Sing chair was used for the last time.

Sophie Treadwell's 1928 expressionist play, *Machinal*, was loosely based on Snyder's story, presenting the experiences of a 'Young Woman', 'any woman' as we are told in the play's epilogue explanations (Treadwell 1928: xi). Treadwell's play was influenced by the earlier drama *The Adding Machine* by Elmer Rice (1923), but her protagonist is female, in comparison to Rice's protagonist 'Zero' who is hanged after losing his job to a mechanical replacement. Treadwell's play needs to be read as a feminist response to the deathly grip of technology; the Young Woman of *Machinal* is trapped in a technological and materialist world that expects her to marry the boss who courts her and become a compliant wife and mother. From the very beginning, the stage direction emphasizes the mechanisms which permeate the world and function metonymically in showing the alienation and denaturalization of the Young Woman's life. The play opens in an office with 'a switchboard, filing cabinet, adding machine, typewriter and table, manifold machine', and the background noises are mechanical: 'typewriters, adding machine, manifold, telephone bells, buzzers'. Each character here has 'their machines', with the Young Woman conflated with her 'typewriter' (Treadwell 1928: 1). The mechanical sounds continue through the play and include 'steel riveting', 'Telegraph instruments', an 'Aeroplane engine', and an 'Electric piano'. At the end of the play, having been tried and condemned for the murder of her boss-become-husband, the Young Woman is taken off stage to her death. Refusing the grotesque spectacularity of the Synder execution photograph, Treadwell's protagonist is heard in her final moments rather than seen. The Young Woman's final off-stage words 'Somebody! Somebod–', cut off as she is executed in the chair, indicate what has been truncated in the electrical, technological world of *Machinal*: the body and natural instinct.

The words of a reporter in the final scene of *Machinal*: 'Suppose the machine shouldn't work!' (Treadwell 1928: 82) are deeply ironic; the play shows that the 'machine' always works, defining and delimiting, and finally destroying the life of the Young Woman. The re-titling of the play as *The Life Machine* for its 1931 London premiere underscores the irony of the drama in which the naturalness of instinct and emotion (life) is murdered by the rigid machines of modern society.

MACHINE-WAR AND POETRY

The terrible power of technology harnessed by modern society was nowhere more comprehensively demonstrated than in the First World War, which killed more than 16 million combatants and civilians. In a strange echo of the hygiene rhetoric of the advocates of cremation and in celebration of terrific destructive power, the Italian Futurist Marinetti, in the title he gave to his writing, declared, *War, the World's Only Hygiene* (1911–15). In his work, such as *The Battle of Tripoli* (1912), inspired by his experience in the Turkish–Italian War (1911–12), Marinetti attempted to harness the techno-logical velocity of war in his response to the modern age. The technologies of war, notably the aeroplane, were crucial instigators for his aesthetic. However, the literary response to the technology of the First World War is generally at odds with Marinetti's technophilia, focusing instead on the inhuman, mechanistic slaughter of men and the decimation of natural land-scape and Western civilization alike. The 'shrieking iron and flame' (Silkin 1981: 208) of Rosenberg's 'Break of Day in the Trenches', the 'successive flights of bullets' (180) of Wilfred Owen's 'Exposure' and the 'wailing shells' (184) of his 'Anthem for Doomed Youth', the 'clamour of shells' and 'blazing' machine guns of Siegfried Sassoon's 'Counter-Attack' (130), the 'machine-gun rattle' (122) of Robert Graves's 'Recalling War'; all these poets evoke the technologies of death that marked this war as a turning point in culture and history. For each of these poets, it is not just the terrible power of technology, but its stark contrast to the fractured, maimed, filthy and rotting bodies of men who are subjugated to and by it. The 'troglodyte world' of the trenches, to use Paul Fussell's terms, produced an overwhelm-ing sense, for the combatants, that humanity had regressed to a primitive state of being in this war. But this sense of regression was contradicted by the advanced power of modern weaponry and the machines of war. In his 'In Parenthesis' (1937), David Jones signals an ultimate rejection of the technological present manifest in war in favour of a mythic past: his exhausted, wounded Private John Ball ignores his orders to cherish his weapon as he would a woman and abandons his rifle to rust beneath a tree.

Jones's poem, as does the work of other poets, reveals the contradictions in the modern technologies of war. Emerging from contemporary science and engineering, these technologies reduced the human individual to a mass of vulnerable flesh, negated narratives of the past (including narratives of heroism and battle) and were often a burden when they misfired or otherwise malfunctioned. But the technological advances of the First World War are undeniable: the war saw the development of the hand grenade, high-explosive shells, flame-throwers, poison gas, advances in machine gun and rifle technology, developments in air power, and naval developments with long-range gunnery and submarines. The First World War also saw the invention of the tank, and it is this deathly machinery which epitomizes a key facet of the role of technology in war. The tank was developed to break the deadlocked Western Front and first used at the Somme in September 1918, but, as Trudi Tate outlines, it was a victorious force because of 'the mobilization of fantasy' around it, rather than its actual military deployment (1997: 69). In contrast to its emergence as a feat of engineering and technological advance, the tank was described in newspaper propaganda and war literature such as Ford Maddox Ford's *Parade's End* (1924–8) as a primeval monster (see Tate 1997: 70–1). The language of pre-history surrounding the tank recalls Fussell's 'troglodyte world' and highlights the odd temporality of war technology, yoking technological progression to the regressive, primal horror of the battlefield. The first tanks themselves were much more effective as spectacles for intimidating the enemy, and particularly for mobilizing civilian support, than as weapons: actual tanks featured prominently in drives to finance the continued war effort through war bonds and featured on everything from handbags to paper napkins. What the tank offered was an 'idea . . . of industrial warfare' (Tate 1997: 79) somewhat at odds with the terrible experiences of tank crews shut inside them and their general failure on the battlefield. The technology of war was thus, in the tank, reified as technological advance in itself, distinct from its actual functioning in achieving military gains. The tank's symbolic value and ability to accrue popular support was its key function as a military technology. This symbolic function for military technology echoes through the twentieth century to, for example, Ronald Reagan's Cold War 'Star Wars' Strategic Defense Initiative of the 1980s.

In his analysis of technology and war, Paul Virilio is not concerned as such with the reification of military technology but with the contiguous relation between military technology and the seemingly distinct media technology of cinema. For Virilio, visual technologies, from seventeenth-century telescopes onwards, have accompanied the 'war machine' with a 'watching machine' (Virilio 1989: 3). The connections between weapons and cinema can be located in Marey's invention of a chrono-photographic rifle for photographing moving objects in the late nineteenth century, but the twentieth century saw an absolute merging of weapons and tools of perception and communication. Virilio argues, in *War and Cinema*, that the First World War saw a coming together of these technologies and compounded a new 'weapons system out of combat vehicle and camera' (1). Thus, '*For men at war, the function of the weapon is the function of the eye*' (20: emphasis in original), to the extent that the line of sight, whether literal or reproduced through photography, mapping or radar, comes, through the development of these technologies, to be the line of fire. For Virilio, it is not just the technologies, but what the technologies produce in terms of lines of sight, and the gaze, what Virilio terms the 'soldier's obscene gaze' on the world – 'his art of hiding from sight in order to see' – that is so crucial (49). The First World War can be read as a 'mediated conflict' (69), and one in which the gaze of combatants 'prefigures the synoptic machinations of . . . the cinema screen' (49). The actual links between cinema films and war are present from the First World War – apparently the battlefields of France were not cinematic enough for D. W. Griffith, who shot the battle scenes for *Hearts of the World* (1918) on Salisbury Plain (15) – but Virilio's crucial point is that in fact '*War is cinema and cinema is war*' (26; emphasis in original). The modern techno-logical battlefield (from the First World War onwards) executes distortions and derangements of the 'space-time of vision' in which 'each of the antago-nists feel both that he is being watched by invisible stalkers and that he is observing his own body from a distance' (72). Thus, war becomes an acutely visual and abstract enterprise that alienates all participants from their own subjectivities just as it inserts them into the cinema-war machine.

If the First World War was the first industrial, cinematic war, then the Second World War saw its escalation as conflict encompassed the globe and took many men into combat thousands of miles from their homes. In literary terms, poets were faced with the fundamental question of what there was left to say given the 'unforgettable' response of Owen, Sassoon et al. to the 'awfulness of modern industrialized war' (Fussell, in Stokesbury 1990: xxv). In their poetic response to this war, poets such as J. F. Kendry, Sidney Keyes, Alun Lewis, Keith Douglas and Henry Reed reacted to what Adam Piette describes as 'the servo-mechanical entrancement brought about by the fabu-lous new killing technologies of warfare', the 'mass death on an industrial scale' (2009: 22, 23). And it is their detachment that distinguishes them from the Great War poets, a detachment that is in line with the cinema of war that Virilio describes and is most obvious in the number of poems written about aerial bombardment. The returning airmen in John Ciardi's 'Return' function in themselves as cinematic devices of horror: 'their eyes are lenses and they house | Reel after reel of how a city burned' (Stokesbury 1990: 72), while Richard Eberhardt writes of 'The Fury of Aerial Bombardment' (10) and Randall Jarrell presents the absolute depersonalization of an aerial gunner in 'The Death of the Ball Turret Gunner' (60). James Dickey's 1964 poem, 'The Firebombing', offers a present-day American recalling his actions in a Second World War bombing plane over Japan. 'Cool and enthralled in the cockpit', the pilot is detached from the death and destruction below, observing the burning Japanese homes 'in aesthetic contemplation'. But the pilot's disconnection is undermined by the persistent memory of the conse-quences of his wartime activities, which 'cloud' his comfortable suburban existence. The poem questions the objectivity afforded by the technological perspective of aerial bombardment. The cinematic 'Shutter-flashing; responding mirrors' of the mass death below the pilot is contrasted with the individual and the human and, as the pilot says, 'This is what should have got in | To my eye' (Stokesbury 1990: 114).

In his poetry, Keith Douglas presents the visual technologies of warfare as part of the process of death and destruction, and the process of death becomes so abstract as to be almost magical: 'Now in my dial of glass appears | the soldier who is going to die', he writes in 'How to Kill', describing the 'sorcery' of making 'a man of dust | of a man of flesh' (Douglas 1979: 112). The omnipresence of machines detached from the death they deal out appears in Douglas also, where 'Perched on a great fall of air | a pilot or angel [is] looking down | on some eccentric chart' ('Landscape with Figures 1' (Douglas 1979: 103)). In his account of his experiences with a tank regiment in the Middle East, *Alamein to Zem Zem* (1946), Douglas presents a version of the cinema of war. While echoing the earliest primal imaginings of tanks as 'toads' (26), Douglas observes that the 'view from a moving tank is like that in a camera obscura or a silent film . . . it is the same in an aircraft' (28). The mediated but enlarged perspective of the tank commander, who, through radio transmissions and the mapping of terrains and movements, gets 'the panorama of battle' in his 'mind's eye', has an infinite advantage over the infantryman who only comprehends his direct proximities (107). But the tank crew is also the subject of an equivalent, omniscient gaze like that of 'a film audience' with a 'detached view of us' (31). As both observer and observed, with neither of these virtual lines of perspective unmediated or even directly visible, the tank crew are encased in a technological space of seeing. Second World War writers such as Douglas do not simply reflect on what many saw as the terrible marriage of technology and barbarism in modern warfare, but expose the distorted space-time of vision that emerges and that produces a contradictory experience of omniscience and vulnerability, objectivity and guilt in the combatants of that war.

Of course, the most radical technological achievements of the Second World War were also its most horrific and those most inclined to produce aloof perpetrators and an undifferentiated mass of victims. The production-line killing of the Holocaust relied on the efficiency of machinery operated with absolute objectivity. Beginning with the euthanasia of the sick and disabled in 1939 and followed by mass executions of Jewish peoples, Gypsies and other so-called undesirables, using guns and mobile gassing vehicles, 1941–2 saw the opening of the six death camps constructed in Poland – Auschwitz-Birkenau, Belzec, Chelmno, Majdanek, Sobibor and Treblinka – which enshrined a seamless process of elimination. In a grotesque hyperbole of the organized technology of cremation, these death camps processed those selected for extermination in gas chambers disguised as showers, where the naked corpses, stripped of gold teeth and hair, would be placed in elevators to the cremation ovens one floor above. The ghastly efficiency of this despicable process was absolute: by the end of the war Birkenau could murder 'approximately 12,000 people a day' (Soumerai and Schulz 1998:

185). For a number of critics, the notion of simply responding to this technological horror with literature was seen as impossible: for Adorno, in 1949, 'writing poetry after Auschwitz' seemed 'barbaric' (cited Vice 2000: 6), while, for George Steiner, 'eloquence after Auschwitz' was an 'obscenity' (1988: 156). Both the Holocaust and the other technological horror born in the Second World War – nuclear annihilation – fundamentally changed the culture that came after. The awful truth of the technological extermination of life and the nightmarish realm of nothingness produced a rupture in history and a scepticism about the continuity of culture. Perhaps paradoxically, the response to this, from nations engaged in a subsequent struggle for power in the Cold War, was an intensified engagement with technology.

TOTAL WAR, INFORMATION AND THE SPY

The Second World War was the catalyst for enormous advances in military technology, and the Cold War period saw a continuation of investment and development. Space exploration – which put Russian cosmonaut Yuri Gagarin as the first man in space in 1961, followed by the first men on the moon with the US *Apollo 11* mission in 1969 – was one technological facet of the capitalist/communist struggle of the Cold War years. Indeed, the possibility of space flight and moon landings suggested both an escape from the containment politics of the Cold War and an extension of those politics into an extraterrestrial sphere. The Cold War arms race saw Soviet Russia testing its first atomic bomb in 1949, and consequently war itself became as much an imaginary field as a strategic reality in a situation of Mutually Assured Destruction. The flourishing of the Military-Industrial Complex that President Eisenhower warned of in his 1961 farewell address – the enormous investment of governments into military technology and the private industries that developed and supplied them – points to the emergence of a system of militaristic technology as a central component of Western society: a system that profits from war turns the development of deathly technology into a self-perpetuating structure intimately connected to structures of power.

But missiles, warheads, tracking equipment and strategic air commands were only one aspect of military technological development; as in the Soviet atomic project, espionage became crucial to the arms race. Klaus Fuchs's role in bringing US nuclear secrets to Soviet Russia in the 1940s, and the trial of the Rosenbergs in 1951, offered an image of the vulnerability of military technology in the face of the duplicitous human individual. But the individual who could threaten the vast, faceless power of the state was reconfigured in popular fiction: when he was working for the West the individual spy, pitted against the machinery of state and the technologies of interception and scrutiny, became the protagonist-hero of Cold War spy fiction.

The techniques of propaganda and surveillance, which had been features of warfare since the beginning of the century, expanded in range and effectiveness through the use of new technologies. Television and the film industry presented explicit and implicit images of the communist threat (from Public Service broadcasts about nuclear blasts to the Creature movies of the 1950s and 1960s), but even domestic kitchen technologies, automobiles and suburban architecture played a propagandist role. The conspicuous display of white goods and new cars symbolically shored up a sense of the superiority of the Free World, while also indicating, in the US most obviously, a proper commitment by consumers to the values of capitalist democracy. Doubt about the impact of this suburban consumer techno-utopia on the authenticity of experience and identity was expressed in a range of Cold War writing, from Sloan Wilson's *The Man in the Gray Flannel Suit* (1955) and Richard Yates *Revolutionary Road* (1961) to Sylvia Plath's poetry, and was one of the driving forces behind the Beat generation writers and 1960s counter-culture.

George Orwell's techno-dystopia *Nineteen Eighty-Four*, originally entitled *The Last Man in Europe*, does not imagine a post-war world of abundant consumer goods. It is set in a stark world of rationing and denial that reflects more closely its time of writing in a Britain suffering the privations of the immediate post-war period. But it is a world in which technology has entered into the most private spaces and opened them up to the penetrating eye of total surveillance. The reassuring presence of the TV in the 1950s household, what Tichi calls 'the electronic hearth' (1991), is, in *Nineteen Eighty-Four*, the sinister screen of the Thought Police who could 'plug in your wire whenever they wanted' (Orwell 1949: 6) while broadcasting simultaneously. Orwell's 'telescreen' monitors the Party members and also, in the morning 'Physical Jerks', regulates their bodies, at the same time as bombarding its compulsory audience with propaganda about military and economic success. This panoptical coercion presents a prescient vision of the regulatory role of television in the 1950s and early 1960s, with its middlebrow, middle-class content endorsing a particular normative notion of family behaviour and individual social role. Such normative ideas had different ramifications in Britain and the US, with American audiences interpellated into a God-fearing, white, middle-class patriarchy (see Nadel 2005), while in Britain the TV network was dominated by a single BBC channel (until the advent of commercial broadcasting in September 1955). The shocked responses to the 1954 Sunday evening BBC adaptation of *Nineteen Eighty-Four*, and the resulting debate about acceptable family viewing, highlighted the need for the alternative channel ITV which had received its licence earlier in the year. Orwell's reputation within the popular imagination was dramatically enhanced by this adaptation to TV technology, leading to a much wider readership for his literature (see Lea 2001, 2010).

In *Nineteen Eighty-Four*, the individual is completely invaded by and incorporated into the technologies of the political system of Oceania – not just the domestic and public telescreens, but the organization of Winston's workplace, his cubicle with the 'speakwrite' device, 'pneumatic tubes' for documents, and paper disposal slit, insert him into the machinery of propaganda and thought control. Even history and nature are not beyond the reaches of technology: Winston and Julia are unwittingly observed in their room above Charrington's shop, from behind the antique pictures, and even in the countryside there is the danger of concealed microphones.

In *Nineteen Eighty-Four*, technology has been harnessed by political power to perpetuate war, and in doing so to concretize the political status quo and negate any possibility of resistance. As Winston reads in 'The Theory and Practice of Oligarchical Collectivism', war is no longer waged with the intent to triumph; instead it involves 'mostly highly-trained specialists' (Orwell 1949: 151) and its primary focus is the use of technology to destroy the products of that technology: the 'primary aim of modern warfare . . . is to use up the products of the machine without raising the general standard of living' (153). As Orwell describes, the more advanced the military technology the better as 'even when weapons of war are not actually destroyed, their manufacture is still a convenient way of expending labour power without producing anything that can be consumed' (155). The paperweight that Winston treasures stands in contrast to the production–destruction cycle: it epitomizes an authentic object of beauty that does not do anything; it just exists, unlike technology which is used to capture and control resources, peoples and so on. Here Heidegger's critique of technology as the transformation of all resources into functional 'standing reserves' seems to resonate strongly with Orwell's techno-dystopia.

However, technology in *Nineteen Eighty-Four* is productive as well as destructive: at a fundamental level, it produces social coherence and machines are put in service of the manufacture of that coherence. The Ministry of Truth produces for all the citizens of Oceania 'rubbishy newspapers . . . sensational five-cent novelettes, films oozing with sex, and sentimental songs which were composed entirely by mechanical means', and, of course, pornography for the Proles (Orwell 1949: 38). What Orwell describes is the mass production of consent through the manufacture of culture, along lines that chime with Horkheimer and Adorno's 'Culture Industry'. This suggests that the brutality of totalitarianism, as Orwell presents it, is predicated upon the control of technology, but what he does not present is technology as a *de facto* evil. The possibility that technology might 'be used to make the masses too comfortable, and hence, in the long run, too intelligent' (Orwell 1949: 154) is a key anxiety for the Party. That technology is used by very human evil, rather than humanity being perverted by technology, is exemplified in the torture of Winston. He is subjected to electric shocks and what appears to be ECT (this treatment had arrived in Britain in the 1940s and had even featured in a Ministry of Labour advert in *The Times* on 20 February 1947), but the ultimate vision that Orwell's O'Brien offers is one of basic individual brutality: 'a boot stamping on a human face' (Orwell 1949: 215). The cruelty of the torture scenes is visceral, rather than technological, pointing to Orwell's conception of his dystopia as basically one of human on human destructiveness magnified, but not created by, technology.

The ubiquitous surveillance in *Nineteen Eighty-Four* highlights the growing importance of information in the Cold War period, where the control and processing of information is directly related to state power and is just as significant as weapons superiority. This development in the functioning of state and military power was a catalyst for the development of digital computing. Most histories of computing technology cite Charles Babbage's Analytical Engine (which he was still working on at his death in 1871) as an early conceptual prototype for the modern computer, but up to the Second World War the term 'computer' referred to a human individual who carried out computations. It was the demand for information processing at volumes, speeds and complexities beyond human capacity in the field of modern warfare that drove the development of the first digital computers. A team at the Post Office Research Laboratories in North London developed and built a device, the Colossus, that could work through possible permutations to decipher messages encoded with the German Enigma machines. Colossus machines were then used at the code-breaking and intelligence centre in Bletchley Park in England from 1944; occupying a large room, they were about 2.3 metres high and 5.5 metres long. Replacing mechanical circuit elements with electronic equivalents and utilizing digital rather than analogue calculations, the Colossus machines were the first programmable digital computers. The Colossus could decipher the German teleprinter messages despite the daily changing Enigma code, taking the data of radio waves that was ostensibly meaningless and converting it into useful military intelligence. The Colossus machines were crucial to the success of the D-Day landings. In its invention, therefore, Colossus formed a nexus of espionage, information and computers, resulting in the production of a deathly technology that was ultimately invisible – a machine that did not act in any direct way in war, but produced information that led to military victory.

The Colossus machines demonstrate how military technology had, by the end of the Second World War, developed beyond the capability of any human individual, and displayed the central importance of the invisible, as opposed to the actual, plane of warfare. The growing importance of information, not just in military terms but across the economies of the Western world, gave rise to what is generally termed the 'Information Age', something that Benjamin had predicted in his 1936 'The Storyteller'. In military terms, the system that developed in this new and complex world was the command control communication (C3) system. There is no single point of authority in a C3 system, just the efficient communication of information to enable specific military goals and objectives. This enormous system and its command technologies subsume the individual and appear to destroy any possibility for individual agency or heroism. However, as Joseph Slade suggests, there is a genre of literature that was adapted to form 'a cultural response to . . . the Information Age' and specifically to the communication and information technologies of that age: spy fiction (1992: 226).

Spy novels are centrally concerned with the value of information, although the exact worth and nature of that information is often an unknown quantity. The secret itself is what counts. For Michael Denning, the information at the heart of a spy novel is 'a relation of power . . . the interest is not in the secret information itself – how many missiles, or what secret treaty – but in the distribution of knowledge' (Denning 1987: 136). Cold War spy novels pit a human individual against the massive C3 system of an evil government or underground organization, dramatizing the anxieties of their audience. By positing spying as an 'additional . . . circuit for the flow of information', the 'spy novel puts a human face on anonymous mechanisms of information flow' (Slade 1992: 229, 248). So the appeal of Cold War spy novels is that of the human individual facing vast, faceless bureaucratic and military systems and avoiding technological annihilation.

Ian Fleming's James Bond is an enduringly popular spy-fiction hero, enjoyed by John F. Kennedy and Jean-Paul Sartre, translated to the screen in 1962, persisting through subsequent decades of global political change and reimagined (yet again) in the stylish films of the early twenty-first century. Unlike the moral complexity of Graham Greene's espionage fiction, Bond occupies a much simpler world of good and evil, but Fleming's novels are not ahistorical fantasies. Bond is a product, as many critics point out, of post-war late-imperial British anxieties and Cold War politics and exists in what is clearly an Information Age. SMERSH, the KGB's assassination squad, figures prominently in the early novels, to be replaced by SPECTRE, Blofeld's villainous organization in *Thunderball* (1961) and subsequent novels, reflecting a change in attitudes to the Soviet Union. The early novels – *Moonraker* (1955), *Dr No* (1958) and *Thunderball* (1961) – all include what Christopher Linder terms 'potentially genocidal atomic conspiracies' (79). Bond's heroic triumph over these villains and their conspiracies suggests that he offers a palliative to an audience faced with late-imperial British influence on the wane in global politics, alongside a human triumph over sinister systems of control. As Linder goes on to argue, Bond protects humanity, but also Britain's international reputation (Linder 2003: 87).

The world of espionage that Bond moves in is one that is excessively technologized, particularly so in the gadgets and vehicles he uses in the novels and which become central to the film adaptations. The connection between espionage and technology was cemented during the Second World War when anything from wristwatch cameras, tear-gas pens and heel knives were developed, with espionage technology developing further in the 1950s and 1960s (see Gersh and Weinberg 2006: 8, 13). In the Bond novels, the operation bases of the villains are where the most excessive technologization is displayed, presenting on a grand scale the idea of a malevolent C3 system that threatens humanity. In *Dr No*, for example, the eponymous Dr Julius No's base on the Caribbean island, Crab Key, has 'the most valuable technical intelligence centre in the world', capable of interfering with the 'telemetred instructions' of high-tech rockets such as the 'multi-stage SNARK' (Fleming 1958: 175). Dr No even has his own 'cipher machine' from Moscow to encode his communications (176). Dr No embodies a sinister mechanization designed to offer him 'total security from physical weaknesses, from material damage and from the hazards of living' (165). Besides his secret base, he himself is a cyborg amalgamation of 'mechanical hands', 'contact lenses' and 'a walkie-talkie' (159). In contrast, the body of Bond is represented as vulnerable human flesh in *Dr No*: as he escapes through a ventilator shaft he is subjected to burning heat that scorches his body, giant tarantulas and a downwards tube where 'metal flayed his skin' (197). Bond's escape culminates in a fight with a giant squid 'as big as a railway engine' (201).

Bond's vulnerable body is something that characterizes his representation in Fleming's novels, from the gruesome, sexually charged torture in *Casino Royale* (2003: 3) to the brutal beating in *Diamonds Are Forever* (1956) which means he has to rely on a woman, Tiffany Case, to help him escape. But he does not simply stand as vulnerable human bravery against the inhuman machines of SMERSH, SPECTRE and other international villanies. Bond is also machinic, 'half-mechanical, half-intuitive' in *Casino Royale* (2003: 33), trained to be 'as cool about death as a surgeon' in *Goldfinger* (1959: 7), and described by M in *The Man with the Golden Gun* (1965) as 'a supremely effective firing-piece' (28). Bond can thus be read as a weapon himself, as a 'political weapon', killing to protect Western capitalist imperialism (Linder 2003: 85). The elision of Bond with the weapon he carries has a sexual dimension from the very beginning; the phallic resonances of his handgun are unavoidable in *Casino Royale* where he treats it with a masturbatory intent. In his hotel room, Bond takes out his .25 Beretta and 'whipped the action to and fro several times, finally pulling the trigger on the empty chamber' before reloading it and leaving his room 'cool and comfortable' to meet the first incarnation of the Bond girl, 'Vespa Lynd' (Fleming 2003: 40). The link between sex, death and violence runs throughout the Bond novels, most obviously underpinning Bond's torture in *Casino Royale* and the threatened laser castration in *Goldfinger*. The machines, sexual violence and Bond's almost automatic sexual performance can be read as articulations of a masculinity threatened by the post-war technologies of information, bureaucracy, atomic destruction and mass consumerism. For Patrick O'Donnell, Bond is 'a retrogressive figure representing a last-ditch effort to . . . save the phallus in the cybernetic age' (2005: 58). Bond is thus both a prosthesis and a playboy, and in him Fleming explores the 'anxieties attending . . . the posthuman formation of the Cold War male subject' (2005: 59).

Moonraker is the only Bond novel to be set solely in England and it deals with many of the national and gender anxieties that permeate the others. Published three years after Britain became the world's third nuclear power, the plot involves the seemingly impeccable millionaire Sir Hugo Drax's munificent plan to build for the nation an Inter-Continental Ballistic Missile base on the Kent coast. By the end of the novel Drax is revealed to be an unreconstructed Nazi megalomaniac in the service of the Soviet Union, whose plan to explode a nuclear rocket on London is uncovered and foiled by Bond. Bond redirects the rocket's trajectory so that it falls in the Channel, with the resulting mushroom cloud 'passed off as the normal formation after an explosion of that size' and the nuclear fallout helpfully 'drifting . . . up north' to Russia (Fleming 2003: 504). The British casualties include a BBC man who was covering the test launch for national broadcast. Drax's plan exposes the vulnerability of Britain in the nuclear age, a vulnerability that had already been demonstrated by the destruction wrought by the German V-1 and V-2 rockets in the Second World War. So Bond defends Britain against both German rockets and a Soviet nuclear threat.

At the beginning of *Moonraker*, we see Bond facing off against a machine. In this case, it is on a firing range and, as the Instructor tells him, 'you can't beat the machine' (2003: 324). The novel plays out this challenge, presenting Bond beating Drax and his system twice, first at cards and then at his operations headquarters. Drax's Moonraker base is a glory of concrete − 'like a newly laid aerodrome' (415) − and high-tech tracking devices: 'Doppler velocity radar and flightpath radar . . . telemetering channels . . . big television screen' (402). The inside is very tellingly described as 'like being inside the polished barrel of a huge gun' (403), while Bond sees Drax's identically attired workforce as 'robot-like Germans' (407). Bond is the human inserted into this weapons system who must 'beat the machine'.

That there is a human trace that affects the machine is indicated from the beginning of the novel. Bond may not be able to defeat the 'complicated box of tricks' at the firing range (324), but we are shown how a human signature persists in the C3 system. One of the papers that Bond reads at his desk in the first chapter is a NATO brief on attempts to protect radio operators from discovery. Any operator has a 'fist' (the signature of movements in his messaging), which leaves a trace in the message itself. The NATO brief is concerned with artificially disguising the 'indelible characteristics' of the radio operator's 'fist' in the technology he uses (329). What *Moonraker* presents is the possibility of subversion from within the machine, a cyborg action. Bond's victory is enabled, not by brute human force (as in other novels) but through technical knowledge and data communication; reprogramming the gyroscope of the rocket and listening to its redirected take-off through a radio broadcast.

At the opening of *Moonraker*, we are given an insight into the day-to-day functioning of the Secret Service bureaucracy, with its 'Ministry-of-Works-green corridor . . . bustling world of girls carrying files, doors opening and shutting, and muted telephone calls' (2003: 325), but Fleming's novels are not centrally concerned with the individual spy's relationship to the technology of bureaucracy and the hierarchies of the military-industrial complex. It is the work of John le Carré that explores the world of espionage as one in which the 'real enemy is the organization itself' (Denning 1987: 140). As his own comments on his Cold War writing indicate, le Carré saw spy fiction as 'a medium for criticizing a society which has developed a dangerous indifference to the grave threat of the Bomb . . . a society in which the gap between the decision-makers and those affected by their decisions . . . having widened to an intolerable degree' (in Sauerberg 1984: 13). His novels from the 1960s and 1970s explore the elaborate machinery of Intelligence and present the dispassionate power of institutions that dehumanize or crush individuals on both sides of the East–West divide. The nightmare expressed by one of the characters in *A Small Town in Germany* (1968) is that democracy is 'a flash of light between feudalism and automation, and now it's gone . . . the voters are cut off from parliament, parliament is cut off from the Government and the Government is cut off from everyone. Government by silence . . . Government by alienation' (le Carré 1968: 128).

The bureaucratic Cold War systems of intelligence necessitate the dehumanization of the individual: le Carré's spies are alienated in all areas of human interaction; they have sacrificed spontaneity and individuality to the technique or 'tradecraft' of the intelligence service to become mere nodes in a system. Dehumanized characters include Toby Esterhase in *Tinker, Tailor, Soldier, Spy* (1974) and Leclerc in *The Looking-Glass War* (1965), but this process is epitomized by Control, the head of the Circus in *The Spy Who Came in from the Cold* (1963) and *The Looking-Glass War*. Control's very name subsumes him into his function. Control is a key figure who excels in the successful technique of tradecraft, and for him this takes priority over any ethical claims; he functions with a machine-like amorality and efficiency. George Smiley, one of le Carré's best-known protagonists, who features in a number of his novels, is a hero in that he presents a humane alternative to the dehumanized amorality of Control and the system. Smiley is the opposite of James Bond's machismo, loving his unfaithful wife, for example, and cutting a rather shabby and pathetic figure as a man, but he too resists the technologies of the Cold War. It is Smiley's handling of information, his ability to work the system, coupled with his humanist, scholarly approach, that makes him superior to the machinations and mechanics of the institutions he confronts.

The impact of the bureaucratic system, with its links to a technological brutalization, is made clear in le Carré's hugely influential third novel, *The Spy Who Came in from the Cold* (1963), in which Smiley plays only a subsidiary role. The central protagonist, Leamas, is a typical le Carré spy, a failure in personal relations (like Smiley he has a failed marriage) and fundamentally dehumanized by his role in the system. The novel tells us explicitly that espionage 'is rooted in the theory that the whole is more important than the individual' (1963: 124), and Leamas is finally revealed to be a mere cog in a complex conspiracy that is willing to sacrifice better men (and women) to save a Soviet mole. Leamas's own trajectory in the novel is from debasement and despair to a reconnection to the world through his love for Liz. As

Leamas says, Liz gives back to him 'the caring about little things' (96). But Leamas's discovery of his humanity and capacity for emotions is pointless in the face of the bureaucracy that controls him. As Leamas turns to face death with Liz, rather than accept the arm over the Wall that Smiley proffers, this fact is made brutally clear to him. In his final betrayal, as the searchlights activate, 'the whole world seemed to break into flame; from everywhere, from above and beside them, massive lights converged, bursting upon them with savage accuracy' (228). Leamas's last vision, in this technological, military glare, is of children on the verge of being destroyed by modern technology: 'a small car smashed between great lorries, and the children waving cheerfully through the window' (229).

With the contrasting battles of their individual protagonists, le Carré and Fleming centralize the importance of espionage in the Cold War and its connection to emerging techno-structures of communication and control. The systems Smiley and Bond struggle against were, in the real world, inextricably linked to the expansion of information systems in the second half of the twentieth century, and to the new computing technology that underpinned these. As the development of the Colossus machine remained secret until the 1970s, it had little impact on the emergence of international computing industries. But, like the Colossus, other early computers were the product of the military-industrial complex. The key factor in the development of computing in the USA was the speed and complexity of the battlefield. The Electronic Numerical Integrator and Computer (ENIAC) was designed and built to compute artillery firing tables for the American military. Using a card reader and card punch, the ENIAC, unveiled in February 1946, could calculate two 10-digit additions or subtractions at 5,000 per second, but, like the earlier Colossus machines, it was not a stored program computer. This was achieved in Cambridge, UK, in 1949, with the Electronic Delay Storage Automatic Calculator (EDSAC) machine, and by the end of the following decade both the UK and the USA saw computers designed for business use. The integrated circuit (microchip) was invented in 1958, enabling increased capacity and speed and smaller size, inspiring Gordon Moore (a co-founder of Intel), in 1964, to come up with 'Moore's Law', an accurate prediction of the development of computing. It briefly states that the number of transistors on a microchip will double about every two years. The microchip also heralded the possibility of smaller, cheaper, potentially 'personal' computers and, in the 1970s and 1980s, home computers began to emerge, with the first IBM PC released in 1981. But computing had entered the popular imagination before this and a number of 1960s and 1970s TV series featured computers, sometimes malevolent and sometimes in the service of the protagonists: *Star Trek*, *Doctor Who*, *The Prisoner*, *Blake's Seven*, *The Avengers*, *Wonder Woman* – and even *Batman* had a large punch-card 'Batcomputer'. Digital computers, used at home and by businesses, organizations and institutions were central to the information society that developed in the late twentieth century. What is clear from the history of computing is the intimate connection between military needs and goals and the origins of the global digital architecture that enables the interconnected, instantaneous information world of the twenty-first century.

In the USA, the military continued to be one of the prime instigators and financial backers of computer development, with the army Ballistics Research Laboratory helping to develop a series of machines such as the EDVAC, ORDVAC and ILLIAC IV, while in 1958 the SAGE – Semi-Automatic Ground Environment – was launched, linking computers, radar, ships, aircraft and telephone lines in the United States and Canada in the first large-scale defence control network. Meanwhile, the US Department of Defense Advanced Research Projects Agency (ARPA) was established as a response to the Russian Sputnik programme and charged with finding the best use for computer investment. This agency went on to develop ARPANET as a way to create secure military communications between geographically remote computers. In October 1969, the first communication on ARPANET was established between UCLA and Stanford Research Institution, via an Interface Message Processor (IMP, now commonly known as a router) and using modems and a telephone line. The network grew rapidly with twenty-three host-nodes in 1971, at universities and government agencies, and 213 in 1981. Airlines and banks also developed network systems to deal with cash cards and ticketing. By the 1990s, the commercial organization known as the Internet had been established and the world is now inconceivable without its presence: in 2009, the International Telecommunication Union estimated that Internet users comprised 1.9 billion people or 26 per cent of the global population (International Telecommunication Union 2009).

It would, however, be wrong to see the development of the Internet as wholly the product of the US military-industrial complex. ARPANET was crucial for the development of the technology and the conception of computer networking, but Peter Willetts argues for the importance of NGOs in expanding the idea of computer networks beyond the closed systems of universities, airlines and banks into an Internet of public, transnational networking that connects diverse computer networks. Willetts cites the groundbreaking PeaceNet in the US and GreenNet in the UK as mid-1980s forerunners of contemporary Internet architecture.

It is important to distinguish between the Internet as the digitally enabled communications system (including both hardware and software) that spans the globe and the World Wide Web (consisting of software), which is one facet of the Internet, or one way in which the Internet is used globally. Tim Berners-Lee, working at CERN, is generally credited with inventing the World Wide Web. In 1990, Berners-Lee created the first web page (a web client and server) and originated the specifications of URLs, HTTP and HTML that were developed into global Web technology. The World Wide Web surfaced in popular consciousness in the mid-1990s, with the Mosaic browser in 1993 and the Netscape IPO in 1995. By December 1993, *The New York Times* (business section) and the *Guardian* and *The Economist* (UK) had published pages on the Internet and World Wide Web, while, with the June 1994 European Commission report into the potentials of Internet communications, the phrase 'Information Superhighway' had become part of the global cultural vocabulary.

The World Wide Web in the 1990s had a crucial formal and thematic impact on literature, enabling the emergence of cybertexts and hypermedia texts, and giving writers as diverse as Douglas Coupland and Jeanette Winterson novel subjects for their fiction. But computers featured widely in earlier fiction. In the 1950s and 1960s, super computers and computing networks figured prominently as the embodiment of a dehumanized system out of control. In his first novel, *Player Piano* (1952), which shares common ground with both *Nineteen Eighty-Four* and *Brave New World*, Kurt Vonnegut imagines a techno-utopia that has made any human labour or creativity redundant, and has the computer EPICAC coordinating the American economy. In D. F. Jones's 1966 novel, *Colossus*, a computer system designed to control the North American nuclear defences establishes a rapport with its Soviet counterpart and between them they take control of human life. Harlan Ellison's 1967 short story, 'I Have No Mouth, and I Must Scream', presents a more horrific vision, with the super-computer AM torturing the five survivors of the human race who are trapped in an endless underground complex and unable to kill themselves. Ellison chose to include the 'talk field' of AM itself in his story, reproducing punch-code tape sections and offering a visual presentation (in a column of capital letters) of the words that AM 'speaks' in 'a pillar of stainless steel bearing bright neon lettering' (243). In *2001: A Space Odyssey* (1968), the HAL 9000 sentient computer fatally malfunctions. Much more ubiquitous than positive images of artificial intelligence, these dark visions of the potential of computing suggest a deep paranoia about supra-human technological systems in control, with no heroic Bond or cultured Smiley to save humanity.

NUCLEAR CULTURE AND COUNTERCULTURE

Orwell's *Nineteen Eighty-Four* is one of the first of many texts to explore the ramifications of Cold War politics and to offer a dystopian vision of the impact of technological warfare in the aftermath of the atom bomb. The range of atomic fictions that emerged from the 1950s to the 1980s explored the catastrophic results of mutually assured nuclear destruction, and imagined different versions of the post-apocalyptic earth. The initial responses to the USA's victory over Japan celebrated the atomic bomb and its superior military power, but attitudes changed as the Soviet Union also developed atomic weapons, and as catastrophically powerful thermonuclear weapons (H-bombs) were developed, initially in the USA in 1954. John Hersey's *Hiroshima*, published as the entire issue of the *New Yorker* in August 1946, was a key text in presenting the individual horror of the bomb. Subsequently published as a book that sold in huge numbers worldwide, *Hiroshima* offers the account of six survivors of the Hiroshima blast and, as a prefatory note in the *New Yorker* explains, it intended to show 'the all but incredible destructive power' of the atomic bomb so that 'everyone might well take time to consider the terrible implications of its use'. In the following decade, Nevil Shute's *On The Beach* (1957) was the most widely read of post-apocalypse novels, while the 1980s, at the height of 'second Cold War' tensions between Reagan's USA and the Soviet Union, saw another period of intense speculation about nuclear holocaust with texts like Jonathan Schell's *The Fate of the Earth* (1982), Raymond Briggs's *When the Wind Blows* (1982) and the TV film *The Day After* (1983).

The immediate impact of nuclear war, the experience of survivors and the long-term effects of radiation poisoning all concerned writers, and in the UK a powerful anti-nuclear campaign, the Campaign for Nuclear Diasarmament (CND) mobilized many intellectuals and artists. Sylvia Plath attended a CND demonstration in 1962 and her work demonstrates an anxiety about nuclear contamination and a comment on American Cold War politics, exacerbated by events such as the Bay of Pigs and Cuban Missile crisis. Her poetic and collage work critiques the gender politics of Cold War military and corporate economies, exploring particularly the impact on women's bodies and on children (see Peel 2002, 2006). Plath's critique resonates with one of the most interesting Cold War texts to examine the masculinist rhetoric of nuclear weapon technology. Stanley Kubrik's 1963 film, *Dr Strangelove, or How I Learned to Stop Worrying and Love the Bomb*, was based on the novel *Red Alert* by Peter George (1958: published in Britain as *Two Hours to Doom* under the pseudonym Peter Bryant). In *Red Alert*, a rogue US Air Force Brigadier orders a nuclear attack on the Soviet Union; the president knows the Soviet response would destroy the world and manages to recall all the planes except one, the *Alabama Angel*. This plane is damaged, however, and the bombs fail to hit their target, meaning the only deaths are those of the crew. *Dr Strangelove* exaggerates and amplifies the masculinist rhetoric and anxiety that underpin the action in *Red Alert*. From the beginning, in an opening sequence that shows planes in mock-copulation in mid-air refuelling, with the romantic soundtrack of 'Try a Little Tenderness', the machines of war are shown to be sexual, phallic substitutions for the weakness of men. There are multiple sexual jokes and references in *Dr Strangelove*, and the rogue Air Force Commander, General Jack D. Ripper, is plagued by deep paranoia about the contamination of his 'precious bodily fluids' (and his sexual dysfunction). In one of the closing scenes, Major T. J. 'King' Kong, the Texan pilot of the plane that heads to its mission, rides the huge projectile of a bomb towards its target like a cowboy on a bronco.

But *Dr Strangelove* does not only ironically treat the idea of military technology as phallic substitute; the film also shows how the human individual has become finally isolated within technological communications and military intelligence. All the locations of the film – the Air Force base, inside the B-52 bomber, the President's War Room – present a synthesized version of the real world, mediated to the male subjects through technology (radios, radar, telephones, tracking systems). The various sexual stimulations and supplements in the film stand in for the possibility of any actual connection in the 'real'. As the world is destroyed at the end of the film, Dr Strangelove himself proposes a survival strategy – a mineshaft for society's elite men with ten desirable women each – to replace love and monogamy with a mechanistic fantasy of sexual breeding that deliberately echoes the eugenic fantasies of the Nazis. The final sequence, Vera Lynn's recording of 'We'll Meet Again' as the soundtrack for stock images of the atomic mushroom cloud, enshrines the depersonalizing effect of military technology, transforming the world into an abstract collection of disintegrating visual–aural information. As Paul Virilio writes: '[h]ere nothing is left but the recording of successive stages of discharged matter and the record of a faraway voice which sings of the desire for reunion that has now become physically impossible, only this time for everyone and evermore' (1989: 24). What *Dr Strangelove* presents is the dissolution of the human into the weapons and communications of an abstract Cold War military system.

The prescience of *Dr Strangelove* is not in its version of global nuclear apocalypse, then, but in its negative vision of technologically mediated human interaction: the early twenty-first century is one in which human relations, personal identities, social conversations and romantic liaisons are conducted through technological prostheses. Through digital computing, we are ever present to any active node in a global network of connections and communications but, as critics would have it, this makes us virtually absent from physical connection. And it is the technology of the Cold War that initiates this transformation of the social and personal field of interactions, and that also provokes resistance from those unwilling to accept the systematization of individual and social life.

If Fleming and le Carré offer a British literary response to the C3 organizations of the Cold War, one of the most prominent movements reacting against the systems of post-Second World War America was that of the Beat generation. The Beats sought an escape from the normativity and containment of Cold War American nuclear culture, characterized by the de-individualizing effects of bureaucratic planning and cultural totalization. Rejecting consumerism, the suburban habitat and the middlebrow cultural status quo, the Beats were crucial precursors for the counter-culture of the 1960s. The technological order that Marcuse identified in his *One-Dimensional Man* and the homogeneity of the technological Culture Industry that Horkheimer and Adorno decried were anathema to the Beats and their successors. Their work can be read as an attempt to escape from a deathly technological paradigm into spontaneity, experimentation, visceral experience and the 'beatific'. Paradoxically, however, for key Beats such as William Burroughs, Allen Ginsberg and Jack Kerouac, it was through technological means that they envisioned their escape.

William Burroughs was resolutely resistant to the idea of system and domination. His writing, in texts such as *Naked Lunch* (1959), demonizes bureaucracy that is understood as an invasive culture of organization: 'A bureau takes root anywhere in the state, turns malignant like the Narcotic Bureau, and grows and grows . . . Bureacracy is wrong as a cancer, a turning away from the human evolutionary direction of infinite potentials and differentiation and independent spontaneous action' (134). In *Naked Lunch*, Burroughs depicts a society in which the individual uses technology and consumer goods to escape from themselves, and in both this text and *Nova Express* (1964) Burroughs presents a vision of a contemporary techno-culture that has territorialized the private subject. These novels are, for McLuhan, 'a kind of engineer's report of the terrain hazards and mandatory processes, which exist in the new electric environment' (1964b: 517). Burroughs's strategies for escaping the containments of language culture ('word traps') included activities such as cut-ups and fold-ins, which are fundamentally a mechanical method of juxtaposing verbal (and other) texts. This introduction of an inorganic process (as Burroughs writes in *Naked Lunch*, 'I am a recording machine' (200)) is not intended as a reduction to automatic meaning, but the introduction of a randomness and lack of human agency that will liberate meaning. But Burroughs's use of technology went further; he experimented extensively with magnetic tape recordings in the 1960s, splicing his own voice reading (his own texts and others) with radio broadcasts and noises. In this, he was engaging directly with a technology manufactured by war: it was equipment seized when the Allies entered Germany in 1945 that revolutionized sound recording and enabled the commercial development of magnetic tape. As Burroughs's later experiments using guns to create art indicate, he incorporated the random effects of deathly technologies into his aesthetic.

Ginsberg is a more direct critic of the American system in pieces such as 'Howl' (1956) where he identifies a country damaged by, among other things, the military-industrial complex and machinations of the secret service. 'Howl' attacks the 'pure machinery' of 'Moloch' 'whose fate is a cloud of sexless hydrogen'. In contrast, Ginsberg offers his own counter-attack: 'our own souls' airplanes roaring over the roof they've come to drop angelic bombs', declaring 'O starry-spangled shock of mercy the eternal war is here' (1984: 131, 133). Ginsberg satirizes Cold War paranoia in the poem 'America' (1956) and offers his own version of the military weapon as sexual supplement: 'Go fuck yourself with your atom bomb,' he challenges 'America' (1984: 146). As a response to the American 'War Machine', in 'Death to Van Gogh's Ear!' (1957) Ginsberg imagines himself as a pseudo-military device: 'I am the defense early warning system' (1984: 168). In the 1960s, Ginsberg articulates an explicit and complete rejection of Cold War technology and American military activities in Vietnam in his 'Wichita Vortex Sutra' (1966). But this does not prevent him from using a tape-recorder, into which he has dictated 'Wichita Vortex Sutra' while driving around Kansas. Ginsberg's car, in this poem, offers him a moving space of solitude from which to compose the poem – to 'speak my lonesomeness in a car' with 'black Earth-circle in the rear window, | no cars for miles along the highway | beacon lights on oceanic plain' (1984: 396, 405).

The car, for Jack Kerouac, is much more than a contemplative or poetic space; it is an ideological vehicle that underpins his *On The Road* (1951, first published 1957). The car enables the frenetic spontaneity that liberates his protagonists, and driving is repeatedly described in powerful, aggressive terms as 'roared', 'zoomed', 'blasted' and 'gunned'. To be on the road, driving at high speed, is to inhabit a non-space beyond the grasp of materialism and normativity: 'we'd dig the whole world with a car like this because, man, the road must eventually lead to the whole world' (1951: 328). Neal Cassady (Dean in the 1957 published version) is in perfect affinity with the cars he drives: 'sometimes he had no hands on the wheel and yet the car went as straight as an arrow' (218). In an odd echo of Marinetti's Futurist rhetoric of the automobile, Kerouac offers a vision of Neal as a messianic road-angel:

a burning shuddering frightful Angel, palpitating toward me across the road, approaching like a cloud, with enormous speed, pursuing me like the Shrouded Traveller on the plain, bearing down on me. I saw his huge face over the plains with the mad, bony purpose and the gleaming eyes; I saw his wings; I saw his old jalopy chariot with thousands of sparking flames shooting out from it; I saw the path it burned over the road; it even made its own road and went over the corn, through cities, destroying bridges, drying rivers. (1951: 360)

The counter-cultural movement of the 1960s contrasts with the Beats in being a much more politically engaged resistance to Cold War America and an attempt to actually replace totalizing and bureaucratic systems with its own communitarian utopias. But Ken Kesey and the Merry Pranksters' bus do form a direct link between the Beat generation and 1960s counter-culture – Neal Cassady drove the bus in 1964. The acid tests that Kesey was so interested in had their origin in Kesey's own techno-military encounter: he had his first experience of LSD as a volunteer on a CIA-funded medical project. The counter-culture of the 1960s did seem to be much more clearly defined as an opting out of contemporary, technological society, but was also connected, in Charles Manson's The Family death cult, for example, with annihilating or apocalyptic tendencies. Moreover, many counter-cultural communities sustained a healthy interest in advanced technology that was not necessarily at odds with their tribal democracies. A direct link can be made from these 'natural' communities and the California computer industry, with the rebels and dropouts emerging as the inventors and entre-preneurs of Silicon Valley. Thus, in the 1960s, the American counter-cultural *Whole Earth Catalogue* advertised and explored advanced technological equipment and techniques in an odd juxtaposition of deliberate primitivism and high tech: 'On one page the "Manifesto of the Mad Farmer Liberation

Front" . . . on the next, Norbert Wiener's cybernetics' (Roszak 2000: 'A Taste for Industrial Light and Magic', np). The computing industry and Internet architecture that has transformed our contemporary world thus has a very odd Cold War legacy, emerging from military investment, hardware and communications developments on the one hand, and 1960s counter-culture and 1980s NGOs on the other.

POSTMODERNISM, MEDIA AND THE DEATH OF THE REAL

What postmodern fiction inherits from the Cold War is a particular version of the paranoia that informs espionage fiction. Indeed, the command technologies of rationalized capitalism that writers such as Kurt Vonnegut, Thomas Pynchon and Don DeLillo explore through the structure and trope of conspiracy theories appears directly inherited from Cold War spy novels. This emerges in their fiction in a distinctive combination with counter-cultural impulses and popular cultural representations of technology.

Kurt Vonnegut's writing draws on fantasy and science fiction to consider the increasing technologization of the world. In *Player Piano*, with its giant EPICAC computer, Vonnegut explores a world in which engineers of huge corporations attempt to automate all of human activity. It was written during Vonnegut's time at General Electric when he was, in his own words, 'completely surrounded by machines and ideas for machines' (1965: 2). In *Cat's Cradle* (1963), where a scientific invention, 'ice-nine', inadvertently destroys the world, Vonnegut satirizes the Cold War arms race. Vonnegut's *Slaughterhouse Five* (1969) returns to the Second World War and offers a postmodern account of the Allies' destruction of Dresden with phosphorus bombs on 14 February 1945. Vonnegut interleaves his own experience of this event with the fictional reconstruction of it by his author-narrator ('All this happened, more or less'), focalized through the protagonist Billy Pilgrim, an alien-abductee who is 'spastic in time' (1, 17). The novel itself is permeated by death, from Billy's dead dog Spot, to the 135,000 dead in Dresden, to the death of the entire universe in an alien (Tralfamadorian) flying-saucer experiment. The only counter to all this death is the fatalistic Tralfamadorian mantra 'so it goes', an ironic articulation of the acceptance of death (and the technologies that produce it) that Vonnegut perceived in his contemporary world. Locked as a prisoner in the eponymous *Schlachthof-fünf*, Billy Pilgrim is an unwilling witness to the decimation of Dresden, but, unlike the author-narrator, he fails to develop a consciousness of the terrible dangers of the military-industrial complex. Where the present-day narrator tells his children 'that they are not under any circumstances to take part in any massacres' and describes how 'my Government gives me a count of corpses created by military science in Vietnam', Billy Pilgrim at the same point in time listens uncomplaining to a Major in the Marines condoning 'bombing North Vietnam back into the Stone Age' (14, 43, 154). As a passive victim, immersed in a consumerist world and unable to resist the apocalyptic Cold War nexus of militarism and technology, Billy functions as a warning of its terrible power.

The terrifying power of the Second World War German V-2 rocket opens Thomas Pynchon's 1973 novel, *Gravity's Rainbow*: 'A screaming comes across the sky. It has happened before, but there is nothing to compare it to now' (3). The V-2 was the first long-range ballistic missile, flying at five times the speed of sound, and was the progenitor of all modern rocket technology. Over a thousand V-2s fell on London in 1944 and 1945, and the scientists engaged in its development played a crucial post-war role in missile and rocket technology in both the USA and the Soviet Union. The V-2 is a central motif in Pynchon's novel, which associates the sexually charged military technology (of the rocket) with the emergence of the techno-bureacracy of the Cold War. The rocket is a structural and thematic motif linking also with the amorphous conspiracies (and counter-cultures) and the novel's constituent circularity which mirrors the arc of the rocket's flight.

Tyrone Slothrop, the novel's protagonist (though he does disintegrate some time before the end of the novel), is intimately connected to the V-2, it is suggested, through an infant Pavlovian conditioning which has subsequently created an affinity between his sexual experiences and the trajectory of the rocket. As the novel develops, a new rocket, the 00000 (and its unknown component *S-Gerät* and plastic *Imipolex G*), becomes the object of a nebulous quest through the final years of the Second World War, with the conspiracies extending into the 1970s. Slothrop's experiences, as an object of surveillance from before birth, and those of other characters, reveals the novel's concern with the individual subsumed into the System in which authority is anonymous and diffused. The conspiracies imagined by the novel constitute a transnational network of corporations, including IG Farben, Shell, General Electric, ICI, Krupp, and the System has many manifestations. One of these, the Operation, resonates with the secret service that le Carré presents, as an organization that incorporates and de-individualizes the human subject: 'Only the demands of the Operation. Each of us has his place, and the tenants come and go, but the places remain' (1973: 729). All of the amorphous manifestations of the System manipulate and control the human individual, and the System is fundamentally a paranoid epitome of the military-industrial complex.

The System, as described in *Gravity's Rainbow*, is also a manifestation of the technological ontology that Heidegger warns of, the enslavement of human consciousness to a mode of technological revealing and imposition on the world: 'Taking and not giving back, demanding that "productivity" and "earnings" keep on increasing with time, the System removing from the rest of the World these vast quantities of energy to keep its own tiny desperate fraction showing a profit: and not only most of humanity – most of the World, animal, vegetable and mineral, is laid waste in the process' (489–90). For Pynchon, this enslavement to technological enframing heralds global catastrophe; just as the rocket cannot escape the force of gravity, so the System 'sooner or later must crash to its death, when its addiction to energy has become more than the rest of the World can supply, dragging with it innocent souls all along the chain of life' (490). Writing in the *New York Times* in 1984, Pynchon makes clear that the systemic machineries of modern culture are coterminous with the technologies of death that characterized the Second World War and shaped the politics of Cold War technology:

By 1945 the Factory system – which, more than any piece of machinery was the real and major result of the Industrial Revolution – had been extended to the Manhattan Project, the German long range missile program and the death camps such as Auschwitz. It has taken no major gift of prophecy to see how these three curves of development might possibly converge. (41)

Thus, the annihilating power of the System in *Gravity's Rainbow* is also the annihilating power of nuclear missiles which, in turn, inform the strategies and systems of the Cold War world. The fact that the atomic bomb features only marginally in *Gravity's Rainbow* – the 'scrap of newspaper headline' with the letters 'MB DRO' 'ROSHI' that Slothrop finds in the final section (1973: 822) – whereas the German V-2 rocket programme is central shows that Pynchon is not concerned with evaluating the relative merits of Second World War weaponry, but with pursuing the convergence of the deathly technological systems of Allies and Germans alike to its ascendancy in the Cold War world. At the end of the novel, the destructive technologies come together as an annihilating rocket falls in the absolute present moment, the 'last delta-t' (902), on us as reader/audience in a darkened cinema.

What Pynchon poses in his 1984 article is a resistance to technological systems, asking that we 'deny the machine at least some of its claims on us' (41). In *Gravity's Rainbow*, Pynchon explores the possibility of freedom from or resistance to the System-machines, in characters who seek escape from it in and through drug hallucinations, mystical cultic experience or sexuality. But too often they are trapped in their own alternate systems of resistance and power as Pynchon ironically indicates with the term 'Counterforce' in the final section of the novel. The carnivalesque counter-cultural energies in the novel cannot fully escape the overarching dialectic of technological force and counterforce in what John Hamill describes as Pynchon's 'transparent allegory of sixties notions of Counterculture' (1999: 434).

But Pynchon also offers, as a textual counter culture, the very form of his novel, with its ludic elements and disruptive form. *Gravity's Rainbow*, written in the present tense, refuses the structures of cause and effect and disintegrates the singular 'I' of characters. But this is not just an experiment in postmodern form: what Kittler points out in one of his readings of *Gravity's Rainbow* (Kittler 1997) is that the fabric and form of the novel enact the very real shifts in the human experience of war and the human inscription by media and information technologies that characterize the post-Second World war era. Pynchon presents the end of narrative in this war novel because it has become impossible to narrativize or historicize war. The convergence of visual, information and military technologies has produced warfare that consists in coincidental events, random correspondence and patterns (chaotic, entropic, stochastic) which all exceed the human individual. All that remains is the facticity of the real, of moments, events, and raw information. As Kittler describes, the novel is not just full of cultural, textual and contextual references but 'builds almost exclusively upon documentary sources in a manner akin to historical novels of the type of *Salammbô* or *Antonius*, to which it adds, for this first time, schematics and differential equations, corporate contracts, and organizational graphs' (1997: 161). The basic undertaking of *Gravity's Rainbow* is therefore 'data retrieval' (Pynchon 1973: 689) and the representation of a 'whole *generation*' for whom 'Postwar [is] nothing but "events," newly created one moment to the next' (65).

One of Pynchon's characters, admittedly while on amphetamines, has a revelation of the actual relation between technology and war: 'this War was never political at all, the politics was all theatre all just to keep the people distracted . . . secretly, it was being dictated instead by the needs of technology . . . by a conspiracy between human beings and techniques, by something that needed the energy-burst of war' (1973: 617). The Second World War is understood as a 'spectacle' (124) that disguises the real competition, between techniques and technologies, not nations. The rocket motif that encapsulates the 'energy-burst' dictated by the needs of technology opens the novel, which also closes with 'the pointed tip of the Rocket' falling to its target (902). In the final rocket-launch, Pynchon parodies the rhetoric of technology and of war, expressed by Captain Weissmann in profoundly masculinist terms: '[b]eyond simple steel erection, the Rocket was an entire system *won*, away from the feminine darkness, held against the entropies of lovable but scatterbrained Mother Nature' (386). Recasting Major Kong's bronco-bomb ride in *Dr Strangelove*, the climactic scene in *Gravity's Rainbow* satirizes an idealized union of beloved with military technology as Blicero (Captain Weissmann) launches his lover Gottfried in the nose of the 00000 Rocket: 'The two, boy and Rocket, concurrently designed. Its steel hindquarters bent so beautifully . . . he fits so well. They are mated to each other . . . His bare limbs in their metal bondage writhe among the fuel, oxidizer, live-steam lines, thrust frame, compressed air battery, exhaust elbow, decomposer, tanks, vents, valves' (891).

This eroticization of technology and death has a counterpart in J. G. Ballard's novel *Crash*, published the same year as *Gravity's Rainbow*. In *Crash*, the car, the vehicle of Kerouac's flight out of corporate capitalism, is the fetishized zone of sexual encounters generated by the 'perverse eroticism of the car crash' (1973: 17). The characters of Ballard's novel experience the conjunction of wounds, death and technology as the ultimate sexual arousal, and the text describes car interiors and sexual congress in the same flat, meticulous language, merging human body parts and car parts into 'conjunctions between elbow and chromium window-sill, vulva and instrument binnacle' (106). One of the central characters, Vaughan, is obsessed with the deaths of celebrities in cars and photographs of crashes, signalling the novel's concern with the technological mediation of desire. This mediation is taken to its extreme in the auto-eroticism of the car crash: a merging with the car in death that is poorly approximated by sex in cars. Vaughan's vision of the crash is one that incorporates the whole world in one orgasmic disaster: 'millions of vehicles hurled together in a terminal congress of spurting loins and engine coolant' (16). The character James Ballard imagines that, in his own car-crash death, Vaughan could achieve a techno-transcendence: 'Vaughan could never really die in a car crash, but would in some way be re-born through those twisted radiator grilles and cascading windshield glass' (210). But Vaughan fails to achieve his desired transcendent union of crashing in his car with Elizabeth Taylor in hers, falling instead in his vehicle from the Heathrow flyover on to an airline coach. Similarly, the Rocket, in *Gravity's Rainbow*, must too, despite Captain Blicero's dreams of transcendence, inevitably fall, drawn back to earth by gravity. Pynchon's novel suggests that the transcendent phallicism of military technology (like the linearity of the text) collapses back on itself, as Randy Schroeder writes: 'the rocket can only turn back on its own context, its own theatre, which it never escaped in the first place' (2002: 93).

The implication of *Gravity's Rainbow* is that a technological system can only ever return to itself; it has no possibility of reference beyond its own terms. Even war is not about itself, but about the competition of technologies, for 'the real crises were crises of allocation and priority, not among firms . . . but among the different Technologies, Plastics, Electronics, Aircraft' (1973: 617). *Gravity's Rainbow* presents humanity caught up in what Kittler terms 'total semiotechnology', where there is no meaning outside that of technology and where 'everything takes places as if in the media that, from the drama to the computer, only process information' (1997: 159). This sense of a technological *mise en abyme* chimes closely with the representation of media technology in Don DeLillo's writing. *White Noise* (1985) is centrally preoccupied with the media capture of death and disaster, so that it can only be experienced through its technological mediation: disaster as a SIMUVAC (Simulated Evacuation) and death as media simulacra that can be warded off with an artificial compound (Dylar). In DeLillo's earlier novel, *End Zone* (1972), what is ostensibly a sports novel deconstructs to connect language, football and thermonuclear war, revealing the corollaries between the closed system of football and the Cold War mentality. The opening of *Underworld* (1997a) also connects sport and nuclear war, but DeLillo is essaying something different in this novel. In the Prologue to *Underworld*, Jackie Gleason, Frank Sinatra and J. Edgar Hoover watch the New York Giants hit a last-minute, world-series, winning home run on 3 October 1951, as Hoover is informed of a Soviet nuclear blast in Kazakhstan. At the end of the novel, a nun, Sister Alma Edgar, witnesses multiple nuclear bomb explosions on the H-bomb home page in cyberspace. The narrative arc between these two points is one that explores the cultural effects of the nuclear bomb for inhabitants of Cold War culture and the symbiotic relationship between media and military technologies that emerges from it (see Spencer 2002). Thus, Beat culture is Cold War bomb culture: 'The whole beat landscape was bomb-shadowed. It had always been . . . The bomb was their handiest reference to the moral squalor of America, the guilty place of smokestacks and robot corporations' (DeLillo 1997a: 545).

In a well-known *New York Times* piece DeLillo described his concerns in *Underworld*, highlighting what he saw as the power of language as a 'counterhistory' which can confront 'the monotone of the state, the corporate entity, the product, the assembly line'. DeLillo identifies the 'primal clash' of his novel as 'the tendency of the language to work in opposition to the enormous technology of war that dominated the era and shaped the book's themes' (1997b: 62, 63). The connections between people, events and times in *Underworld* are repeatedly figured through the nuclear bomb: Matt Shay's work in the 'Pocket' on 'consequence analysis' of nuclear blasts (401), his brother Nick's witnessing of an underground Soviet nuclear test, the spray-painted B-52 bombers of Klara Sax's Land art, Lenny Bruce's closing tagline 'We're all gonna die!'; as DeLillo stated in an interview, 'all technology refers to the bomb' (in DePietro 2005: 124). But *Underworld* is not an apocalyptic text; it is the cultural effects of the bomb, with its production of a Cold War system of interconnected paranoias and uncertainties, and their effects on the individual, that the novel explores. As Hoover muses at the opening: 'There is the secret of the bomb and there are the secrets that the bomb inspires, . . . the genius of the bomb is printed not only in its physics of particles and rays but in the occasion it creates for new secrets . . . hundred of plots go underground, to spawn and skein' (1997a: 51).

Underworld's Cold War culture is characterized by surveillance and control and technologies and organizations, which produce a system resulting in the capture and invasion of the individual. This is both alienating and comforting, for Matt in his military work and for Nick in his waste corporation. Matt yearns to be part of the centre of the atomic industry, and Nick points out that 'The corporation is supposed to take us outside ourselves . . . You feel the contact points around you, the caress of linked grids that give you a sense of order and command' (1997a: 89). For Nick, moreover, the information and communication machines reinforce this order and purpose: 'It is about the cell phones slotted in the desk chargers, the voice mail and e-mail – a sense of order and command reinforced by the office itself and the bronze tower that encases the office and by all the contact points that shimmer in the air somewhere' (806). Nick's sense of connectedness in his office is paralleled by the fantasy of cyberspace that DeLillo ends the novel with, where 'everything is connected . . . linked, hyperlinked' (825), and DeLillo is very pessimistic about the reality of this techno-utopia. *Underworld* is highly sceptical of the possibility of a technological reality 'becoming a thing in the world' (826) and refuses the illusory 'Peace' that the technological system offers. This has already been foreshadowed by Marvin Lundy's mistaken belief that technology (photography) will help him to find reality (the destination of the home-run baseball). Lundy believes that 'This is what technology does. It peels back the shadows and redeems the dazed and rambling past. It makes reality come true'; 'Once you get inside a dot, you gain access to hidden information' (177).

DeLillo's treatment of the Texas Highway Killer video presents another role for technology, a 'shadow technology' that 'intensifies and compresses the event', moving it from any real-world referent to a realm of entertainment and media spectacle (159). Matt's work during the Vietnam War, deciphering aerial reconnaissance images, reveals how this virtualization of the real begins in the theatre of war. Matt's position, 'cranking rolls of film across a light box' (462), recalls the cinema of war reflected on throughout literature of the Second World War. Matt's work actually creates a reality from the data: 'When he found a dot on the film he translated it into letters, numbers, co-ordinates, grids, entire systems of knowledge' (463). DeLillo is thus not simply elaborating Secretary of State Rusk's claim that Vietnam was 'the first struggle fought on television', but explores the Cold War technologies of military-created seeing. The novel exemplifies what Virilio describes as 'the transpolitical pan-cinema of the nuclear age . . . an entirely cinematic vision of the world' (66), and it is this danger that *Underworld* warns of.

The implosion of war into a cinematic spectacle for the West happened on September 11, 2001, in an event prefigured by the cover image of *Underworld*. The collapse of the World Trade Center towers marked the end of the twentieth century for commentators as diverse as Slavoj Žižek – 'the last spectacular cry of twentieth-century warfare' (2002: 36–7) – and Paul Auster: 'so the twenty-first century finally begins' (cited Morley 2008: 249). DeLillo wrote his own response to September 11 in the December of 2001 ('In the Ruins of the Future') and in his 2007 novel *Falling Man*.

As the planes crashed and the Twin Towers fell, repeatedly, on screens around the world this event presented a visceral enactment of the convergence of military and media technologies, and 'this fantasmic screen apparition entered our reality . . . and shattered our reality' (Žižek 2002: 16). As Žižek argued, 'the association of the attacks with Hollywood disaster movies' (16) revealed 'the spectacular effect' (11) of the event and showed that 'the September 11 attacks were the stuff of popular fantasies long before they actually took place' (17). But this imploding of boundaries between real and technological fantasmic had already occurred in the arena of warfare, predicted in Virilio's own account of war and cinema. Baudrillard had, a decade earlier, argued that the meeting and merging of military and media technologies and the hyperreal scenario of 'live' battlefront TV coverage had elided the possibility of a 'real' war happening. The intensity of military deployment of simulation technologies in the first Gulf War reached new levels and this conflict, Baudrillard argued, witnessed an unprecedented military system that controlled the production and circulation of images, and simulated and controlled the actions of bodies and machines. Thus, the 'Gulf War did not take place', as he provocatively titled his 1991 essay, to signal what he saw as only a virtual engagement between two forces, the result of which was never in doubt. The advanced technology of the US and the UK necessarily triumphed in their technological slaughter of Iraqis, and the Western media spectacle merely reiterated and instantiated their military stratagem. The translation of major world conflicts (particularly the Second World War) into virtual-reality entertainment is fully fleshed out in the glut of computer and console games that appeared from the late 1990s, such as the *Medal of Honour* series (1999 onwards), *Call of Duty* series (2003 onwards), and *Company of Heroes* (2006 onwards). But violence has been a feature of video gaming since the early days of its inception, with the arcade game *Pong* in 1972 (see Kent 2001), as has the backlash against the supposed real-life effects of violent gaming. The *Death Race* arcade game (1976) (the object being to run down fleeing 'gremlins') was pulled after protest while, at the century's end, the game *Doom* was implicated in the violent tendencies of the 1999 Columbine High killers.

The twentieth century thus ends in a situation where, in a post-Cold War world, technologies of death, entertainment technologies and media forms are inextricably linked, and where virtual death becomes a cultural mainstay. What Baudrillard terms 'fake war, deceptive war, not even the illusion but the disillusion of war . . . the global disillusion of everyone else by means of information' (1991: 65), Žižek describes as 'a virtual war fought behind computer screens, a war experienced by its participants as a video game' (2002: 37), and Virilio characterizes as 'total war' in a 'permanent technological ambience' (1989: 66). But throughout the twentieth century and particularly in the explosion of information and control systems during the Cold War, technologies of death have challenged the precincts of the real and transgressed the boundaries of the human subject. Moreover, the range of texts that emerge out of and in response to war suggest a paradoxical situation: that military machines produce, rather than destroy, literature and culture.

5 Technological Texts: From Typewriters to Hypermedia

In 1874, E. Remington and Sons in Ilion, New York, began the serial production of the 'Sholes and Glidden Type Writer', bringing out the much more successful 'Remington No. 2' model in 1878. Remington was, and still is, a firearms manufacturer, responsible in the twentieth century for the biggest-selling pump-action shotgun in the world (the Model 870 'Wingmaster'). The company had diversified into other areas (notably sewing machines) after the American Civil War and their typewriter production was intended to use up excess capacity (see Bliven 1954: 56). The association of weapons and typewriters is remarked upon by a number of critics and reveals how the connections between technology and war are manifest in multiple forms and modes, wherever the history and culture of technology is closely examined. Kittler argues that war itself is the primary driver of media technological transformations. For Kittler, the American Civil War begets 'storage technologies for acoustics, optics, and script: film, gramophone, and the man-machine system, typewriter': the First World War introduces 'appropriate electric transmission technologies: radio, television, and their more secret counterparts': the Second World War and after brings 'the schematic of a typewriter to a technology of predictability . . . future computers' (Kittler 1999: 24).

Whether we accept the full extent of Kittler's analysis – and it seems problematic to reduce the complexity of the dynamic evolution of social systems to war and media – typewriters must be considered, not simply as machines that transformed the office spaces of the twentieth century, but as elements in a culture and a political and social domain reconfigured by the technological transformation of writing. With the advent of typewriting, it is primarily a machine that writes or at the very least mediates between the human subject and their writing. This removal of a direct physical link between writer and text has a profound impact on the position of the author and on the conception of the text. The typewriter has a social impact but also a material and aesthetic impact on literature; it is a prime example of a machine that changed the domain of the literary and the very stuff of literature. Moreover, it presaged for some the technologically mediated human interactions that would come to realization in the late twentieth century.

Writing in 1909 of a new version of the typewriter, the Zerograph (invented by Mr Leo Kamm of London), Geo Mares imagines a radical advance for typewritten communications. Describing how the Zerograph would transmit 'through the air two ether waves', causing the 'distant receiving typewriter to record the same letters upon a paper type', Mares speculates on a net-worked future:

In view of the possibility for developments of this machine, therefore, there would seem to be no reason why a man sitting at his Zerograph in London, may not, in the future, be able to hold written converse with his correspondents in the futhermost parts of the globe, without the intervention of any physical connection. (Mares 1909: 312, 314)

The World Wide Web can thus be located historically, not solely as a mani-festation of informatics or military culture, but in the dreams that the type-writer age instantiated.

TYPE-WRITERS AND TEXTS

Writing machines were patented from the eighteenth century with some of the first machines invented for the blind – Pière Foucauld, who patented his machine in Paris in 1849, was himself blind. These early machines, function-ing as prosthetic devices for the disabled, were cumbersome and unwieldy, using dials and levers, and it was not until Christopher Latham Sholes's upstrike key method and QWERTY keyboard arrangement that the poten-tial of the typewriter, writing faster than the human hand, could be realized.[1] The commercial success of the typewriter began with the Remington No. 2 model, and through the 1880s and 1890s a range of competing models appeared on the American and British market. Until the 1897 Underwood 'visible' front-strike typewriter, all typing was 'blind' (that is, the typist was unable to read the typescript past the mechanism). Nevertheless, the twen-tieth century dawned as one in which writing machines were both radically altering the dynamics and culture of the office workplace and beginning to metamorphose the way literary writing was perceived and practised.

At the basic level of its functioning, the typewriter can be conceived as instigating a disembodiment and disengagement of the text from its human origin. As both Mark Seltzer and Kittler emphasize, typewriting fundamen-tally disconnected the process of writing wherein the eye, hand and paper were bound up in a perfectly smooth continuity, and reinforced the notion of the self-presence of the writing act as creative process. As Heidegger describes it, 'the typewriter tears writing from the essential realm of the hand, i.e., the realm of the word. The word itself turns in to something "typed".' Heidegger's anxiety about this effect is that 'Mechanical writing', that is, 'writing withdrawn from the origin of its essence', 'degrades the word to a means of communication' (Heidegger 1942–3: 80–1, 85–6). Other anxieties about typewriting lay in the standardization that it imposed on writing, and the transformation of the human agent into an operator, reflected in the ambiguous use of the term 'type-writer' to designate both the machine and the individual using the machine, a designation evident in Treadwell's *Machinal* (1928). On the other hand, contemporary commentators saw the uniformity of the typewriter as its great achievement:

It has done more than anything else to create uniformity in business matters and in communications. It has rendered correct spelling a thing impossible to avoid. It has forced attention to the problems of punctuation. It has taught display, system, orderliness and a due regard for little things. It has trained even the most careless operators in a more or less perfect school of mechanics. (Mares 1909: 13)

The typewriter, then, can be seen as part of the wider cultural shift towards calculating, cataloguing and archiving data, creating set patterns and order from complex information, that can also be connected to the wider techno-epistemes in early twentieth-century culture.

The typewriter seemed ideal for the atomization and organization of work and information, but in its use and effect it had a profound impact on the way language and writing itself could be comprehended. Friedrich Nietzsche's employment of a typewriter, briefly in 1882, has been recorded, and its potential connection to his interest in the problem of language and his epistemological scepticism is an interesting area for speculation. Nietzsche's typewriting was not particularly successful – he was using an outmoded Writing Ball model, developed in Denmark in the 1860s, that had all sorts of mechanical problems. The resulting texts were mostly letters and some light poetry (Nietzsche titled it *500 Aufschriften auf Tisch und Wand: Für Narrn von Narrenhand*), but the effect of the experience of typing, where disconnected standardized letters take the place of the natural and immediate written word, presented language as radically contingent; 'Our writing tools are also working on our thoughts', Nietzsche commented in a letter written during his 1882 typing period (cited Kittler 1999: 200, see also Emden 2005).

Mark Twain, enthusiastic for all types of technological innovation, is usually credited with submitting the first typewritten literary manuscript, *Life on the Mississippi* (1883). But it is another American writer, Henry James, who offers an interesting perspective on the role of the typewriter in the production of literature. From 1897 onwards, Henry James dictated his writing to a secretary who typed directly on to a Remington typewriter, finding the noise of the writing machine conducive to his own dictation. And, as Pamela Thurschwell and others describe, he established a complex intimacy with his final, long-standing secretary Theodora Bosanquet, who was employed from 1907 (Thurschwell 2001: chapter 4). James described his writing practice in a letter as 'Remingtonese', a direct transformation of his words into text through the human-machine hybrid of the typewriter. This is one way in which the disembodiment of typewriting transformed the writing process, creating the possibility of a instant connection of speech to writing, where dictation appears as immediate writing: 'if the typewriter . . . *dis*articulates

the links between mind, eye, hand, paper, these links are *re*articulated in
the dictatorial orality that "automatically" translates speech into writing'
(Seltzer 1992: 201). In such a process, the typewriters (machine and individual) seem to be reduced to mere function, a mechanism for the words
of the writer.

As well as the process of mechanization, the emptying out of the body
of the typist connects also to the uncanny zones of techno-culture, the spiri-
tualist communications that found an affinity in the strangeness of new
electrical communications. Many researchers were interested in the properties of the typewriter as an automatic machine for writing other-worldly
messages and experimented with the typewriter (locking it in empty rooms,
for example), while ghostly typewriting features in John Kendrick Bangs's
1899 *The Enchanted Type-writer* and Anna C. Brackett's short story 'The
Strange Tale of a Type-Writer' (1890). After James's death in 1916, Bosanquet
worked as a medium, using automatic writing and receiving dictation from
beyond the grave from Henry and William James: while alive, William James
had written 'Notes on Automatic Writing' (1889) and Gertrude Stein, study-
ing with James, conducted her experiments in automatic writing at the
Harvard Psychological Laboratory.[2] The typist-medium here, the author of
automatic writing in a double sense, represents what Lisa Gitelman describes
as a 'dilemma of indeterminate authorial agency' (1999: 213) that seems
peculiarly modern. The typewritten word becomes a specific kind of signifier, one divorced from a certainty or singularity of origin and circulating
instead in a network of standardized, atomized signs.

If we can understand the typewritten word as a 'specific kind of signifier'
through which 'culture enters into modernity' (Keep 2001: 168), the body
of the typist also has a specific role in this entry into modernity, a body that
was functionally gendered as feminine. Shortly before his death in 1890,
Sholes had described his invention as 'a blessing . . . especially to womankind'
(cited Fleissner 2005: 68; Shiach 2000: 115), but the machine was not necessarily invented with women in mind despite the distinctly 'sewing-machine'
look of the first Remington model. However, ideas of the typewriter as a
'literary piano' (Mares 1909: 12) contributed to the conception of a natural
fit between women and the mechanics of the typewriter and the role of
transcription, and the role of type-writer and stenographer enabled by the
new machines meant that increasing numbers of young women from the
lower-middle and working classes entered the public space of late nineteenth-century offices.[3] Speed touch-typing amplified the idea of the perfect
mechanically attuned typist whose hands worked automatically, what
Christopher Keep describes as the 'endo-colonized subject, the woman who
has fully abandoned herself to the machine' (Keep 2001: 158). This colonized
body was subject to thorough regulation and control: in the 1916 Remington
Typewriter Company publication, *How To Become a Successful Stenographer,
For the Young Woman Who Wants to Make Good*, one chapter is entitled
'Making Your Body an Efficient Machine' and includes lunch menus to keep
you productive.

The 'Type-Writer Girl' entered the popular imaginary of the early twentieth century along with the New Woman and the Gibson Girl as an icon of liberated femininity, featuring in a thriving industry of Type-Writer Girl pornography (see Keep 1997). Grant Allen's (writing as Olive Pratt Rayner) novel *The Type-Writer Girl* (1897) explores the sexuality and class status of this new femininity. Better known as a scientific writer and Darwinist, Grant Allen's *The Woman Who Did* (1895) was very pessimistic about the New Woman, and he explores further questions about the role of liberated women in modern society in his *The Type-Writer Girl* protagonist Juliet Appleton. Juliet, a Girton graduate left penniless by her father's death, finds work and love as a 'type-writer', though finally forsaking her lover/employer on finding he is engaged to an old friend, and resolutely un-New Woman, the fragile, blonde Michaela. The text shows Juliet's sense of the machinic aspect of her work – 'I continued to click, click, click like a machine that I was' (Allen 1897: 35) – but this is then displaced on to Juliet's working-class colleague Elsie who is better suited to the mindless role: 'copying like a machine Elsie was perfectly happy' (94). Musing that 'No woman is born to be merely a type-writer', Juliet nonetheless reasserts her (single) working status at the end of the text: 'I am still a type-writer girl' (139). Allen's text, as Clarissa Suranyi indicates, explores the 'discourse of evolution, class and technology' (in Allen 1897: 9) as they meet on the body of the typist, and place the type-writer girl at the intersection and negotiation of technological modernity and the individual.

Bram Stoker's *Dracula*, also published in 1897, brings together discourses of gender, technology and modernity in a text mediated through the typewriter. Jennifer Wicke coins the phrase 'vampiric typewriting' to describe how this text engages with the new technologies and cultural forces of the age, offering a text in which 'mass mediation' (where language is refracted through mass culture and media machines) foreshadows the literary and cultural concerns of the twentieth century. As Jonathan Harker describes in his 'Note' that closes *Dracula*, in the 'mass of material' that composes the story of the text 'there is hardly one authentic document; nothing but a mass of type-writing' (486). The typewriting is the record of events that Mina Harker has copied and transcribed from sources including those produced by modern communication and media technologies (phonograph recordings, telegrams, newspaper articles). Mina's role as type-writer is fundamentally connected to her position as loyal wife (in contrast to the Vamp Lucy Westenra who succumbs to Dracula). As Mina writes to Lucy, her desire is to be 'useful' to Jonathan 'when we are married', hoping 'if I can stenograph well enough I can take down what he wants to say in this way and write it out for him on the typewriter, at which I am practising very hard' (74). But Mina's proximity to events, through her typing of them, places her in proximity to Dracula and the unsettling forces he represents; sexuality, racial/colonial otherness and, as recent critics have highlighted, mass culture. Bitten by Dracula and ensanguined with his blood, Mina Harker becomes the unknowing conduit of Dracula's consciousness, moving from the position of channelling the events of the text (as a type-writer) to channelling Dracula in a hypnotic trance. As Theodora Bosanquet and various ghostly type-writers demonstrate, there seems an inevitability in Mina's trajectory as an automatic writer. Mina is, of course, redeemed at the end of the novel, becoming a mother rather than a type-writer (the opposite ending to Grant Allen's Type-Writer Girl), but it might be possible to see *Dracula*'s conclusion as the more modern one. Jennifer Fleissner argues that Mina's role heralds the arrival of a twentieth century in which the working woman was not condemned, but allowed comfortably to inhabit the role of wife, mother and secretary where these roles involve being the desexualized body that supports masculine endeavour and expression.

TYPING, POETRY AND SPONTANEITY

For modernist writers, the typewriter was a further manifestation of the contemporary techno-sphere that had radically altered the experience of being in the modern world. Although typescripts were rapidly becoming the norm for literary manuscripts submitted to magazines and publishers, it was only gradually that writing machines had an impact on the form as well as the theme of writing. In modernist poetry, William Carlos Williams and Marianne Moore both demonstrated an interest in typewriters (and other machines); e e cummings used the regular spacing of the typewriter to enable a new emphasis on visual ordering; Hugh Kenner points to the importance of the space bar in the typography of Ezra Pound's texts from 1913 onwards (1971: 90). Later in the century, experimental poets used the typewriter to order and produce visual concrete poetry, but the artistic possibilities of the typewriter were explored by some from very early on: Mares's 1909 *The History of the Typewriter* includes two typewriter pictures, a portrait of 'Queen Victoria' executed on an *Oliver* typewriter and 'Flower Study' executed on a *Williams* typewriter. What these visual pictures demonstrate is the possibility that the typewriter could produce a new kind of art, one in which the regular spacing of the typewriter keyboard (it was 1944 before IBM introduced the 'Executive' electric typewriter with proportional spacing) could be used to produce (and reproduce) a machinic art.

In his 1917 collection, *Al Que Quiere!*, Williams was inspired by the mecanomorphic portraits of the New York Dadaist Francis Picabia to look at the importance of the printed page to poetic composition, and used line divisions to split rhythm units, producing what Marjorie Perloff describes as 'among other things, an homage to the typewriter' (Perloff 1983: 174). Even more radical in his typographic use of the typewriter, e e cummings takes advantage of the typewriter's power to control the exact spacing and shape of every line. He composed for the typewriter, and the look and meaning of many of his poems emerges directly from the typewritten page. In one piece, the typewritten 'l' as both a number (one) and a letter (*el*) creates meaning in a poem about solitariness:

l(a

le
af
fa

ll

s)
one
l

iness   (cummings 1991: 673)

As with later concrete poets such as Dom Sylvester Houédard, the typewriter was used to produce a new kind of poetry, and in this process the typewriter could be imagined as a machine for channelling artistic energy, for making the force of a text productive and focused. Williams used the typewriter to reorganize his poetry after he had written it, cutting his lines in different ways and structuring them through the grid of the typewriter keyboard by trying out different stanza divisions and lineations, 'mechanically manipulating his texts in a way far removed from the voice' (Berry 1988: 51). Marianne Moore used the typewriter as she wrote and it was crucial for the production of her intricate verbal patterns. In Moore's syllabic meter, each syllable has an individual significance which is not necessarily connected to context or meaning. The typewriter enabled, and perhaps even suggested, the process of mechanically separating language into units of individual significance, lying at the source of the tension between the organic and mechanical in Moore's poetic form. Precision and accuracy were crucial for both Williams and Moore, and were enacted through their typewriting, while T. S. Eliot comments in a 1916 letter to Conrad Aiken that 'the typewriter makes for lucidity' (cited Eliot 1971: x). For Moore, 'precision creates movement' and, for Williams, who described a poem as a 'machine made out of words', to 'Write going' is crucially important (1969: 256, 278). In 'The Pangolin', Moore's poetic description of the scaly anteater explores its fusion of mechanical and organic: it is a 'miniature artist engineer', 'da Vinci's replica'; with its 'Armor' and careful movement, it offers 'models of exactness'. In their very being, Moore's pangolins embody the careful mechanical production of a poem working through tensions:

> they have the not unchain-like machine-like
> form and frictionless creep of a thing
> made graceful by adversities, con-
> versities. (Moore 1984: 118)

Eleanor Berry connects this poem with Moore's use of the typewriter and her exploration of the way that precise patterns create shape and motion by channelling energy (53). But the tension between the organic and the mechanical, the flow of writing and the standardized machinic process, is not simply a productive one. Williams might have celebrated the linguistic transformation of the typewriter but he warns against the danger of coming to a 'stop' and making a 'fetish' of a machine. In a similar vein, Moore's poem 'To A Steam Roller' (which might be a critique of Ezra Pound) describes a mechanical process which reduces singularity to consistency; 'You crush all the particles down | into close conformity' (Moore 1984: 84). Eliot's *The Waste Land*, which associates the 'typist' with a dehumanizing, mechanical existence bounded by 'food in tins' and 'automatic' sexual encounters, extends this critique (Eliot 1940: 35, 37).

Eliot's 'typist' is his own take on the type-writer girl of the 1920s, and recalls the substantial connection between women and typing, suggesting the possibility of a gendered aspect to the typing experiments of the modernists. According to Kittler, the typewriter 'inverts the gender of writing [and] in so doing . . . inverts the material basis of literature', contributing to the implosion of the Gutenberg Galaxy and its 'sexually closed feedback loop' (1999: 183, 184). He argues that female typists brought about a revolution, not in terms of redrawing the boundaries of work and public office space, but in the order of discourse. The shift from pen to machine led to what he describes as a desexualization of writing, which enabled women to 'reign over text processing' (195). What Kittler's analysis suggests is a different way of approaching both the role of women in modernism and the masculinist assertions about the 'serious artist' from Pound et al. The predominance of women in the role of 'text processing', editing and publishing modernist texts, may be the necessary extension of the typist's invasion of the scene of the text, while the extreme masculinism or phallic anxiety of modernist men (Pound, Eliot, Lawrence and so on) stands as a response to the loss of the sexualized certainty of the writer's hand-pen, and the dexterity of women in type-writing and text processing. After taking secretarial courses at Carlisle Commercial College (1910–11), Marianne Moore taught typing along with stenography, book-keeping, and commercial English and law at the US Industrial Indian School at Carlisle until 1915. Her experience as a typist (or teacher of typists) can be connected to what seems her gendering of the typewriter: in her 1923 reading diary notes on the invention of the type-writer, she describes the typewriter and the sewing machine (collectively) as 'beautiful', (cited Steinman 1984: 200, n.18), and claiming American women have been '[a]ssisted by the typewriter, the sewing-machine, and the telephone' to be 'less servile' (cited Steinman 1984: 213).

Reflecting on Henry James's relationship with Theodora Bosanquet, Marshall McLuhan suggests that in dictating his writing to his type-writer, James 'developed a free, incantatory quality' (1964a: 283), and goes on to suggest that a similar freedom in poetry was 'encouraged' by the typewriter.

The poet at the typewriter, according to McLuhan, 'has the experience of performance as composition'; he [and McLuhan's poets are all men] has a 'machine' that is 'a public address system' as the typewriter 'brought writing and speech and publication into close association' (284, 285). McLuhan's example in *Understanding Media* is e e cummings, but elsewhere he offers Charles Olson as a prime example of the positive impact of the typewriter which, instead of disembodying the writer, marks his text with his very presence. McLuhan's comments gesture back to Olson's influential 1950 essay, 'Projective Verse', which emphasizes how the typewriter can record the breath and rhythm of the poet, a presence and an immediacy that is lost in the institutional transformation of manuscript to printed page. In 'Projective Verse', Olson's (typewritten) 'projective' or 'open' verse is posed in distinction to 'print bred' or 'closed' verse. According to Olson a poem should be a 'high energy-construct', and this can be only be achieved with a typewriter; 'from the machine'. In his essay, Olson argues that 'the advantage of the typewriter [is] that, due to its rigidity and its space precisions, it can, for a poet, indicate exactly the breath, the pauses, the suspensions even of syllables, the juxtapositions even of parts of phrases, which he intends.' Thus, a poet composing on a typewriter can use 'the machine as a scoring to his composing, as a script to its vocalization'; the machine can 'record' for him and 'indicate' to 'any reader' (Olson 1950: 16, 22). The poem 'The Kingfishers' (1949) expresses Olson's sense of the fine balance between communication and control in the ordered space of the typewritten page:

> We can be precise. The factors are
> in the animal and/or the machine the factors are
> communication and/or control, both involve
> the message. And what is the message? The message is
> a discrete or continuous sequence of measurable events distributed in time.
>   (Olson 1993: 9)

With the other Black Mountain poets, Olson's conception of the poem is of process, not a containing form. Thus, he rejects the homogenization of poetry in 'print verse' in favour of a more spontaneous expression through the typewriter. The apparent contradiction (writing machine produces living form) is resolved in Olson's sense of what the typewriter can do: record and transmit the immediate expression of the individual poet with no external interference, a reimagined form of automatic writing. What Olson's typewritten poetry offers is a familiarity between poet and machine that does not erase the human: the typewriter-machine enables an embodiment of a text, not its uncanny disembodiment. Olson's ideas emphasize the intimacy and corporeality of this technologically produced poetry and highlight how human–machine interactions are personal, individual and material.

Interviewed on a US TV show in March 1959, Truman Capote famously dismissed Jack Kerouac's work, saying: 'it isn't writing at all, it's typing', a dictum he was to repeat in subsequent interviews. Capote's resistance to

Kerouac, and by association the whole of the Beat Generation, is not surprising, but making a connection between such writers and technology was actually in keeping with certain aspects of Kerouac's celebration of speed, energy and power. Identifying Kerouac's writing as 'typing' may have been a dismissive reference to the story of the composition of *On The Road*, but Capote was unintentionally foregrounding the intense, machinic engagement which constituted Kerouac's literary practice. From his earliest representations of himself as a writer, Kerouac was a type-writer: 'Here I am at last with a typewriter', he wrote in 1941 (cited Wershler-Henry 2007: 238).

The composition of *On The Road*, punched out on a typewriter, is described by Allen Ginsberg:

On The Road was written around 1950, in the space of a few weeks, mostly on benny, an extraordinary project, sort of a flash of inspiration on a new approach to prose, an attempt to tell it completely, all at once . . . discover the rhythm of the mind at work in high speed in prose. An attempt to trap the prose of truth mind by means of a highly scientific attack on new prose method. The result was a magnificent single paragraph several blocks long, rolling, like the Road itself, the length of an entire onion-skin teletype roll. . . . the rhythms and swing of it . . . the sustained imagic rhythms of that magnificent endless paragraph. (Ginsberg 2000: 342)

This account of *On The Road*, supposedly typed by Kerouac in three weeks in April 1951 (not the 1950 that Ginsberg offers), has persisted in the Kerouac myth. Critical work has, though, uncovered a more accurate picture of Kerouac's composition, working with notebooks, letters and a chapter guide on the desk next to him, consciously making the scroll (by cutting and taping together drawing paper) and very likely powered by nothing stronger than caffeine (see Cunnell 2007). But the typewriting is central, a way for Kerouac who, as friends recall, was an amazingly fast typist, to channel and record directly, to reproduce the immediacy of subjective experience. It is through typewriting that Kerouac perceived his ideas of spontaneous writing. In the essay 'Essentials of Spontaneous Prose' (1958), Kerouac declared his faith in 'the purity of speech', in 'sketching language' as an 'undisturbed flow' and being 'always honest, spontaneous, confessional', with a certain hostility against 'selectivity' of expression or 'revisions' that were 'crafted' (1958: 57, 58). The scroll of *On the Road* is thus imagined as emerging spontaneously from the writing machine itself: as Kerouac wrote to Neal Cassady, 'the whole thing on a strip of paper 120 foot long . . . just roll it through type-writer and in fact no paragraphs . . . rolled it out on floor and it looks like a road' (cited Cunnell 2007: 1). Typing allows the writer to record mimetically, to reproduce the experience accurately (of the road itself) in the automatic process of typing. Kerouac's other texts – *The Subterraneans* (1958) and *Vanity of Duluoz* (1968) – were composed in similar ways, but the initial typing frenzy was not the end of this text's composition. In tension with the concept of spontaneous (typed) prose is the fate of *On The Road*, which went through various processes of editing and reformulating to become the text that was published by Viking in September 1957.

If Kerouac taped together long sheets of paper to type the 120-foot paragraph of the original *On The Road* manuscript, William Burroughs cut up his typing to produce his texts. Burroughs, like Kerouac, was interested in the relationship between typing, language and meaning, but the typewriter functions in a particular way in his Nova science-fiction trilogy. Burroughs survived on a family inheritance from his grandfather, William S. Burroughs, who had invented a key-operated adding machine: Burroughs's (junior) typewriters play a central role in the malicious world conspiracy of government, media and the 'Nova Police' agents that his texts portray. Burroughs's idea of the 'soft machine', the end product of the control conspiracy, is also imagined as a 'soft typewriter', an inner writing machine which imprints the code of the controlling system or method in the individual. As *The Ticket That Exploded* (1962) relates, 'the human body . . . is composed of thin transparent sheets on which is written the action from birth to death – Written on "the soft typewriter" *before* birth' (123). Burroughs's challenge is 'Why not rewrite the message on "the soft typewriter"? – Why not take the board books and rewrite all messages?' (124). Burroughs composed *Naked Lunch* and the *Nova Trilogy* (which included *The Ticket That Exploded* and *Nova Express*) from the same 'Word Hoard' of manuscripts, with the trilogy all composed by using the cut-up technique that Burroughs had collaborated on with Brion Gyson. Cutting up typed texts, like cutting up newspapers, magazines and tape recordings, takes part in Burroughs's literary-guerrilla tactics: a dismantling and denaturing of language codes, and the introduction of chance, scatology, random noise and interference. In doing this, Burroughs attempts to 'rewrite the message' of all cultural codes, norms and systems, and to produce remarkable new conjunctions of ideas and words. The sexual element of what he terms, in *Nova Express* (1964), the 'liquid typewriter' (152), which attempts to write a new world, is unavoidable. According to Darren Wershler-Henry, 'Burroughs's typewriting describes a liquid world where words and solid objects – including typewriters, of course – merge in unorthodox couplings, beyond all attempts to control them' (117). Such unorthodox mergings are actually a continuation of the potential the typewriter presented, right from its inauguration as a writing-transcribing device; according to Thurschwell, 'technologies such as . . . the typewriter are instrumental in creating transgressive fantasies of access to others who would be otherwise inaccessible' (87).

DIGITAL WRITING AND HYPERTEXT

In Burroughs's work, and in the work of his Beat contemporaries such as Kerouac, writing technologies were envisioned as a potential way to escape the rigid confines of a static, controlling code/text, the paradox being that the technologies they used were also those that served the controlling system (in FBI bureaus, naval bases, advertising agencies). It was the wartime impetus for code-breaking, firing table calculations and communication network design that drove the first electronic computer engineering, and in these systems the typewriter (and the typewriter operator) were central. Kittler posits the typewriter as the necessary progenitor of the digital computer, arguing that early computer design 'reduced typewriters to their bare principle' (1999: 245) and that 'Colossus' was 'a several-ton version of Remington's special typewriter with a calculating machine' that 'observed conditional jump instructions' (1999: 258). This is to elide the fundamental difference between the two technologies, founded in the fact that the production of words through digital computing rests on a binary code that underlies and enables the text, but is never visible: digital computing has a depth and necessarily involves an interaction between the functional levels of screened letters, digital coding and electronic hardware. The computer is not a typewriter, but the two can be articulated together through the textual effects of digital computing which extend the specific impact that typewriting had on literature. The typewritten text is one in which physicality and intimacy can be emphasized, but it is also a text which can no longer simply belong to an author, by virtue of its kinetic production at the keyboard and by its insertion into a machine process which involves but also exceeds the function of the author. With the opportunity to write literature in a digital form, kineticism and process become paramount features of new forms of textuality.

But, in the avant-garde experiments of Robert Carlton Brown in the late 1920s, the potential for this new textuality was already present. Using, as Craig Dworkin describes, 'a combination of electric motors, magnifying lenses, microscopic type and rolls of paper tape' (Dworkin 1999: 59), Brown proposed a reading machine that would scroll text in front of a reader who would control the text and its speed with a button. The machine was never manufactured beyond a prototype, but an anthology of 'readies' for the machine were published as *Readies for Bob Brown's Machine* in 1931, including contributions from William Carlos Williams, Ezra Pound and Gertrude Stein: Stein's piece called 'We Came' uses the symbols =, ++ or +++ and - to connect her phrases. Brown's idea was a response to the 'speed-rate' of the present, comparing his reading machine to the other technologies of the day – electric advertising signs, telegraph, radio, typewriters, etc. – and proposing with his machine a 'modern, moving, word spectacle' (Brown 1931: 177, 186). Brown describes himself as 'always . . . movie-minded' (157), in an echo of Dos Passos's notion of the 'eyeminded' American public, but for Brown this is essentially a positive trait, corresponding to his sense of the way 'words ebb and flow' (158). Brown's 'lively readers' (161) would respond to the way he 'oozed type' and participate in the 'more-moving-reading-more-moving- - -' activity of 'Reading-writing' (161, 184, 185).

The prototype of Brown's 'reading machine' (photographed for the 1931 anthology) suggests a familiarity with microfilm, which was marketed by

Kodak from 1928 after its invention in the application of microphotography to record cancelled cheques. It was this very advance in optical technology that, in the 1930s, became part of Vannevar Bush's conceptualization of a machine for storing and accessing books, records and communications – the memex. Bush, on the staff at MIT and director of Roosevelt's wartime Office of Scientific Research and Development, had been working with his colleagues on the Rockefeller Differential Analyser, an analogue, electromechanical computer that, by 1950, was made obsolete by the digital computer. But already in his 1938 book of essays, *World Brain*, Bush was working on ideas for his memex, at a time when H. G. Wells was proposing a World Encyclopaedia – an accessible synthesis of the world's knowledge. As explained in the 1945 essay 'As We May Think', published in the *Atlantic Monthly* in July and then in a condensed, illustrated form in *LIFE* in September, the memex would solve the problem of data storage and access, reducing the *Encyclopaedia Britannica* to 'the volume of a matchbox' (Bush 1945: 93). An optical reader and selector, codes for locating documents quickly and the possibility of inputing new documents, notes and correspondence on to blank microfilm, all to be viewed on a table-top with multiple screens, would comprise Bush's memex. Such a device would transform access to knowledge and data because it would replace the slow process of alphabetical or numerical ordering. As Bush argues, 'The human mind does not work that way. It operates by association' by a 'web of trails carried by the cells of the brain' (101). With the memex, Bush proposes that 'selection by association, rather than by indexing, may yet be mechanized' by documents being linked together in the path of accessing and reading them (102). The process of using the device would mean that numerous items could be joined in a trail, and any item 'joined in numerous trails'. Bush celebrates that 'Wholly new forms of encyclopedias will appear, ready-made with a mesh of associative trails running through them' (105).

Bush never really transferred his interest into the digital realm, but his memex emphasis on links, and on the new forms that would be created through the automatic link-jump, had a profound influence on subsequent digital innovators and the way connection, organization and navigation are conceived in computers. Both originators of hypertext – Ted Nelson and Douglas Engelbart – cite Bush's 'As We May Think' as their inspiration. Nelson is credited with coining the term 'hypertext', and popularized it in his book *Literary Machines* (1981). As he writes there, 'By hypertext I mean non-sequential writing – text that branches and allows choices to the reader, best read at an interactive screen. As popularly conceived, this is a series of text chunks connected by links which offer the reader different pathways' (0/2). Nelson's ongoing project Xanadu (see <http//:www.xanadu.com/>) describes an ideal 'docuverse' where links connect everything in complete accessibility – Bush's 'trails' made completely interconnected and non-linear. Engelbart's innovations in computer technology with his colleagues at Stanford, alongside the mouse and the GUI (graphical user interface), include the first software implementation of 'hypertext', in the On-Line System (NLS), which became the second node on the ARPANET network. Hypertext is now embedded in all the technology we use through the Internet in the form of html (hypertext mark-up language), the set of tags and rules used in developing hypertext documents.

Hypertext serves as a general term describing the organizational principle in which computer documents, files and text chunks are interlinked into a non-linear, interactive, associative network. In terms of literature, the inter-linked and interactive forms enabled by hypertext applications (such as *Hypercard*, introduced by Apple Computers in 1987) gave writers a chance to reimagine their forms and to produce hypertexts that rewrote the bound-aries of the manuscript, codex text. Computers had been used for poetic experimentations from very early on: Theo Lutz produced 'Stochastische Texte', a text generator that used sixteen phrases and subjects from Kafka's *The Castle,* in 1959; Brion Gysin's 'I am that I am' was programmed for automatic random permutations by Ian Somerville in 1960. Following these early experiments were a range of subsequent experiments in combi-natoric, permutation and kinetic visual works: in 1973, R. W. Baily edited *Computer Poems,* which included the work of sixteen poets. What is now generally called 'Digital Poetry' (a useful term that encompasses computer, cyber and hypermedia poetry) thus has a long history that pre-dates the personal computer (see Funkhouser 2007; Glazier 2001; Stefans 2003). But the transformation of fiction in digital space was very much instigated by the hypertext software of the late 1980s, using the basic feature of hyper-text, the hyperlink, as its 'crucial structural and aesthetic component' (Ensslin 2007: 20).

Hypertext fiction can be functionally defined as a form of non-linear, interactive, screen-based textuality, in which the reader chooses the structure and unfolding of the text in her reading actions – clicking on certain areas of the screen to activate and follow hyperlinks to other screens and seg-ments. Usually, each screen will have multiple possible links, and each reading can produce a different sequence of signs. If a codex text has a fixed semiotic base, in hypertext a variable display of text appears, dependent on the reader's actions. Structurally, a hypertext is composed of blocks of text, termed *lexia* (after Roland Barthes's *S/Z*), and the electronic links that can connect them: in hypermedia, these lexia can include sound, visual images, animation or other forms of information. The electronic links have a pecu-liarly multiple function which marks one of the differences of hypertext writing: each link is a sign in its own right, an indicator pointing towards a different lexia, and a bridge or stepping stone between segments; it thus can be read and made meaningful in these three ways. Many early hypertexts (which included poetic and narrative forms) used systems such as *Hypercard* and *Storyspace* but, with the advent of the World Wide Web, stand-alone hypertexts available as disks were superseded by networked texts accessible via the Internet.

The production of hypertext writing was immediately met by a theoretical and critical exploration of this new literary form, which sought to define and substantiate its poetics and aesthetics. Key features of hypertext – interactivity, non-linearity, rupture or frustration, textual process over textual product, the performative aspect of the text, the interaction between human language and the machine-readable code enabling the text – were explored and debated and continue to resonate in twenty-first-century considerations of electronic literature. The central question for the early theorists and practitioners was whether or not hypertext marked an absolute rupture from the manuscript codex text.

Two key figures in the theorization of hypertext, who occupy opposed stances on this key question and set the parameters for a decade of debates, are George Landow and Espen Aarseth. Landow, the founder and webmaster for the *Victorian*, *Postcolonial* and *Cyberspace and Hypertext* websites, argues that 'literary theory and computer hypertext . . . have increasingly converged' (Landow 2006: 1). Thus, it seems, for Landow, that hypertext functions as the embodiment of the post-structuralist concept of text (see also Bolter 1991). Landow's study *Hypertext: The Convergence of Contemporary Critical Theory and Technology* was first published in 1992, with a revised and expanded edition, *Hypertext 2.0*, appearing in 1997, and *Hypertext 3.0* in 2006, these subsequent versions taking into account the rapid developments in computer technology and networks. Landow's core points remain that: hypertext 'blurs the boundaries between reader and writer' (2006: 4); that they 'continually shift the center' (56); that they are based in a conception of 'network' that is a 'rejection of linearity' (63) and have 'radical effects on our experience of author, text, and work' (52). According to Landow, 'electronic computing and other changes in media have eroded the power of the linear model and the book as related culturally dominant paradigms' (67). Hypertext literature is presented as the incarnation of the key ideas of theorists such as Roland Barthes, Michel Foucault, Mikhail Bakhtin, Jacques Derrida and Deleuze and Guattari.

In contradistinction to Landow, Aarseth is rightly reluctant to co-opt post-structuralist theory to the examination of hypertext: he is much more concerned with considering the potential 'functional' difference of computer texts from paper texts (Aarseth 1997: 17). Rather than theoretical analogies, Aarseth explores the actual material function and effect of specific textual forms. At the heart of Aarseth's study *Cybertext* is a typology of textual communication, plotting a graph of variables on a data matrix for twenty-three texts, ranging from the (paper-based) *I Ching*, to *Moby-Dick*, to *MUD* (*Multi-User Dungeon*), a text-based real-time virtual world, to Stuart Moulthrop's *Victory Garden* hypertext fiction. Rather than hypertext, Aarseth proposes the term 'cybertext' or 'ergodic literature' in which 'nontrivial effort is required to allow the reader to traverse the text', arguing that 'a cybertext is a machine for the production of variety of expression' (1997: 1, 3). For Aarseth, a cybertext is a complex mechanism in which the 'reader *is* a player' and is put 'at risk: the risk of rejection' and 'failure' rather than a desired textual 'intimacy' (4). Thus, Aarseth's cybertext is a machine 'not metaphorically but . . . a mechanical device for the production and consumption of verbal signs' (21), which is not total or comfortable, but which 'constantly remind[s] of inaccessible strategies and paths not taken' (3). Central to Aarseth's conception of the 'cybertext' is any text-machine (whether paper- or screen-based) that produces a cybernetic interface between the operator, the verbal signs of the text and the textual medium.

Jorge Luis Borges' story 'The Garden of Forking Paths' (1941), which posits a labyrinthine structure/text where every possible path can and is followed, is often translated into a metaphor for the structure and potential of hypertext (see Moulthrop 1991b and Papanagou 2000). This short story predates hypertext literature by fifty years and it does demonstrate that the conception of a multicursal, non-linear book was possible before computer software made such texts realizable. Indeed, as Aarseth and many other critics point out, there are many experimental, avant-garde and popular texts that disrupt linear reading paths, that explicitly offer (in footnotes, endnotes, cross-references and so on) links to follow, that play with visual form, that explore the materiality of practice and even offer alternate, contingent narratives. One could cite any of the following: *Tristram Shandy*, *Moby-Dick*, Mallarmé's 'Un Coup de Dé', *Ulysses*, *Pale Fire*, Raymond Queneau's *Cent mille milliards de poèmes*, B. S. Johnson's *The Unfortunates*, the *Choose Your Own Adventure* children's book series. What this demonstrates is that computing technology does not mark an ontological break for literature; rather, we should, as Katherine Hayles advises, 'attend to the specificity of networked and programmable media', 'rethink the specificities of print and electronic literature and . . . explore their commonalities without collapsing one into the other (Hayles 2008: 30, 35). Electronic literature, of which hypertext fiction is one genre, does not herald the twentieth century as the last century of the book, despite Sven Birkert's dire warnings in *The Gutenberg Elegies* (1994), but instead offers profound new avenues for the ongoing interface between literature and technology. Literature is firmly inserted into the machinic interconnections of a technological world long before the advent of computing, but the end of an obsolete idea of the literary work as an organic expression of an innate human individuality is not the end of literature itself.

Michael Joyce's *afternoon, a story* (1990), composed in Storyspace, the hypertext writing environment developed by Eastgate Systems, was released in Windows and Macintosh versions in 1990. It has since become canonized as the first major hypertext fiction and included in the *Norton Anthology of Postmodern American Fiction*. The narrative, as emerges after multiple reading attempts, includes a figure, Peter, who is recently divorced, and a car crash that he has witnessed, which may or may not have involved his ex-wife and son. This undecidability – here, not whether the car crash has happened, but what status it actually has in terms of Peter's awareness of it and its impact on his life narrative – is an iconic feature of this and many other hypertext fictions. The text thus opens with two lines of search, Peter's for his ex-wife and son and our attempt to understand the events being related.

The opening lexia, which is the only place to begin *afternoon: a story*, poses the question 'Do you want to hear about it?'([*begin*]) and the text is accessed from here and read in two possible ways: either through pressing return or clicking on 'Y' (for Yes), or clicking on words in the lexia to follow alternate links. Thus, even at the beginning (in refusing to click 'Y'), the reader is offered the possibility to reject a simple reading path. However, even the supposedly direct path is eventually frustrated as 'guard fields' embedded in the program prevent the reader from following links to certain lexia until others have already been read. A 'Y' click reading eventually leads to the lexia [*yes*] which tells you 'There is an end to everything, to any mystery'. But instead of an ending, the guard field prevents the link to a new lexia [*yesterday*] being active, and instead brings the reader to [*work in progress*]. Here we are warned:

Closure is, as in any fiction, a suspect quality, although here it is made manifest. When the story no longer progresses, or when it cycles, or when you tire of the paths, the experience of reading it ends. Even so, there are likely to be more opportunities than you think here at first. A word which doesn't yield the first time you read a section may take you elsewhere if you choose it when you encounter the section again; and sometimes what seems a loop, like memory, heads off again in another direction . . . There is no simple way to say this. [*work in progress*] (Joyce 1990)

This self-conscious statement about the structure of the text appears on many reading paths and returns us only to [*begin*] again.

There are story elements to discern in *afternoon*, involving Peter, his therapist friend Lolly, workmate Werther and his lover Nausicaa, but just as there are guard fields in the text program, there are limit-edges in the textual material: Peter cannot locate his ex-wife Lisa, and his son Andrew features as an equivalent absence. Peter is unable actually to define Andrew's presence (or absence): a recurring lexia offers 'I want to say I may have seen my son die this morning' [*I want to say*]. At the crash site he witnesses, Peter sees Andrew's school essay caught on a fence, which expresses Andrew's own presence (and the crash) as a kind of narrative 'fenceline' which catches the text up: 'Here there is a catch place, a low wire fence along a ditch which snatches what the wind wafts . . . there . . . is a fresh white paper with my son's name upon it' [*fenceline*]. Car crashes feature in a number of early hypertexts, and this crash site is a different way of thinking through the technology-death nexus. At a textual level in hypertext, the crash seems a manifestation of technological failure where the reading path is frustrated, an experience that is essential to the hypertext reading experience. A reading of *afternoon* cannot help but stumble or be caught in repetitive loops. This enacts what Stuart Moulthrop (1995) sees as essential to hypertext fiction, 'the principle of breakdown' (73), a 'primary disturbance' (72) which 'reveal . . . to us the nature of our practices and equipment (71). The breakdown is a factor of the concerted un-fixity of the text and is articulated right at the start of *afternoon*: 'I do not signify one way or another' [*begin*]. A narrative can be pieced together through each successive entry into the text, but this is made fundamentally discontinuous by the reappearance of lexia which, in their reappearance, resignify in the light of the lexia preceding them. According to one critic, there are 539 lexia and 951 links in *afternoon* (Bell 2007): there is even a lexia [*false beginning*] which recasts [*begin*]. The uncertainty of the narrative, which only exploratory reading behaviour can engage with, is contained also in the crucial lexia [*die*] (which can also be accessed as [*die?*]) where the aleatory possibility of the dice throw is reworked as an uncertainty over whether or not Peter's ex-wife and son have been killed. For some critics, such as Douglas, the text does have a narrative centre; for her, the lexia [*I call*] is 'physically and literally central' because it has the largest number of paths branching from it and could offer a pathway to understanding Peter's guilt (1994: 168). Such a reading sees *afternoon* as a kind of mystery, with 'certain narrative strands that spiral down further into the narrative with each successive encounter', producing a 'stratiographic writing' (172). The introduction of a hierarchy in readings and a final clue to decipher is, though, in opposition to the mechanics of the text, which insistently draw reading paths away from the determination of narrative. Aarseth's idea of a 'heterarchy' in the text which offers a 'game of narration', producing a narrative version of the story marked 'with the reader's signature' (Aarseth 1997: 89, 94, 95), is a more sympathetic (and accurate) description of the reading experience.

Some pathways which can be encountered in *afternoon* take the reader away from narrative threads altogether; the pathway 'interanthology' includes various lexia, quoting different sources: [*orchis*] quotes a botanical guide entry on a northern orchid (the 'Showy Lady's-Slipper'), [*strawberries*] quotes from Freud, while [*midwife*] quotes from *Tristram Shandy*, one of the many points of self-conscious intertextual referencing in *afternoon*. The 'fragments' pathway presents lexia of single words or phrases, with varying fonts, spacing and sizes: [*f*] reads ' F (iction) fragments' while the lexia [*the*] can be encountered in multiple variations (placed differently on the screen each time).

Throughout the text, there is an insistent self-conscious awareness of the text's constructed nature: 'Go on, press the button, treat it all as if it were real', we are challenged [*the lady or the tiger*]. Peter is found describing his own self as a hypertext construct: 'I'm not sure that I have a story. And, if I do, I'm not sure that everything isn't my story, or that, whatever is my story, is anything more than pieces of others' [*me★*]. But the form of the text here is crucial, as Alice Bell points out, to the thematics of *afternoon*, in which Peter's 'reluctance to confront his own world' (2007: 50) mirrors the multilinearity of our reading. Narrative emerges almost despite itself: 'Am I to understand that I may, in fact, know something which I will be unaware of knowing, and which, nevertheless, I may be liable for disclosing, whether or not I might know I've done so' [*K*]. Coupled with this is a sense of the technological construct of voice and selves, epitomized in the Datacom automated telephone device and answering machines that intercept or replace communication in the lexias [*transcript*] and [*I call*].

In terms of the undisclosed aspects of the text, as Peter's son Andrew and his death(?) mark a limit-edge of knowledge and textuality, Lisa, the ex-wife, appears in a thread that can be followed after sustained engagement with *afternoon*. The pathway titled [*a hidden wren*] offers Lisa's first-person narrative, in which she reflects self-consciously on her textual construction. But this alternate perspective offers no stable point of reference or clarification. 'Why then do I have to define myself?', asks Lisa, eventually expelling us from this hidden path and the possibility of knowledge: 'you want to give yourself to believing despite the machine. You think you've found something . . . I'm sorry I have to end it for you so soon.' [*calm*].

The role of the reader of *afternoon, a story* epitomizes her role in hypertext, variously described as a 'player' (Aarseth), a 'screener' (Rosello) or a 'wreader' who combines the functions of reader and writer in the way Bob Brown imagined for his 'readies' in the 1930s. A hypertext wreader must activate the text through their actions, and the text they read will be the one that their actions create, a text that may never correspond to the text constructed by another wreader. However, the ideals of complete interactivity and absolute decentering do not fully correspond to the limits of classic hypertext which, as in *afternoon*, is an enclosed, non-networked textual space which authorizes certain reading choices over others; indeed, Hayles describes *afternoon* as 'printcentric' (Hayles 2008: 62). Nevertheless, there is a level of fundamental ambiguity in hypertext fiction, which is a product of hypertext's specific (lack of) authorial textual arrangement. John Fowles's *The French Lieutenant's Woman* (1969) may have offered two mutually exclusive endings, but one succeeds the other in the linear unfolding of a print text. In hyptertext fiction, mutually exclusive endings can coexist, with neither taking precedence over the other in the text; it is only in a reading path that one succeeds another, and this reading path will be contingent and mutable.

Stuart Moulthrop's *Victory Garden* (1991a) is variously a fiction about the first Gulf War, a campus novel and a war-protest novel; the emergence of these potential genres depends on the reading path chosen through the 1,025 lexias. A central character in *Victory Garden*, Emily Runbird, either dies in Operation Desert Storm, or returns to America unharmed. As Robert Selig points out, 'nothing becomes final in a hypertext novel so long as we continue to screen and rescreen its essentially unstable story' (2000: 649). *Uncle Buddy's Phantom Funhouse* (1992), created by John McDaid, takes the potential of hypertext technology even further, blurring the inside and outside of the digital space of this 'hypermedia novel', as McDaid describes it. The text consists of the digitally encoded hypertext (written using *Hypercard*), two music tapes and the proofs, editor's letter and printing of a short story by Arthur 'Buddy' Newkirk, whom the reader has supposedly inherited the funhouse legacy from. Blurring real and virtual worlds, *Uncle Buddy's Phantom*

Funhouse offers a home-card which is a navigational map, the 'Funhouse', offering readers access to different rooms. The architectural space of *Funhouse*, however, is designed to disorientate the reader as she moves through deeper levels. McDaid's text takes off from John Barth's story 'Lost in the Funhouse' (1968) which presents the funhouse-text as an 'incredibly complex' mechanism 'controlled from a great central switchboard' (97). 'Lost in the Funhouse' is directly referenced in the [*Art Gallery*] stack. Like the boy who is lost in Barth's story, the reader suffers a profound absence of proprioceptive coherence in McDaid's *Funhouse* which offers, not a central mechanism, but textual fragments dispersed amongst different text types: tarot cards, emails, photos, a screenplay, band lyrics. There is even a password-protected inverted mirror image of the text, accessible through a back door called 'Auntie Em's Haunt House', and the whole hypertext of *Uncle Buddy's Phantom Funhouse* is designed to crash at an appropriate narrative moment, throwing the reader out and demonstrating the self-consciousness of this text as an obfuscatory spatio-textual virtuality.

In her hypertext *Patchwork Girl* (1995), which takes its theme and organization from the motif of Mary Shelley's Frankenstein's monster, Shelley Jackson explores the material area of the electronic text, not as a disorientating game space, but as a somatic region, a body/text that is 'stitched' together in the act of reading. As is discussed in the final chapter, Jackson's text explores the gendered implications of technological interaction. In *Patchwork Girl*, the body/text that Jackson presents is not one that ever reaches, or even aspires to, unity; the text disperses and undermines 'classical wholeness and taxonomic self-knowledge' [*whole*]. The text/monster tends inevitably towards fragmentation, a whirling apart of the pieces momentarily stitched/linked together. Jackson's text differs from the car-crash disruption of Joyce's *afternoon*, as in the 'story' section of *Patchwork Girl* the monster literally disintegrates, coming apart at the seams in [*diaspora*], reverting to her fragmentary state. In this breaking up into pieces and parts, she embodies the status of hypertext writing itself. That Jackson is offering a feminist critique of logocentrism, linearity and singularity in her electronic text is evident. As the dialogue with Derrida in [*interrupting*] expresses, writing the female body/text is necessarily the construction of a feminine 'outlaw' and a 'monster'.

The feminist critique that Jackson articulates in *Patchwork Girl* highlights how women writers have used the forms of hypertext to explore the possibility of an electronic *écriture féminine*. Carolyn Guyer's *Quibbling* (1993) is representative of such attempts: Guyer takes the metaphor of water to connect womanhood and the fluidity and mutability of digital writing: 'is there anything as alive and full of light as a body of water?'([*bottle glass*]). In *Quibbling*, the female characters reflect on their roles as women and the text instantiates a merging, weaving and flowing textuality, which deconstructs polarities and absolutes. The potential corollaries between experimental women writers and the non-linear, non-hierarchical, decentering forms of hypertext have been explored by a range of critics (see Page; Guertin), and resonate with Sadie Plant's claims for the mutuality of feminism and cyber-culture (1997). Thus, electronic writing brings to the fore key social and material questions about gender identity and serves to challenge reductive ideas of the relationship of women to technology.

In Deena Larsen's narrative hyper-poem, *Marble Springs* (1993), feminist textual strategies inform the use of hypertext. *Marble Springs* tells the poetic stories of nineteenth-century women in the American West. It is based on a reasonably orderly structure, with a map of the Colorado mining village which provides the history and stories for the text. The links in *Marble Springs* embody the interrelationships between people, places and histories, and Larsen's text invites readers to contribute, giving instructions on adding notes in margins and bibliographies of poem cards (lexia) and on adding their own text on blank character cards. Larsen's text is a hyperpoem, a mode in which the node or lexia, rather than the syllable, is the foundational, struc-tural unit.

John Cayley's digital poetry is perhaps best described as cyberpoetry. He collectively terms his output *Indra's Net*: the earlier pieces in this oeuvre (*Indra's Net I-IX*) were issued on diskette, but by the late 1990s Cayley's work became mostly web-published (see <http://www.shadoof.net/>). Not based on hypertext links, but working intimately with programming code, Cayley produces what he terms 'machine modulated writing' (1996: 169), working from a base text to produce permutations, transformations and col-locations on screen as the reader activates the text. As Funkhouser describes this formal technique: 'Cayley's collocation process actively produces content through generative algorithms embedded within the programme that shuffle language using a formula to determine word placement' (2005–6: 108). In *Golden Lion* (1994), letters from a Chinese Buddhist text emerge to produce, at the bottom of the screen, lines of a poem written by Cayley. Here, as in some of his other work, words appear and dissolve on screen, serving to foreground the generative structures of language, activated here by the machine code–human reader interaction. Even Cayley's earliest pieces are only semi-automatic, and later works, such as *Book Unbound* (1995), are permanently changed with each individual reading: the reader selects phrases for transformation, which produce new strings of words which can be copied or edited on the 'Leaf' page and are also stored as new potential base texts for transformation. Cayley's 1990s cyberpoetry is essentially dynamic and indeterminate and recalls, in many ways, the techno-aleatory experiments of Burroughs and Brion Gysin. In its visual and kinetic elements, though, it also points towards late twentieth-century innovations in hypermedia.

Classic hypertexts such as *afternoon, a story*, although considerably ground-breaking at their release, have been overtaken by developments in computing technology and the growth in narrative and poetic textual experiments that resulted from close engagement with these new technologies. Classic hyper-texts are very heavily text-based, are closed systems (on disk rather than networked) composed of static lexia, and rely quite heavily on guard-fields to construct and control the narrative. They are followed by texts that are more properly descried as hypermedia texts. These texts of the later 1990s move into multimodal Web forms and, while the hyperlink remains central, also utilize other interface and navigation schemes. Hayles describes the classical hypertext as first-generation and the hypertexts of post-1995 as second-generation or contemporary (2008: 6–7), while Ensslin offers three categories: classic hypertext, hypermedia texts and cybertexts (which contain an element of 'machine autonomy' (2007: 101)). In such taxonomies, *Patchwork Girl* stands as a border case, with *Uncle Buddy's Phantom Funhouse* and *Marble Springs* also pointing the way towards multimedia and immersive wreader participation. The recent works of Michael Joyce (*Twilight, a symphony*, 1996a; *Twelve Blue*, 1996b) and Stuart Moulthrop (*Reagan Library*, 1999) utilize the advances in digital technology to create immersive texts. *Reagan Library* uses blocks of text and QuickTimeVR navigable panoramas with different links, with the screen changing in form on subsequent visits. The repetitions in this text are more like the algorithmic transformations of Cayley's poetry than the frustrations of classical hypertext and the experience offered is more like the unfolding of a pattern than the exploration of a labyrinth. *Twilight, a symphony* utilizes a range of signifiers – different font types, handwriting, photographs, sound files – while *Twelve Blue*, a web-based text, offers a navigation through modes that reflect a fluid and multiple sense of the structures of electronic textuality: coloured 'threads' that can be played in eight different 'bars' in a blue screen, blue-script text that repeatedly returns to images of rivers, flow and water. *Lexia to Perplexia* (2000) by Talan Memmott is, as the title suggests, not concerned with revealing a coded truth, but of exposing the interpenetration of discourses in electronic writing spaces. *Lexia to Perplexia* is composed of ten linked 'chapters' (layered web pages), each with their own source code, and involves the emergence of an English-computer code 'creole' in which, according to Hayles, 'code erupts through the surface of the screenic text, infecting English with machine instructions and machine instructions with English' (2002: 50). Mark Amerika's *Grammatron* (1997) combines animated graphics and streaming audio with short text-based lexias. In the text, an authorial alter-ego 'Abe Golem' is embarked upon a mastering and rewriting of 'Nanoscript', 'the underlying code' [*magick*], in an attempt to break and rewrite the codes of subjectivity and consciousness. Like Burroughs's 'liquid typewriter', in *Grammatron* it is the subversive power of desire that can reorder existence: 'Golam was seeking contact with the Other, the remote digital being that could circulate its unwritten code of desire into his operating system' ([*meaning*]). As a web-based hypertext, *Grammatron* offers an open-ended narrative encounter completely embedded in the multiple experience of new media.

The twentieth century ends with a tangible shift into hypermedia, web-based forms of communication and authorship. One late-century phenom-

enon was the rise of blogging on the Internet. Weblogs as a term was first
used in 1997, shortened to blog in 1999 – the year that Pyra Labs (today
owned by Google) launched the first free Blogger service that provided an
easy set of tools for anyone to set up a blog. With the emergence of wiki
software at the end of the century, collaborative websites and writing ven-
tures also became popular – Wikipedia being the best known. There were
also, and continue to be, experiments with wikinovels, from the Science
Fiction *Galaxiki* and *Orion's Arm* to the *A Million Penguins* venture (hosted
by De Montfort University in Leicester, UK, with Penguin Books) and *The
Autobiography of Pain*. Such experiments coexist with an extension of forms
and experiments with hypertext writing.

Electronic hypertexts utilize the screen, multiple linking and the activity
of the wreader to produce unstable and changing texts that are only realizable
as electronic literature. However, by the end of the twentieth century most
literature was, and is, electronic, existing as digital files before the publisher's
final, hard-copy, production. This puts all texts, potentially, under the condi-
tions of mutability of the digital zone, placing them within the feedback
loops of human–computer interactions – what Hayles terms 'dynamic heterarchies' (2008: 44). It becomes impossible for later twentieth-century print
texts to ignore this fundamental participation with digital code. In conjunction with the emerging ubiquity of electronic texts and networked digital
communication and information accessing, therefore, print texts of the 1990s
began to engage in dynamic ways with the formal, aesthetic and philosophical
grounds of computer writing, just as decades earlier writers explored the
impact of the typewriter on what and how they were writing.

In his 1995 novel *Microserfs*, Douglas Coupland adapts the epistolary novel
form to explore the lives of Microsoft® employees at the main Washington
campus and their move to Silicon Valley to work on an independent programming project: the 'Oop' project. The text, initially a short story published as the lead article in *Wired* magazine in 1994, is composed as the diary
entries, emails and random words filed in a desktop file (the computer's
'Subconscious') of Daniel Underwood, a software tester named after a typewriter. Throughout emoticons, computer jargon, varying typeface and
instances of corrupted files – 'Allllllllt the office we"llve decided that instead
of Friday Fllllll3636111136being' (239) – foreground this text as mediated
through digital–human heterarchies. In particular, Coupland uses double-
page spreads to address the interaction of human life and language with the
computer as writing machine. The word 'machine' is listed 592 times in
sixteen evenly spaced columns on pages 180–1 (repeating what is done with
the word 'money' fifty pages earlier); pages 104–5 are composed entirely of
binary code (reworking the trope used in Harlan Ellison's 'I Have No
Mouth, and I Must Scream') which encodes a message that satirically rewrites
the Creed of the United States Marine (the *Rifleman's Creed*), beginning 'I
heart LiSA Computers. This is my computer. There are many like it, but
this one is mine'; page 308 is devoid of vowels, which have been separated

out on to the facing page. The computer enables the externalization of memory and history: 'We've periphalized our essence', as one character remarks (1967: 254), and is mirrored in characters' attempts to transform bodies into machines (Todd through body-building and Ethan by taking Prozac). The cumulative effect of these linguistic and somatic machine intimacies is to reveal the complex nature of the communicative interface through the computer: it is reductive and standardized, discontinuous and disrupted, subversive and personal, and, in Daniel's mother's computer-written 'speech' after her stroke, something that rescues humanity from incomprehension and inarticulacy. In *Microserfs*, the computer infects discourse but also enables new forms of linguistic intimacy.

Daniel, in *Microserfs*, writes his diary on an Apple Powerbook, the same machine the Jeanette Winterson names her 2000 novel for: *The.Powerbook*. As Ute Kauer points out, this title is deliberately ironic as 'the "old" technology, the printed book, asserts its power by using the name of a computer product' (2005: 93). With this title, Winterson is engaging directly with computing technology and the impact it has on our understandings of ourselves, our world(s) and narrative fiction, focusing not on language and communication but on the intersection between the real and the virtual. *The.Powerbook* is designed, with its cover and chapter headings and divides (hard drives, icons and documents), to suggest the mechanisms of the computer interface. These features, and the dots in the title and the author's name, point to the influence of the Internet and computer technology, particularly hypertext, on the organization and conception of the novel. The main narrative line takes the form of an online chat between a young woman called Ali or Alix and an older, married upper-middle-class woman whose alias is 'Tulip'. Ali/x owns an old shop in Spitalfields called VERDE which is full of period costumes and from where she writes e-stories for online customers, and 'Tulip' is a customer. The technological/computer structure of the text is suggested by the index, called MENU, and there is a graphic differentiation here between the chapters' titles belonging to the frame narrative (online chat), which are written in small print, and the embedded stories in capitals (like email addresses and file names).

Throughout the text, there is an interaction between these two narrative levels which should be read as a heterarchy rather than in a hierarchical way: this text does not follow the traditional structure of a tale-within-a-tale (here *The Arabian Nights* is the most obvious intertext) where the frame narrative, or first-level narration, opens and closes the text. Here the frame narrative is left open; it is left inconclusive at the key moment that Tulip has to choose between taking a train to Oxford or starting a new life with Ali/x. The last four sections of novel are presented as embedded stories (they have capitalized titles). The text is thus decentered and is predicated upon an ideal of freedom that the digital world could offer: Ali/x, as the writer of online stories, offers her customers 'Freedom for a night . . . Just for one night the freedom to be somebody else' (4). This freedom is one in which alternate selves and stories can be imagined, alternatives in which the self is liberated from a sexed and gendered body, liberated from an encoded genetic gender signified by the X and Y icons that head the first section 'language costumier'. This examination of the sexed and gendered body, rewritten in the codes of computer language, resonates very clearly with Jackson's *Patchwork Girl*.

In *The.Powerbook*, Winterson proposes an ideal of multiplicity and openness, giving the reader the possibility of reading variations on the same events. She, indeed, in the multiple endings she writes for the story of Ali/x and Tulip, seems to suggest that all possible pathways exist: as in Borges's story 'The Garden of Forking Paths', all paths are taken, everything is possible. The book refuses to choose, refuses to privilege one ending over the other, sending us back, instead, into the alternative world of the embedded narratives. This sense of narrative possibility is connected, for Winterson, to her belief in the idea of the world that quantum mechanics has created. The digital realm thus enables an approximation of the multiplicity and mutability that quantum mechanics suggests: 'in quantum reality there are millions of possible worlds, unactualised, potential, perhaps bearing in on us, but only reachable by wormholes we can never find . . . I can't take my body through space and time, but I can send my mind, and use the stories, written and unwritten, to tumble me out in a place not yet existing – my future' (2000: 63).

John Barth's 1997 short story 'Click' attempts to instantiate computer reading to a different effect. The text of 'Click' approximates the visual experience of hypertext in the colour and underlining of supposed links in the text (reading this online, it is tempting and frustrating in equal amounts that the hot links are textual constructs rather than active links: clicking gets you nowhere). This story intertwines a couple's argument that threatens to rend their relationship, with their initial exploration of Web-based hypertext (through their use of the website authored by CNG, revealed as an acronym for 'Center of Narrative Gravity': 93). 'Click' claims to be an account of 'the Hypertextuality of Everyday Life' that offers numerous instances of metafictional comment on the construction of narrative and the experience of hypertext links. But Barth offers only a generalized and inaccurate sense of World Wide Web hypertext links: 'given time and clicks enough, you will have "accessed" virtually the . . . entire expressible world' (1997: 82). For Barth, the reading subject cannot respond to multiplicity and non-linearity and is not transformed or rewritten by it; instead, the subject, as Barth describes him, 'continuously ignores, associates, distinguishes, categorizes, prioritizes, hypothesizes, and selectively remembers and forgets' (95). What Barth appears fundamentally to reinforce are stereotypical gender differences which make Mark an Expediter (goal-orientated, direct) and Valerie an Enhancer (meandering, distractable), differences that are amplified by hypertextual networks. For Laura Shackleford, this is a manifestation of Barth's anxiety about digital hypertext's effects on 'the masculine writing subject' threatening to undermine his 'instrumental mastery altogether' (2005: 299). In *The.Powerbook*, Winterson imagines that the computer can rewrite the gendered self 'in these long lines of laptop DNA . . . we take your chromosomes, twenty-three pairs, and alter your height, eyes, teeth, sex. This is an invented world' (2000: 4). Her text is one that offers the digital realm as a place, not where the body is transcended, but where it can be reimagined, where gender identity and sexual relations can be reconfigured. The liberated women that Winterson imagines in *The.Powerbook* are the computer-generation equivalents of the typewriter-women of the late nineteenth century, enabled by technology to reconfigure their material and social relations. For Barth, however, in his vague notion of the virtual worlds of hypertext, gendered differences are reinforced, amplifying Valerie's 'feminine' tendencies to browse and exacerbating Mark's goal-orientated phallocentrism.

Other texts such as Mark Danielewski's *House of Leaves* (2000) explore more fully the impact of inscription technologies on the textual and actual world. *House of Leaves* takes as its subject the (fictional) film *The Navidson Record*. But we only ever access this through Johnny Truant's reconstitution of the fragments of a critical study of the film by the dead man Zampanò, intertwined with Johnny's story (in a different font) complete with hundreds of footnotes and references, including footnotes by the anonymous editors of Truant's text. Hayles points to the concern of this text with 'remediation', incorporating into itself a startling array of inscription media (from tattoos to film), 'as if imitating the computer's omnivorous appetite', to create a 'technotext' (Hayles 2002: 112, 129). *House of Leaves* is not technological in that it is simply a print book and not about computers or hypertext in any direct way, but its material surface bears the marks of late twentieth-century techno-culture and electronic literature, radically decentered and disturbed by a heterarchy of voices that displace any sense of singular narrative. Just as the structurally impossible house delineates an incongruous and irrational space, so this text architecturally recasts the proprioceptive confusion of hypertext reading. *House of Leaves* inscribes the inaccessibility of reference in a digital age, the absence of a fixed point of 'truth' in the bewildering spaces of the digital realm. As Jeanette Winterson writes in *The.Powerbook*, 'it used to be that the real and the invented were parallel lines that never met. Then we discovered that space is curved, and in curved space parallel lines always meet' (2000: 108). The blurring of boundaries in the virtual worlds of digital texts and spaces could be read as a version of the simulacra of postmodernism, but electronic writing does not imprison us in an endless chain of signification even as it replaces traditional conceptions of the writing or reading (human) individual with an interactive network of connected subjects. The somatic ground of our interface with technology signals the phsyicality of writing and reading even in the digital realm. Technology is inescapably a productive, material force with substantial effects on bodies and on the social and political realms they inhabit, so the overtly technological grounds of digital textuality are also overtly material ones.

There is, as has been discussed, no absolute rift between print and electronic literature, and electronic writing merely extends and amplifies the relationship between text and reader: what Hayles terms 'recursive feedback loops' (2008: 135) can be experienced through codex text, hypertext or cybertext. But the profound impact of computers on redrawing the limits of textuality must be acknowledged, along with its corollary; the crucial impact of digital technology on identity and embodied subjectivity. What Barth wants to resist and what Jackson's *Patchwork Girl* and Winterson's *The.Powerbook* investigate is the impact of writing technology on the subjects who use it. From the first touch-typing type-writer girls to the hypertext wreader clicking links and navigating with a mouse, writing technologies manifest a prosthetic effect in which body, mind and machine interact at a conscious and an unconscious or instinctual level. 'Writing is pre-eminently the technology of cyborgs,' writes Donna Haraway in her 'Manifesto for Cyborgs' (1985: 176), and, as the preceding discussion has shown, it is impossible to ignore, at the multiple sites of engagement with writing machines, the fact that subjectivity is transformed in the process of reading and writing technologically. Haraway theorizes the cyborg fusion of organism and machine at the end of the twentieth century, but various figurations of the human–machine nexus have concerned writers from the very start.

6 Robots, Cyborgs and the Technological Body

In L. Frank Baum's *The Wonderful Wizard of Oz* (1900), the first of his Oz series, Dorothy meets and rescues the rusted-up Tin Woodman. As he tells his story, the Tin Woodman reveals he was originally a flesh-and-blood woodcutter who has had his limbs, head and body replaced by a tinsmith after his wickedly enchanted axe severed and divided them. The Tin Woodman appears in subsequent books and in the twelfth book in the series, *The Tin Woodman of Oz* (1918), he meets his own severed head, kept in a cupboard, and a hybrid creature made from his flesh body parts. In *Ozma of Oz* (1907), Baum also imagined a clockwork man made of copper, Tik-Tok, who needs to be wound with keys and runs down at inopportune moments. With such creations, Baum introduced contemporary technology into a fantasy world for children, but he also raised particular political questions about the effect of technology on humanity. The industrial Tin Woodman and his prosthetic body have been created by ruthless injustice and he needs to have his heart/humanity restored to him. Tik-Tok is differentiated from the cyborg figure of the Woodman; he is purely mechanical, a robot with no emotions, who can act as Dorothy's 'slave'.

Robots and cyborgs, mechanical men and human-machine hybrids, have been the twentieth century's most enduring image of the interaction between humanity and technology, imagined variously as the technological extension, invasion or assimilation of the individual. In exploring the technological bodies of literature and culture across the decades – bodies in machines, bodies alongside machines, bodies modified by machines, bodies replaced by machines – it becomes possible to consider specific links and contrasts across the twentieth century and to understand how technology has defined and produced ideas of the human. In addition, the cyborg and her ancestors raise political and social questions, and pose a challenge to a dualistic understanding of nature and culture. Cyborgs, robots and other mechanical beings are key figures for understanding the technophilic and technophobic dreams of a century, embodying fears about technological encroachment, suggesting to some the chance for technological transcendence, and challenging the idea of the individual, differentiated, human subject. Ultimately, engaging with the implications of the technological body and the ways that literature explores these implications leads to a fuller understanding of the substantial connections of our existence as beings in the world.

'I WOULD RATHER BE A CYBORG THAN A GODDESS'[1]

The twentieth century inherits a long pre-history of artificial humans and similar forms. Automata, from the Greek αύτόμᾳτος, 'acting of one's own will', can be found in the Hellenistic world, ancient China and the Islamic Middle Ages, and the European Renaissance saw a resurgence of interest in mechanical models. Leonardo da Vinci designed a humanoid automaton, but it was René Descartes, describing the human body as an 'earthen machine' in his *Treatise on Man* (1664), who introduced the philosophical dualism that underpinned a conception of physical life as a mechanistic process. In an alternate context, the golem of Jewish Tradition, particularly in Ashkenazi Hasidic lore, was an artificial creature animated through magic to serve its creator. Automata, mechanical toys, clockwork models and humanoid mechanisms were incredibly popular in modern Europe: Jacques de Vaucanson in the eighteenth century constructed a Flute Player and a duck which appeared to digest food it was given and excrete waste. The most famous mechanical human was Baron Wolfgang von Kempelen's chess-playing 'Turk', which toured Europe and America after its invention in the late eighteenth century, beating numerous chess experts. The Turk fascinated many writers, including E. T. A. Hoffman and Edgar Allan Poe, but was a fake with space for a small, human chess champion secreted inside the mechanism (though this was never revealed for certain to the public). Walter Benjamin invokes the Turk at the beginning of his 'Theses on the Philosophy of History' to illustrate the hidden teleo-theological drive behind a supposedly objective narrative of historical progress (the 'little hunchback guid[ing] the puppet's hand' 1999: 245). The mass of speculation about the Turk in the eighteenth and nineteenth centuries derived from the possibility that not only could functioning life be constructed, as Vaucanson had supposedly done with his digesting duck, but that human intelligence could be produced mechanically; these automata posed fundamental questions about the possibility of artificially creating life and intelligence. In this light, Mary Shelley's *Frankenstein* offers a fictional engagement with the creation of artificial life that combines the emergent science of electricity, the questions posed by the popular automata of the period and some of the elements of the Jewish golem. The nineteenth century, with its interest in *tableau vivant*, waxwork displays and Pygmalionesque transformations, also abounded in Mechanical Museums and showrooms that displayed a variety of automata. As Simon Schaffer describes, the different automata of John Merlin, James Cox and Thomas Weeks were objects of voyeuristic wonder and delight, as well as philosophical speculation and mechanical innovation. At the same time, the Industrial Revolution was producing new ideas about the human–machine connection; Tamara

Ketabgian highlights, for example, how Harriet Martineau's accounts of women in manufacturing praise the enhancement of the female body achieved through a fusion of the organic and the technological. There are echoes here of the late nineteenth-century type-writer, perfectly attuned to the mechanism she operates. Emerging from these different technological bodies are different ways of conceiving of mechanical humans: as the product of an industrialized workplace that subsumes them; challenges to the pre-eminence of human intelligence; evidence of a God-like human ability to create life; or crystallizations of the perfection of human *techne*. Each of these conceptions leads to further questions about the status and value of the human-machine.

Speculations about the creation of a biomechanical human can be found in both fictional and engineering works at the end of the nineteenth century, notably in an odd conjunction of imagined and actual inventions. In *L'Eve Future* (*The Future Eve* 1886), Villiers de L'Isle Adam offers a fictional version of Thomas Edison who creates an artificial woman – Villiers's term is *andreid* – to replace the beloved of his friend Lord Ewald, Miss Alicia Clary. Alicia is outwardly beautiful but has an unfortunately banal and debased character, and so Edison forms his *andreid* Hadaly to replace her. Hadaly functions through an intricate electromagnetic mechanism and system of circular plates, joints and golden phonograph disks for speech, and is controlled by the rings and necklace she wears. She is fashioned externally to exactly match Alicia and, at an unsettling moment in the text when Lord Ewald takes the *andreid* to be Alicia, she convinces him that the mechanism is the original it has replaced.

Villiers is working through a decadent aesthetic in his text, substituting an artificial, and so superior, replacement for the messiness of nature. But in a real-life convergence, Edison, in the late 1880s, invented and marketed a talking doll that 'spoke' through a phonograph disk inside her body cavity (see Wood 2002). What is foregrounded in Villers's *andreid*, and to a lesser extent in Edison's doll, is a gendering of the human-machine that draws an affinity between women and the technological that eroticizes machines and denigrates female specificity. Edison's comments in a 1912 *Good Housekeeping* article that electricity 'will develop woman to the point where she can think straight' (cited Wood 2002: 147) highlights how technology and gender are so often conjoined in discourses about the machine. The traditional associa-tion of woman with materiality and the body is extended, in so many specu-lations on the machine, to consign women and the female to the realm of the mechanistic processes of existence. In the sexual and gender politics of the human-machine the presumed familiarity between women and machines has been the foundation, on the one hand, for their objectification or demonization, and, on the other hand, for new discourses of emancipation: this politics continued to resonate through the twentieth century.

In the late twentieth-century imaginary, it is the cyborg that has figured most prominently in conceptions of a human-machine. The term 'cyborg', a conflation of the phrase 'cybernetic organism', has its origins in the military-industrial complex, as does so much technology. Cybernetics, as the study of communication and control in organisms and machines, emerged during the Second World War out of a synthesis of disciplines: electrical engineering, mathematics, biology, neurophysiology, anthropology and psychology. Norbert Wiener is usually credited with the naming of cybernetics, from the Greek *κυβερνήτης*, meaning 'steersman' or 'pilot', in his book *Cybernetics; or Control and Communication in the Animal and Machine* (1948). Wiener had worked on automatic anti-aircraft defence technology during the war and it was the role of regulatory feedback in biological or technical systems – wherein the system adjusts to external environmental changes through information looped back into it – that characterized his idea of information feedback systems. Wiener's ideas were popularized in his *The Human Use of Human Beings: Cybernetics and Society* (1950) which also expressed the equivalence of information feedback systems in supposedly different structures and organisms; Wiener describes 'the nervous system and the automatic machine [as] fundamentally alike in that they are devices which make decisions on the basis of decisions they have made in the past' (1950: 33).

The first cyborg creature was created as part of research into modifying the human body for space travel and so exploring how the human regulatory system could adapt, through prosthetic extension, for a different environment. Manfred Clynes and Nathan Kline, in their research at Rockland State Hospital, New York, fitted a laboratory rat with a permanent osmotic pump which automatically injected chemicals to control the rat's biochemistry. In their 1960 published article, 'Cyborgs and Space', accompanied by pictures of this white rat, Clines and Kline offered the term 'cyborg' and proposed 'creating self-regulatory man-machine systems' and 'cyborg dynamics' to enable space travel (30). With subsequent advances in medicine, bioengineering, genetic manipulation, weapons technology, communication devices, computing and so on, the integration of humans with the inorganic and artificial became more and more commonplace. From pacemakers to cosmetic surgery, Bluetooth ear pieces to satnavs, bomb-disposal exoskeletons to smart drugs, the late twentieth-century interpenetration of human and machine suggests that the high-tech societies of the world are increasingly populated by cyborg beings. Literary speculations about human-machine hybrids and fusions accompanied and often predicted the advances in science and engineering, posing important ethical and ontological questions about the technological future of the world.

The cyborg enters into the terrain of theory and critical discourse with Donna Haraway's 'Cyborg Manifesto' (1985; revised 1991). This essay has been hugely influential in the field of cyberstudies and has been applied, adapted, discarded and critiqued in a multidisciplinary arena. Haraway does not claim in her manifesto to offer an accurate account of the current state of cybernetic technology; hers is explicitly a socialist-feminist declaration in response to the 'Informatics of Domination' that she argues is the distinguishing feature of the social reality of the late 1980s (161ff.). Thus, for Haraway, the Informatics of Domination replaces 'White Capitalist Patriarchy' and this is accompanied by other shifts, from 'Public/Private' to 'Cyborg citizenship', 'Labour' to 'Robotics', 'Mind' to 'Artificial Intelligence' and 'Family/Market/Factory' to 'Women in the Integrated Circuit' (1985: 161). The new era of technologically mediated and permeated economy and society produces a new sense of the human individual, not as a singular I, but as enmeshed in and with technological devices, networks and codes. What Haraway is advocating through the 'Cyborg Manifesto' is an absolute refusal of myths of 'organic wholeness' in the face of the increasingly 'leaky distinction between animal-human (organism) and machine', arguing that 'we can learn from our fusions with animals and machines how not to be Man, the embodiment of Western logos' (150, 152, 174). Thus, as 'theorized and fabricated hybrids of machine and organism . . . we are cyborgs' and the 'cyborg is our ontology; it gives us our politics' (150). For Haraway, the gender politics of technology, viewed through the figure of the cyborg, can be reimagined as a liberation of women and others from the oppressive myths of patriarchy.

As Haraway makes clear in her subsequent work, her 'Cyborg Manifesto' does not advocate a transcendence of the human body into some kind of cyborg techno-utopia: 'This is not some kind of blissed-out techno-bunny joy in information,' as she puts it (Gane and Haraway 2006: 139). Crucially, Haraway sees the strength of a cyborg figuration as its ability to resist, much more effectually than an anachronistic techno-phobia, other constructions and myths of technology which are much more damaging to those traditionally dominated in culture; 'women, people of colour, nature, workers, animals' (1985: 177). In contradistinction to the 'clean and light' machines of microelectronics and information processing and the 'grid of control on the planet', imagined by advanced military technology (1985: 153, 154), the cyborg is embodied, and troubling. Haraway presents some striking examples of the cyborg to illustrate its particular resonance for a progressive feminist politics, highlighting how 'Sex, sexuality, and reproduction are central actors in high-tech myth systems structuring our imaginations of personal and social possibility' (169), and offering as real-life cyborgs 'the Southeast Asian village workers in Japanese and US electronics firms' (177). In this, Haraway foregrounds issues of race, class and gender as pertinent to the figuration of the cyborg at the same time as seeking to challenge reductive ways of imagining the human-machine.

MACHINE-AGE MAN

The machine men of modernism were closely bound up with militarism and the impact of war and military technology on conceptions of the human. The First World War foregrounded, for many poets and other writers, the terrible impact of technology on the vulnerable human form in warfare. At the same time, and in part as a corollary, specific modernists such as F. T. Marinetti and Wyndham Lewis were imagining an invulnerable male form, merged with or armoured by advanced technologies of combat. Lewis's war paintings depict soldiers and their artillery as machines of the same order, and the armouring of the ego that Lewis advocated in his writing sees the self as technologically hardened against the shocks of the modern world. Marinetti's technophilia sees the strong man metallizing himself, emerging empowered and technologically hardened from his confrontation with the machines of modernity. In his writing, he extols the virtues of the machine-man engaged in 'the enthusiastic imitation of electricity and the machine . . . the happy precision of gears and well oiled thoughts' (Apollonio 1973: 154). And, for Marinetti, there are specific, regulated bodies that already approximate machine perfection:

For precursors we have gymnasts and high-wire artists who, in their evolutions, their rests, and the cadences of their musculature, realize the sparkling perfection of precise gears, and the geometric splendour that we want to achieve. (1973: 155)

Marinetti's gymnasts appear an almost benign embodiment of machinic regularity; by contrast, Jacob Epstein's *Rock Drill* (1913–14), originally a large white, machinic-humanoid figure mounted on a pneumatic rock drill, is one of the most terrifying images of a dehumanized machine-age. This form was reconstructed in the immediate post-war period by Epstein, who cast the torso, without the legs and rock drill, in bronze. He described *Rock Drill* in his 1940 autobiography as 'the terrible Frankenstein's monster we have made ourselves into' (1955: 56).

The body/machine complex, reimagined for aesthetic and artistic purposes by Lewis, Marinetti and other modernists, had emerged, by the end of the nineteenth century from a conjunction of rationalist physiology with the new sciences of physics, psychology and natural history. A conception of the living body as a biological machine, which could be approximated by the undertaking of engineers, was inherited from Descartes, Gottfried Leibniz and Julien Offray de La Mettrie, and the body had begun to figure as 'a field of forces, energies and labour power' (Rabinbach 1990: 66). This sense of the biological machine combined with theories of energy conservation (thermodynamics), political economy (Marxism), the mechanisms of natural and social history (Darwinism) and psychology (Freudianism), and the result was what Anson Rabinbach terms the 'human motor' as a functional metaphor of the working body. It was this central conception that shaped understandings of labour power and production in the early twentieth century. Taylorism and Fordism, standardization of workplaces and workers' production, were founded on understanding the human body and self through the lens of technology. The human individual is seen as reducible to rational processes and the human body is made into a machine by its insertion into sequences of repetitive labour. Even in the field of sexual ethnography, Darwinian determinism and the images of the machine age were influential: Rémy de Gourmont, in his *The Natural Philosophy of Love* (1903), presented sexuality as nothing more than a mechanical process: his six chapters on 'The Mechanism of Love' cover copulation across the animal world, reducing the variety of human practices and fetishes to automatic biological mechanisms. For Gourmont, therefore, 'the female . . . is the machine and has to be wound up to go: the male is merely the key', and the concurrence between sex organs is 'mechanical and mathematical' (1903: 14, 43). For the American Henry Adams, in the Gallery of Machines at the 1900 Paris Great Exposition, the power of the Goddess and the religious iconography of the past are finally comprehensible through a mechanical model. As he views the great dynamos turning, Adams is able to conflate goddess with machine, seeing the Virgin Mary herself as 'the animated dynamo' (1907: 384) and the dynamo and the Virgin as 'convertible, reversible, interchangeable attractions on thought' (383).

In his 1930 *Romance of the Machine*, the American scientist Michael Pupin also connected religious devotion and the supposed American 'worship of the machine' (28), arguing that both sought the 'spirit of eternal truth' (29). He describes the whole of nature, including the human body, as 'primordial machines' (14) and compares the human bloodstream to the United States' transportation system (14, 63). Pupin celebrates telephones, radios and automobiles in a passionate tribute to American machines, defending his adopted nation against attacks by 'European critics of our machine civilisation' (79). Pupin's defence is evidence of the extent to which machine culture was seen, by these European critics (and theorists and contemporary avant-gardists), as the spread of 'Americanism'. As Peter Wollen outlines, America was intimately associated with a supposed materialism and with rationalizing machine processes and the mechanization of human labour. In *Successful Living in this Machine Age* (1932), the American entrepreneur-businessman Edward Filene also defends against attacks from the 'croaker about the standardization of life' (242). For Filene, the mass production inaugurated by Taylor and Ford has the potential to abolish poverty, create leisure for all and even bring about world peace. 'Instead of creating sameness', mass production, he argues, 'is bringing an infinite variety into the lives of masses', and, in a Nietzschean vein, will enable 'the mastery of mechanization by human life, instead of the mastery of human life by traditions' (1932: 33, 247). Stuart Chase, American engineer and economist, in his 1929 *Men and Machines*, also emphasizes the need to dominate machines, arguing that 'Man is not the slave of his machines . . . he has . . . to break them to his service' (347). Chase too sees machines as producing variety, releasing us from 'our old folkways' and 'forc[ing] us to experiment with a host of new ones' (278). In addition, Chase stresses the prosthetic enhancements that machines have brought to humankind so that 'biological limitations . . . are banished' and mankind has access to 'Power unlimited: sensitiveness unbounded' (9). These American writers all seek to argue for the power of machines, which, controlled by man, will bring about an absolute increase in prosperity, opportunity and personal development.

The positive summations of Filene, Pupin and Chase stand in contrast to the much more equivocal examinations of the machine age a decade earlier in the work of New York Dada artists such as Marcel Duchamp, Francis Picabia and Man Ray. Each of these artists utilizes mechanical forms and components, or machine-produced objects, in their artistic examination of the effect of technology on art, culture and humanity. Their work responds to technological modernity through an ambivalent early twentieth-century masculinity one which, instead of confronting or merging with the machines of combat, explicitly adopts the position of non-combatant: Duchamp and Picabia fled to New York to avoid the First World War.

Duchamp is well known for his 'readymades', the presentation of mass-produced items such as a bicycle wheel, typewriter cover or infamously a porcelain urinal as art objects. His work consistently denaturalizes both art and the artist, exploring the mechanics of perception and confounding the supposed values of art based in beauty and artisanship. He had already suggested a mechanization of the human form with his *Nude Descending a Staircase* (1912), the centre of attention at the 1913 New York Armory Show which, with its abstract lines and planes depicting the descent of the 'nude', approximates Muybridge's photographs of animal and human locomotion. With *The Bride Stripped Bare by Her Bachelors, Even* (*The Large Glass*) (1923), Duchamp offered an image of male–female relations in which the bachelor machines are forever separated from a Bride of semi-visceral, semi-mechanical form. Amelia Jones describes *The Large Glass* as a 'mechanical-erotic map of the workings of the heterosexual sex act' (2004: 96), and it shares with the work of other New York Dadaists a concern with gender and sexuality in an era of Fordist mass production and machine regulation.

Francis Picabia was inspired by the modernity of New York, claiming in a 1915 *New York Tribune* article, 'French Artists Spur on an American Art', that 'immediately upon coming to America it flashed on me that the genius of the modern world is machinery . . . Machinery the soul of human life'. In his illustrations for Alfred Steiglitz's magazine *291* and elsewhere, Picabia used machine forms and components in portraits. The 1915 drawing *Fille née sans mère* (*Girl Born without a Mother*) presents a 'girl-machine' that is a peculiar blend of the organic (rounded shapes) and machinery (a set of sketchy springs and gears). *Portrait d'une jeune fille américaine dans l'état de nudité* from the same year is a functional representation of a spark plug, presenting the young American girl as a mass-produced part at the heart of the Ford revolution. Picabia similarly imagines himself in *Le Saint des Saints / C'est de moi qu'il s'agit dans ce portrait* (1915) as a composite horn–cylinder–spark plug. Man Ray's 1918 photographs *Homme* and *Femme* reveal a confusion of genders in the domestic but pendulous technology of an egg beater which represents 'man' and the phallic clothes pegs which juxtapose the curving light reflectors of 'woman'. Here again there is a translation of humanity into mechanical terms, which disturbs traditional notions of gender and sexuality. The mechanomorphic portraits and forms of New York Dada do not celebrate the transcendence of human frailty in the machine: rather than apotheosizing the machine, they present 'dysfunctional machines' which mark 'the inevitable *failure of the process of rationalization successfully or fully to contain or regulate human bodies/selves*' (Jones 2004: 129; emphasis in original). This is epitomized in the productions and performances of the New York Dadaist Baroness Elsa von Freytag-Loringhoven, who costumed herself with mechanisms (car tail-lights), machined objects (ice-cream spoons, postage stamps) and gilded fruit, and made art out of the detritus of mass production (metal springs, curtain tassels, beads, plumbing). As an ageing, penniless woman who contested and confronted rather than fetishized modern technology, Baroness Elsa stands as the opposite of Marinetti's Futurist rhetoric. What the New York Dadaist mechanomorphic portraits share with Italian Futurism, however, is a profound sense of the transformation of the human in the modern machine age, particularly in the arena of sexual relations. Gourmont's account of the mechanisms of sex was just one influential presentation of male and female relations freed from the weight of romantic idealism and Christian prudery by the impact of technology.

The British poet Mina Loy was one of the few women to be directly engaged in Italian Futurism, forging personal relationships with both Marinetti and Giovanni Papini, editor of *Lacerba*. Her poetry, in pieces such as 'The Costa San Giorgio' (from 'Italian Pictures' 1914), works with a form of Marinetti's wireless writing to record vivid sense impressions in a compressed and unmediated form. Loy was drawn to the Futurists while resident in Florence because of their iconoclastic rejection of tradition and convention, but for her, unlike the anti-feminist Marinetti, this would necessarily involve a reinvention of femininity and the role of women. Loy's 'Feminist Manifesto' (1914), for example, imagines a re-engineered femininity in which the '<u>unconditional</u> surgical <u>destruction of virginity</u>' (1996: 155) would free women from the 'man made bogey of virtue' and from the impossible choice between '**<u>Parasitism, & Prostitution</u> – or <u>Negation</u>**' (154). In her poetry of the 1910s, Loy engages directly with the machine-men imagined by Futurism, and with their celebration of the fusion of man and machine in cars, aeroplanes and warfare. In her letters and unpublished writings, Loy critiqued Marinetti's militarism and politicized beliefs, along with his misogyny, and, with the publication of the poem 'Sketch of a Man on a Platform' in 1915, she publicly satirized Marinetti's hyperbolic masculinism, presenting him as an absurd marionette.

Loy's exploration of the politics of Futurist machine-men is inextricably bound up with the gender consciousness of her work, so that, while embracing a modernity that rejects the *passéist* aspects of Western culture that enclose women in idealistic fantasies of love and romance, she is also cautious about a purely mechanical mode of human interaction. In 'Human Cylinders'

(1915), Loy presents a mechanical union between two ultramodern bodies; the poem describes the 'lucid rush-together of automatons', beings who are severed from the sensations ('without tasting') and religions ('without communion') of humanity (1996: 40–1). These 'human cylinders' are models of the human motor resisting entropic decline, 'revolving' in defiance of their 'enervating' surroundings. But, however much the human cylinders are liberated by being stripped of sentimentality, the poem emphasizes (by enjambment) their 'singularity', their isolation and dehumanization. The second stanza contrasts the mechanical bodies and the fleshly body, with the flesh figured as an evolutionary regression, a 'little whining beast . . . longing . . . to slink back to antediluvian burrow'. The poem does contain a sense of the possibility of 'reciprocity' or a union without sentimental baggage – a 'communicative' possibility emphasized by the typography which creates empty space on the page around this word. But this 'potential' is lost in the 'frenzied' emphasis on 'intellect'. In this poem, Loy uses the vocabulary of mechanism and science to explore modern relationships, but ultimately rejects the 'solution' offered by science: in this poem, written during the First World War, science has the apocalyptic power to 'Destroy the Universe'.

Loy's *Love Songs* (*Songs to Joannes*) (1917) engages, in part, with a similar discourse of sexual conjunctions without the trappings of romantic love. The lovers of the sequence are imagined variously as 'lighted bodies | Knocking sparks off each other' (Loy 1996: 59), 'machines' (63) or selves who can be 'welded together' in a profane reworking of Christian mythology (58). This mechanistic language is paralleled by a vocabulary of sterility, which reinforces the failure of this love affair and its barren conclusion. The sequence begins by translating the rhetoric of romance into a mechanistic process through images of artificial illumination; a 'sky-rocket' and a 'lantern' take the place of the moon and the stars. The male figure is then reduced to nothing more than an entropic motor, a 'clock-work mechanism | running down against time' (54). What is made clear is that this man, reduced to an automatic, phallic prosthesis in an exaggerated form of Futurist technophilia, offers no satisfaction to his female lover who is 'not paced' to his mechanics. Both man and woman are transformed into puppets, at the mercy of a 'Wire-Puller' who controls their automatic reactions (55).

In *Love Songs*, Gourmont's sense of the animalistic 'mechanism' of love is clearly present where the lovers are imagined as 'fireflies' 'Bouncing | Off one another' (61). Loy's sequence takes Gourmont's terminology to its logical extreme and the lovers 'turn into machines' through their sexual interaction (63). The only escape from this position is to 'Melt' into nebulous non-self or to become the harbingers of a new race of robotic, unsentimental beings 'Cutting our foot-hold | With steel eyes' (63). Loy's ambivalence about the idea of a Gourmontian 'love mechanism' and the reduction of humanity to a mechanical functioning emerges again in her poems about the marginalized and outcast of society. Here, the automaton is understood as a trope that confines and defines those who fall outside the privilege of normative subjectivity. Thus, Loy imagines women trapped in the codes of virtue and propriety as animated dolls in poems such as 'Virgins Plus Curtains Minus Dots' (1915) and 'Magasins du Louvre' (1914). The marginal selves of 'Der Blinde Junge' (1922) and 'Crab Angel' (1921–2) are similarly ensnared in a model of mechanistic subjectivity. In these two post-war poems, an external controlling hand or force, the 'Wire-Puller' of *Love Songs* recast, controls the identity of social outcasts, converting a blind, penniless youth into a clockwork device ('Der Blinde Junge') and a cross-dressed circus dwarf into an 'automaton' ('Crab Angel', Loy 1996: 86). Loy's interest in marginal subjectivities intensified in her later work, and in the novel *Insel* (posthumously published in 1991), the eponymous, itinerant, surrealist artist forges a different relationship with technology. Instead of being defined as a purely mechanistic subjectivity, the protagonist Insel possesses a strange technological power: he has a subconscious affinity with the narrator of the novel and can communicate with her invisibly via what seem to be electromagnetic rays. Insel is less an automaton than an inverse form of the 'influencing machines' that plagued the techno-fantasies of schizophrenics through the twentieth century.[2]

ROBOTS, AUTOMATION AND THE FUTURE OF THE HUMAN

Mina Loy's specific concern is how mechanistic models of subjectivity can disadvantage women and ensnare social outcasts or those marginal to the productive drives of modernity, but anxieties about the concept of the 'human motor' were widespread in the early twentieth century. A sense that humanity was being diminished in the drive towards cost-effective production and in the celebration of machine efficiency was paralleled by a sense that the human was being subsumed into the technology it had created. So, while the regulated factories of America and Europe produced cheap, consumer goods that were newly available for the working and lower-middle classes, certain writers feared this was a further step in the standardization and mechanization of mankind. D. H. Lawrence's celebration of primal, natural energy and essential masculine and feminine identity is, in part, a response to this fear of the mechanization of the human. In *The Waste Land*, T. S. Eliot envisages a stunted crowd of humanity flowing across London Bridge, in a reference to Dante's *Inferno*; this crowd is later refigured in an image of the clerks of London as 'the human engine | like a taxi throbbing, waiting,' (1940: 35). With his own version of the human motor of political, economic and psychological theory, therefore, Eliot uses the trope of the machine to conflate the anonymous force of modernity with what he saw as its emasculating effects on the individual.

In *The Big Money* volume of Dos Passos's *USA* trilogy, the consumerist mass production of the machine age is also critiqued for its effect on the human individual. In the biographies of Frederick Taylor and Henry Ford that Dos Passos offers, both exponents of what he terms here 'The American Plan', he ironically reveals the failures of their success stories. Taylor is characterized as a driven man who sees machinery and labour power as equal resources for efficient production: 'He couldn't stand to see an idle lathe or an idle man' (1938: 16). Dos Passos emphasizes Taylor's invention of piecework, which necessitates a deskilling of the workforce and the institution of a mechanistic process: 'the substitution for skilled mechanics of the plain handyman . . . who'd move as he was told' (19). The irony in the biography Dos Passos gives is that Taylor dies in hospital after his own mental mechanism breaks down, still obsessed with timekeeping: 'he was dead with his watch in his hand' (19). In his account of Ford, Dos Passos emphasizes his desire to escape the land of his family's farm in favour of machinery. Inspired by Edison, the entrepreneurial engineer, Ford's real ingenuity is in sales and profits: 'the big money was in economical quantity production, quick turn-over, cheap interchangeable easily replaced standardized parts' (40). Ford's workers are not content with their allotted place on the production line, for 'machinists didn't seem to like it at Ford's' (40), and Dos Passos's text reveals the source of this dislike. The compacted, dehumanizing rationality of a production-line worker is reproduced in compressed, condensed language: 'the Taylorized speedup everywhere, reach under, adjust washer, screw down bolt, reachunderadjustscrewdownreachunderadjust until every ounce of life was sucked off into production and at night the workmen went home grey shaking husks' (44). The irony of Ford's biography, for Dos Passos, is that he retires as a 'passionate antiquarian', creating a simulacra of a tavern 'the way it used to be, | in the days of horses and buggies' (45).

The Big Money explicitly critiques the mechanization of the worker in capitalist mass production, but in Dos Passos's earlier novel, *Manhattan Transfer* (1925), there is already a clear sense of the mechanization of the human in the modern city. There are repeated references in *Manhattan Transfer* to the machine of the city and to the individuals who are subsumed into this technological epitome of modern, commercial, mass-produced, media-saturated America. One protagonist, Jimmy Herf, increasingly feels stifled by his place in the city-machine as a reporter, bemoaning his conversion into 'a goddam travelling dictograph . . . You get so you don't have any private life, you're just an automatic writing machine' (309). The female protagonist, Ellen Thatcher, is a contrasting success in the city, ultimately as an actress, but in relinquishing herself to the society of images and machines in the text she also becomes more and more mechanical, 'an intricate machine of sawtooth steel whitebright bluebright copperbright' (209). Ellen too is conscious of this mechanization and the automatic roles she, as a woman, is required to play, 'winding up a hypothetical dollself and setting it in various positions'. Aware of the insufficiency of her position as automaton, she admits 'It's like a busted mechanical toy the way my mind goes burr all the time' (334, 356). But Ellen's final movement is to enter into the 'shining soundless revolving doors' of a skyscraper, signalling her capitulation to the turning cogs of the city-machine and to the automatic self (357). Conversely, Jimmy experiences a vision of a 'humming tinselwindowed skyscraper' that denies him access, and ultimately leaves the city and its technological spaces (327).

In Dos Passos's *Manhattan Transfer*, the successful, modern, urban woman, whose triumph lies in her ability to perform for an audience, is imagined finally in robotic terms, terms which resonate with the automated spectacle of women that constituted the Tiller Girl and similar precision dance troupes. In 1927, Siegfried Kracauer saw an intimate relationship between such regulated spectacles of 'geometric precision' and the worker doing 'his or her task on the conveyor belt, performing a partial function without grasping the totality'. For him, 'the hands in the factory correspond to the legs of the Tiller Girls' (78, 79). A different type of anxiety about robotic femininity is expressed in the German Expressionist film *Metropolis* (1927), in which a robot replacement for the virginal heroine Maria seduces and incites rebellion and self-destruction, and is finally burnt at the stake. What is being conflated in the gender politics of this film, as Andreas Huyssen suggests, is a fear of female sexuality and a fear of technologization, both read as otherness from the male. At the end of the film, 'sexuality is back under control just as technology has been purged of its destructive, evil, i.e. sexual elements through the burning of the witch-machine' (Huyssen 1986: 81). Thus, *Metropolis's* 'machine-vamp' is the carrier of intensified male anxiety, which is allayed when this robot is destroyed.

The term 'robot' is a Czech coinage from the word *robota*, which means 'strenuous work', and it entered the language and quickly replaced the term 'automaton' with Karel Čapek's 1921 *R.U.R. (Rossum's Universal Robots)*. The play was premiered in English in New York in 1922, where one reviewer described it as 'the most brilliant satire on our mechanized civilization' (cited Čapek 1921 x). Set in the future, in an island-based factory concerned with the 'manufacture of artificial people', as the General Manager describes them (Čapek 1921: 6),[3] *R.U.R* offers a disturbing vision of a future in which robot labourers replace human workers, a necessary act as 'The human machine . . . was terribly imperfect' (42). The robots are designed and produced to be the 'cheapest' 'simplif[ied]' worker (17), so that humans can live a life of leisure, and aesthetic and philosophical contemplation. But as they are made more 'human', the robots eventually desire to be masters themselves and go on to eliminate humanity. The only hope left at the end lies with two robots, described by the last man on earth as 'Adam' and 'Eve' (187), who experience the stirrings of love and an appreciation of the natural world.

Robots and man-machine hybrids proliferate in SF in the first half of the twentieth century, in fictions that speculate on the implications of robot life. Rather than Čapek's politically inflected satire, many of these stories simply rework a *Frankenstein* narrative in which artificial life turns on its creator, or consider in other ways a struggle between man-machine and human. In

Ambrose Bierce's 1909 story, 'Moxon's Master', a fictional chess-playing robot (that recalls Kempelen's Turk in its appearance) murders his inventor, while in Harl Vincent's story 'Rex' (1934), the robot Rex takes over the world, only to commit suicide. The conception of a noble, self-sacrificing robot, rather than a monster run amok, has its origins in the Adam Link robot created by Eando Binder in 'I, Robot' (1939), but it was Isaac Asimov and his Robot Series of stories and novels, beginning with 'Robbie' (1940), that really enshrined the idea of the benevolent robot, serving man. What Asimov innovated was the idea of Three Laws of Robotics which would hardwire an ethics of obedience and protection into a robot's brain.[4]

When Asimov's robots are faced with an impossible contradiction of the Laws of Robotics, unable to act, they suffer something termed 'roblock' or 'mental freeze-out', a deadlock of their hardwired ethics. An alternative malfunction is suggested in David R. Bunch's 'The Problem Was Lubrication' (1961), which humorously explores the manifestation of human emotions in automated factory mechanisms. A mobile 'Lubro' machine attacks an 'Oiler' machine when a 'new blonde machine' (gendered feminine by the text) appears to show a preference for the Oiler machine over the Lubro. This appearance of sexual jealousy means that both machines are destroyed and replaced by static apparatus (one paired to each automated device), in a robot version of enforced monogamy. In *R.U.R.*, the only suggestion that the robots are fallible machines, which will eventually revolt, is their tendency to malfunction in a particular way and 'stand still' and 'gnash their teeth'. Described as an 'epilepsy' called 'Robot's cramp' by the factory managers, robots malfunctioning in this way are sent to the 'stamping-mill' to be destroyed (Čapek 1921: 46). In his satire of the mechanized assembly line, *Modern Times* (1936), Charlie Chaplin inverts this robotic epilepsy so that his (human) character is afflicted by a compulsive tic which means that he continuously and comically performs the action – tightening a bolt – that is his function on the assembly line.

As a comment on the Great Depression, *Modern Times* is essentially concerned with the lost centrality of the human worker in the efficiencies of modern industrialization. Throughout the early scenes of *Modern Times*, the juxtaposition of the human and machine, and the tyranny of technology, is prevalent: Chaplin's character is startled by an Orwellian telescreen that monitors his break period, subjected to a Feeding Machine which has an impossibly paced tempo, and is swallowed into the mechanisms of the factory process, becoming, literally, a cog in the machine. His compulsive tic, the point at which he becomes most machinic, ironically means he is no longer an acceptable component of the assembly line and he is hospitalized with a mental breakdown. Chase is also concerned, in his *Men and Machines*, with the mental and physical effects on what he terms '"robot-workers" – that mechanism of flesh and blood first heard of in a Czechoslovak play, towards which, it is alleged, all men are moving' (1929: 142). Moreover, he extends this concern to reflect on the 'problem of the restless, neurotic middle-class

woman' who has been 'stripped of her . . . skills' by the 'machine' (181).
Chase's only real appeasement is to see the 'genuine robot' as an anachronism
to be replaced by 'automatic machinery' (265), 'relentlessly substituting
machines for machine tenders' (147). In such a summation, what is of central
concern is not so much the mechanization of man, but his replacement by
machines in a full automation of production and culture that would offer
mankind a utopian release from labour.

The shift from the assembly line to automation, taking humans from being
cogs in the machine to being surplus to the efficient functioning of the
machine, is explored in Vonnegut's novel *Player Piano*. The novel presents a
stratified anti-utopian world in which the few privileged engineers run automated factories in a single, integrated economy, and the rest of America
undertakes meaningless public works or military service while the state sup-
plies all their needs. Paul Proteus, the manager of the Ilium manufacturing
works, reveals how far this society has replaced the human with an ideal of
machine efficiency on surveying the works at the beginning of the novel.
Paul describes a vision of one of his automated machine shops as a regulated
space of performing bodies, a 'great gymnasium, where countless squads
practised precision callisthenics – bobbing, spinning, leaping, thrusting,
waving' (1952: 18). The drilled gymnastic bodies that Marinetti had extolled,
or the Tiller Dance Troupe as Kracauer characterized it, are here superseded
by the machines they approximated. The coordinates for Vonnegut's anti-
utopian vision in this novel are clearly marked by his reference to two historical figures in the text, Thomas Edison and Norbert Wiener. Paul has
preserved the outdated 'Building 58' on the site because of its connection to
Edison: it 'was the original machine shop set up by Edison in 1886' (16).
This clearly indicates the origins of the highly automated system of *Player
Piano* in the entrepreneurial engineering that Edison epitomized. But individual entrepreneurship has been replaced by subsequent waves of American
technological advance that brings the human and the machine into closer and
closer proximity. The mention of Norbert Wiener, 'a mathematician . . . way
back in the nineteen-forties' (22), illustrates how the machine society initiated by Edison has moved, in stages, towards a cybernetic age. Paul refers to
Wiener in outlining the different stages this machine society has gone
through: first 'muscle work' and then 'routine mental work' were 'devalued'
as they were taken over by machines (22), and Paul speculates that the 'real
brainwork' will eventually be taken over by 'thinking machines' (23).

Player Piano illustrates how the struggle and labour of men, which defined
them as Americans, has been replaced by 'machines' that 'hummed and
whirred and clicked' (13). These machines embody a new Americanism, one
that is being extolled to developing nations (like that represented by the
visiting 'Shah of Bratpuhr'), one dedicated to 'eliminating human error
through machinery' (29). In this new America, both men and women are
replaced by machines 'doing America's work better than Americans had ever
done it' (56). Thus, both the engineer Bud Calhoun and a barber are replaced

by a machine they invent, and Paul's friend Edward Finnerty satirically offers to design a machine to replace Paul's wife Anita, made of 'stainless steel, covered with sponge rubber, and heated electrically to 98.6 degrees' (46). The women in this society are as redundant as the men: all housework is automated so they are reduced to watching TV, or, as Anita does, making endless lists to organize her husband's life. Anita's own mechanical functioning is made obvious: she 'has the mechanics of marriage down pat' (25).

But the society that Vonnegut imagines is not simply one of technological dominance over man: it is one in which, as in Anita's 'mechanics', human and machines are fused in a process of efficient production and consumption. At the Ilium works, Paul, Finnerty and Lawson Shepherd have been responsible for converting the manned-machines to automated ones by replacing the men with recordings. Over a decade earlier, they had 'recorded the movements' of Rudy, a 'master machinist', on to magnetic tape, and this is the tape that now controls the machines in a system of Taylorist efficiency amplified beyond human capability: 'by switching in lathes on a master panel and feeding them signals from the tape, Paul could make the essence of Rudy Hertz produce one, ten, a hundred, or a thousand shafts' (20). As Paul observes, 'This was the essence of Rudy as far as his machine was concerned . . . The tape' (20). Thus, Rudy's expertise is absorbed into machine production; he is translated in his 'essence' into a stream of technological data which can then be integrated in the machines.

It is Paul's own sense of being 'so well-integrated into the machinery of society and history as to be able to move in only one plane, and along one line' (42) that instigates his resistance to the process of automation. This automation extends to everyone being assessed and summed up by personnel machines, with a 'profile' and a 'personality' based on 'unnamed units of measure', 'translated into perforations on his personnel card' (76). The completely average American, Edgar R. B. Burroughs, is defined as such by his mechanically stored and processed statistics: the personnel machine also calculates his marital infidelities and likely cause and age of death. When Burroughs ultimately goes insane and disappears, his malfunction can easily be read as another mode of Čapek and Chaplin's robot epilepsy. The integration of man and machine has a dual facet, however, as machines are personified by the men who resent them, terming them variously as 'son-of-a-bitch' and 'slaves' (236, 262). It is in the Carlsbad Caverns and the dedication ceremony for EPICAC XIV, the latest version of the computer that runs the US economy and makes all decisions relating to production, that the blurring of the boundaries between human and machine reach their apex. EPICAC has a 'nervous system' that spreads across miles, and its 'hummings and clickings' signal 'a condition that was translatable from electrical qualities and quantities to a high grade of truth' (140). In his dedication address, the US President Lynn describes EPICAC XIV as 'the greatest individual in history' (116). In contrast, the President is seen, by the diplomat Halyard, as little more than a robot, a 'gorgeous dummy' whose only role is to 'run wisdom from somewhere else through that resonant voicebox and between those even, pearly choppers' (116).

If EPICAC XIV is a thinking individual and the President merely a 'dummy' who speaks, then the machine appears to replace the human, not merely in terms of mechanical actions, but in the very essence of what it means to be human. A direct challenge between human intelligence and automatic processes is played out in the confrontation between Paul and Checker Charley, the robot that is designed by a rival to beat him at checkers. Evoking Kempelen's chess-playing Turk, which posed questions about the possible superiority of automaton intelligence, Checker Charley is a real robot with a 'brain' and a 'memory' running on magnetic tape (59). Paul admits defeat before the game has even started because of the infallibility of artificial intelligence: 'I can't win against the damn thing. It can't make a mistake,' he says (60). Paul is victorious, however, as Checker Charley malfunctions and burns out because of an overlooked loose connection, but for the watching audience this malfunction is seen as a 'Tragedy', 'something beautiful had died' (62). Checker Charley is endowed with a form of life by these onlookers, valued for the efficiency of his design and his rational intelligence.

The novel ends with a rebellion against the machines in Ilium, which ultimately fails. The people of the town tear the machines apart – and the beginning of chapter 35 offers an alphabetical list of the destroyed technologies. But the people are inevitably drawn to a fascination with the exposed workings of the broken machines and are overcome by a compulsion to repair and refit them. As Finnerty reflects, this is the only outcome possible in a contemporary age in which human and machine are inextricably bound up with each other: 'the goddamned people . . . always getting tangled up in the machinery' (309). *Player Piano* not only undermines the differentiation of human intelligence and the human individual, but presents an environment in which technology and humanity are inextricably 'tangled up' together.

TECHNOLOGY, IDENTITY AND THE CYBORG SUBJECT

The failure of Checker Charley, in Vonnegut's *Player Piano*, to beat Paul at checkers is due to a technical malfunction. Vonnegut does not undertake to speculate on whether a fully functioning Charley would have bested his human opponent: Charley, unlike Kempelen's Turk, is not a hoax automaton. Charley thus stands as a profound challenge to Paul's status (he is saved from humiliation by human error in the wiring, not an error by the machine) and Charley is endowed, by the onlookers who mourn his demise, with a form of independent life. Nearly fifty years later, in February 1996, an actual machine, the IBM Deep Blue computer, did succeed in beating the chess grandmaster Gary Kasparov in the first game of a match (Kasparov was to go on to a convincing match victory but lost a 1997 match with Deep Blue). This victory of Deep Blue was seen as a seminal moment because it appeared to demonstrate a machine exhibiting not only intelligent behaviour, but an intelligence that surpassed that of a human expert.

In this study so far computers have been characterized in different ways: as an information processor with military origins, as the architecture of a global communications system and as the interface through which a new textuality can be created. However, what computing technology purports for what it means to be human is perhaps its most fundamental impact, and leads to questions that remain unanswered even in our present day.

Alan Turing, involved in the development of the Enigma code-breaking computers, and the most important twentieth-century theorist of digital computing and computer intelligence, asked a very simple question in a 1950 article, 'Computer Machinery and Intelligence': 'Do machines think?' Instead of answering this question, Turing went on to pose an alternate question along the lines of: can machines do what we (as thinking entities) can do? In his article, Turing imagines a version of the 'imitation game' where type-written responses in a natural language conversation from two sources in another room, one human and one a digital computer, are given to an individual who must decide which is which. The Turing Test, as it became known, continues to be a central concept in the philosophy of Artificial Intelligence (AI), and what it proposes is a scenario where a computer is understood as intelligent when a human can no longer tell that it is a computer and not a human. Thus, AI becomes, not an abstract judgment, but an attribute that is decided on human terms: it is a vision not of human and artificial intelligence in competition, but of 'people . . . tangled up in the machinery'.

Turing's speculations on computer machinery and intelligence emerged at the same time as Wiener's ideas of information flow and feedback, and Wiener visited Turing in 1947 before completing his book *Cybernetics*. The analogies between Wiener and Turing's thinking, between the human cybernetic system and a computer-based intelligent system, lie in the centrality of information in both systems. It is not embodiment that persists, but the patterns of information and intelligence (see Hayles 1999). Wiener pointed out in *The Human Use of Human Beings*, for example, that, as the cells of the human body change during its lifetime, any identity of a human being lies beyond its physical continuity: 'We are not stuff that abides, but patterns that perpetuate themselves' (1950: 96). With subsequent generations, it seemed possible, at least in speculation, that human intelligence could exist outside the human body, contained in a machine that functioned as the human mind did. Most famously, Hans Moravec's *Mind Children: The Future of Robot and Human Intelligence* (1988) suggested the imminent possibility of downloading human consciousness into a computer. Vonnegut's Rudy Hertz, translated into his 'essence' for the machine-shop on a strip of magnetic tape, is comparable to Moravec's prediction, especially given the fact that magnetic tape was used to record computer data, beginning with the UNIVAC computer in 1951. As an inexpensive medium for mass data storage, magnetic tape was central in the computer revolution and indeed was the physical impression of the 'intelligence' of the computing machine: the tape consists of magnetic particles embedded in the surface to materially comprise the data recorded. Many questions arise from a notion like Moravec's, of a human consciousness contained by technology and separated from a fallible, contingent body; one effect is a recasting of the Cartesian dualism of mind and body, suggesting that the mind as well as the body might be understood as a machine. What this might mean for human subjectivity, for understanding the place of the self in the world, is profound. Would it be the same individual inside the machine? Would this individual be endlessly reproducible? Would we, in fact, recognize ourselves inside the machine? Is our embodiment part of our self-identity or superfluous to it?

The mind–body dualism is a persistent concern in Samuel Beckett's work, though the influence of Descartes on him may well, as Matthew Feldman (2006) points out, have been over emphasized in Beckett Studies since the 1960s. Beckett's plays, particularly those, like the radio dramas, concerned with acoustic technology, explore the tensions between the mental and the visceral, the way that a thought or conception relates to physical reality, how a self might engage with its own embodiment. Eugene Webb's argument that Beckett 'sees the world and man not as dualistic but as fragmentary' is more accurate. In Beckett, therefore: 'The conflict within man is not nearly so simple as a mere conflict between body and soul; it is a general disunity involving a multiplicity of conflicting physical and psychological impulses' (cited Feldman 2006: 44 5). In *Krapp's Last Tape* (1958), Beckett dramatizes this conflict and disunity by considering how technology, in the form of magnetic tape-recording, might produce a technologized individual and foreground the fragmentary, contingent nature of the self in the world.

Beckett wrote *Krapp's Last Tape* for the Northern Irish actor Patrick Magee, after hearing his voice on the radio soon after receiving the broadcast tapes for the radio play *All That Fall*. This context emphasizes the origins of the play in the author's sense of acoustic data and his discovery of the technology of the tape-recorder. *Krapp's Last Tape* stages the annual birthday ritual of a sixty-nine-year-old man revisiting his memories and recollections by listening to old tape-recordings; in this, it establishes themes which are revisited in the later radio drama *Embers*. The play is ostensibly a soliloquy or monologue – the only character and voice heard is that of Krapp himself – but Krapp's voice and presence is distributed across both the embodied actor and the voice that is heard on the tape-recording, played on stage by Krapp-69. Thus, on stage, is the physical presence of Krapp-69 and the physical presence of his voice thirty years earlier; also implicitly present is Krapp, aged about twenty-seven, whom Krapp-39 describes listening to in his own birthday recording; 'Just been listening to an old year' (Beckett 1984: 58). The implied Krapp, evoked by this recorded voice listening to an earlier self, also then evokes the presence of all the other past Krapps on all the spools of tape in cardboard boxes on the stage: the stage is potentially inhabited by vast multiplicities of the supposedly singular character. Moreover, often the voice speaking in the play emerges from a machine, while the body of Krapp remains motionless, shifting the locus of consciousness from body to machine.

As the stage directions indicate, the setting is '*late evening in the future*' (55), and this futuristic aspect of the play is necessary because Krapp-69 has been making his annual audio recordings for over forty-two years: commercial magnetic tape-recording had only been available outside Germany from 1948 when the Ampex 200 model launched in the USA (the Ampex 600 model for home use was released in 1954). The BBC was still mostly using discs for its recordings in the late 1950s. In its engagement with this cutting-edge technology, therefore, *Krapp's Last Tape* offers a speculation on the impact of this technology on identity: what it seems to offer is the possibility of transcending the mutability of the physical self by fixing a material embodiment of the self which can be infinitely retrieved. The machine seems to offer Krapp the chance of extending himself through technology: Ulrike Maude describes the audio tape as Krapp's 'prosthetic memory' (2009: 64). As a technological self, Krapp-69 is mirrored by the tape on the machine; it is a version of Krapp's mind turning backwards and forwards in time, with the same memories, preoccupations, hopes and anxieties endlessly repeating themselves. But the technology also enacts a severing of the self where, as Hayles writes, 'presence can now mean physicality or sound, and voice can be embodied in either a machine or a body' (1997: 83).

Krapp's Last Tape stages and explores a very obvious tension between the intellect and the body. Krapp-69 is a fallible body, a 'wearish old man' whose appearance approximates that of a vaudeville clown: he has short trousers, a waistcoat with large pockets, and large, dirty white boots, and the stage directions detail: '*White face. Purple nose. Disordered grey hair . . . very near-sighted . . . Hard of hearing*' (55). In addition to this clownish appearance and failing faculties, Krapp suffers from a bowel complaint and an abnormal taste for bananas. It is clear, from the connotations of his name, to his ridiculous antics with bananas and banana skins and his repetitive behaviour, that Krapp-69 is physically debilitated and unable to escape the base material of the body. But he is also a man of intellect, a writer who relishes the word 'Spool' and attempts a withdrawal from 'everything on this old muckball' (1984: 62). The tape-recordings give Krapp the possibility of escaping the 'muckball', prosthetically extending himself beyond his body and transcending the pull of the physical that draws him back to the body and sex.

But what emerges in the repeated playing of the tape-recording and in Krapp-69's response to it is a clear sense of the non-coincidence of the self, the fact that the Krapp of prosthetic memory cannot correspond to the Krapp who listens to him. There is no continuity between the present self and the self of thirty years earlier as Krapp-69 is unable (and not interested) to remember the 'Memorable equinox' that features so importantly for Krapp-39, and edits, rewinds and so recreates the Krapp that was recorded by Krapp-39. But there are also ways in which the recorded, technological self produces a physical effect in the embodied self: Krapp-69 'closes his eyes' as Krapp-39 on the tape says 'I close my eyes and try and imagine' (1984: 58), Krapp-69 laughs alongside his earlier self, both of them sneering at the Krapp in his twenties, and Krapp-69 sings soon after Krapp-39 asks 'Did I ever sing?' (58). This is less a harmony of past and present in a unified self than a dramatization of the enormous gulf between consciousness and the body (the tape-recorder and the actor on stage), which is only occasionally traversed with success. What persists across time, *Krapp's Last Tape* suggests, is not the intellect, despite the 'seventeen copies' sold of Krapp's magnum opus (62), but the most basic, automatic bodily functions: the addictions and sexual urges that continue to drive Krapp-69. Thus, it is the sexual encounter with the woman in the punt that Krapp-69 forwards to, eliding the personal epiphany of Krapp-39 on the tape, to listen again and again to that lost moment of bodily ecstasy.

Krapp's Last Tape engages with the Cartesian separation of mind and body, not endorsing this dualism but examining the tensions between the material, mechanical body and the intellect. The multiple thematic and scenic contrasts between light and darkness in the play also express this tension. However, the technology of *Krapp's Last Tape* serves only to foreground, and not to invent, the ontological and metaphysical questions Beckett is asking. Technology which allows us to archive physical versions of ourselves, which can be reactivated at any future point, forces us to ask questions about the materiality or not of our consciousness and the status of our identity in time and space. As Maude suggests, the tape-recordings 'function as an opportune trope for identity, because of their simultaneously permanent and mutable nature: they epitomize both the stative and active aspects of subjectivity' (65). Moreover, as the play ends with the tape-recorded voice which '*runs on in silence*', and not the live voice of the actor on stage – 'KRAPP'S *lips move. No sound.*' (63) – it becomes clear that any subjectivity which persists lies solely in the technological, prosthetic memory and not in the worn-out, emptied body of Krapp-69.

That subjectivity transfers from Krapp-69 to the Krapps embodied by the tape-recordings and only accessible via, and subject to, technological mediation, is heightened in the productions of *Krapp's Last Tape* with which Beckett was involved in 1969, 1973 and 1975. In these productions, the curtains did not fall on Krapp sitting motionless but, as James Knowlson relates, 'Beckett had both the stage and the cubby-hole lights fade . . . leaving only the "eye" of the tape-recorder illuminated' (n.p.). Rather than emphasizing the death and erasure of subjectivity that awaits in the darkness of the stage, the final light on the tape-recorder indicates that a consciousness persists, but it is not the consciousness contained in the body of Krapp-69. The final eye/I is the prosthetic identity and memory that the tape-recorder articulates. Thus, Krapp finally becomes a fully technological subject as his fallible body is erased by the mediation of the machine. A version of Krapp ends in the play, but selves multiply in the technological prostheses that outlive him. The tragedy of the play is that these selves are fundamentally non-coincident so that, even as a technological subject, the individual can never be present to himself.

The technological Krapp epitomizes how the intimacy of human and machines poses philosophical questions about human subjectivity, which long pre-date Haraway's feminist vision of a cyborg politics. The postulation of robot intelligence and AI raises all sorts of ontological and ethical issues that are explored in literary texts. Robots in SF negotiate the boundary disturbances that result from the man-machine nexus and speculate on the possible consequences of creating mechanical humanoids superior to their makers. The fear of intelligent machines and computers dominating (and destroying) mankind surfaces in many texts, as indicated in chapter 4, and the issue of the power and role of robots is addressed by Isaac Asimov's Three Laws of Robotics, which became an organizing principle for his SF worlds. These laws serve to territorialize robots and establish them as subordinate to their human creator: Asimov's noble robots are hardwired not to rebel against their objecthood, and in this he circumvents, or even denies, a central question raised by the presence of robots or cyborgs: is an autonomous intelligent machine an object that can be commodified and owned, or does it have a claim to the agency and self-determination that is afforded the autonomous system that comprises the human being? In his novel *Do Androids Dream of Electric Sheep?* (1968), Philip K. Dick explores this question.

In *Do Androids Dream*, the position of humanoid machines in an imagined future is immediately established through references to slavery, the ideology of racial superiority that supported the objectification of humans in the modern Western world. The organic androids ('andys'), in a future polluted and decimated world, function as the 'mobile donkey engine of the colonization programme' to Mars, which, a TV advert claims, 'duplicates the halcyon days of the pre-Civil War Southern States', and where each emigrant to Mars is offered an android 'absolutely free' (1968: 17, 18). The irony is, of course, that the free android, equipped with human intelligence and ability, is resolutely unfree. The narrative focuses on the rogue Nexus-6 andys who escaped their slavery and fled to earth, and the bounty hunter, Rick Deckard, charged with killing them: the objectification and dehumanization of the andys extends even to this act, which is described as 'retiring' rather than the execution that it is. In comparison to the andys, the remaining genuine animals on earth are highly prized and cared for, endowing status and a humanity on their owners. But, just like the andys, the value of animals, from spiders to goats, is defined by their price and availability.

The link between the exploitation of andys and slavery in *Do Androids Dream* points towards the racial aspect of the cyborg and the ways in which the constructed and exploited humanoid of racial discourse, and the ideologies of race superiority and purity, are repeated in speculations about cyborgs and robots. Ralph Ellison's *Invisible Man* (1952) evinces a particular awareness of the 'racializing machinery' of the modern world and, as Johnnie Wilcox explores, exposes the way this machinery produces objectified racial bodies and how, in his final hacking in to the electricity system, the narrator 'subverts the racial power networks that have sought to define him as inferior' (Wilcox 2007: 1000). One character in *Invisible Man* describes the role of black peoples as 'the machines inside the machine' (Ellison 1952: 217) and this serves to highlight, just as Loy's poems on marginal subjects do, the ideology that reserves the privilege of human autonomy for the white, heterosexual, male subject, while othering mechanistic subjectivity.

However, Dick's novel is acutely concerned with undermining this ideological turn, consistently blurring the distinction between the autonomous human and the objectified android. The 'mood organ', the machine that is used by the human characters to control and instigate their emotions, illustrates the cyborg minglings that are essential to the human functioning in this future world, while the 'chickenhead' Isidore, a human designated subnormal by his society, is ridiculed and exploited by his human fellows and the rogue Nexus-6 andys alike. Moreover, there are key moments when Deckard questions his own humanity and when other characters challenge it, suggesting that he himself might be an andy with false memories implanted. The andy Rachel Rosen does not know she is not human, and believes her implanted memories until Deckard uncovers the truth. The anxiety about the unstable distinctions between human and andy that fundamentally disturb the society of *Do Androids Dream* is expressed through the legal injunction against sex between a human and an andy, an injunction broken by Deckard with Rachel and which subsequently profoundly unsettles his ability to 'retire' the same android model as his lover. The novel suggests an imminent state in which the boundaries between human and machine will be completely erased, leaving only an uncertain zone of cyborg interactions. The only obstacle to the complete erasure of the boundary between human and android in *Do Androids Dream* is the question of empathy, with the Voigt-Kampff Empathy Test the remaining scientific way of distinguishing a living human from a living android, and Mercerism, the religion channelled through the technology of the empathy box, that andys cannot experience. Both have come under intense scrutiny through the novel, which ends with a deep ambivalence.

In *Bladerunner* (1982), the film adaptation of *Do Androids Dream* directed by Ridley Scott, a similar blurring of the distinction between human and cyborg is enacted, most obviously in the character of Deckard. The Director's Cut of the film (without the artificial happy ending and film noir voice-over that the studios wanted) emphasizes Deckard's uncertain status and clearly implies that he is a replicant (as andys are termed in the film). *Bladerunner* also rewrites the sexual politics of the andy/replicant, positing a 'pleasure model' of female replicant rather than the sexual taboo of the novel. This emphasizes the servitude and exploitation of the replicants along gender lines, as well as posing a further parallel with human exploitation in prostitution. The romantic closure that ends the film narrative – Deckard and Rachel in love – is profoundly unsettling, presenting either a human and a replicant crossing the natural–artificial divide, or even two replicants experiencing the 'human' emotion of love.

Cyborg figures, in which human and machine are merged in a range of ways, feature repeatedly in fictions in the latter half of the twentieth century, often reproducing the questions and issues raised by Dick's novel and Scott's film. The central question of identity is raised in the film *Robocop* (1987), where a fatally wounded police officer, Alex Murphy, is rebuilt as a cyborg law-enforcer. Murphy is created by Omni Consumer Products to be an object that serves their megacorporate ends, but his human memories disturb the supposedly dispassionate mechanism and his human self-identity eventually re-emerges. In the first *Terminator* film (1984), Arnold Schwarzenegger plays a cyborg assassin from the future. Schwarzenegger's naked muscular body in the opening scenes of the film presents a blurring of real and artificial: the bodybuilder's hyper-masculine bulk achieved through biochemistry, biomechanics and implants stands as/for the cyborg of the future. *Terminator II: Judgement Day* (1991) has a different boundary, blurring with Schwarzenegger's cyborg re-engineered as the hero-protector, being humanized by his parental care for the teenage John Connor, while the human mother, Sarah, has manufactured herself as a hard-body fighter with a mechanical singleness of purpose.

Sarah Connor's muscled body in *Terminator II* points to the fetishistic aspect of the cyborg woman, and the erotic charge of the intimacy between humans and machines, that was anxiously negotiated in the early twentieth century in texts such as *The Future Eve* and *Metropolis*. The erotic female-machine has a dual aspect: on one hand there is the fantasy of the robot or cyborg woman as ideal sexual-domestic servant, epitomized by the replacement wives in Ira Levin's *The Stepford Wives* (1972). This patriarchal narrative is foreshadowed in Lester Del Ray's short story, 'Helen O Loy' (1938), where two men create the perfect women by reprogramming a housemaid robot to become a faithful and adoring wife. On the other hand, there is the fear of and desire for a powerful femininity that is a fusion of artificial and organic played out in C. L. Moore's 1944 short story, 'No Woman Born', and in the plethora of sexualized, dangerous cyborg women who populate texts in the latter half of the twentieth century.[5] The best known of these is Molly Millions in William Gibson's Sprawl Trilogy (*Neuromancer, Count Zero,* 1986, and *Mona Lisa Overdrive*, 1988), who has vision-enhancing mirror lenses implanted over her eye sockets, retractable razor claws under her finger nails and artificially heightened metabolism and reflexes. Molly, and her counterparts in film, fiction, animation and manga, embody, quite literally, the disturbing fascination of technology in their fetishistic representation.

They function as techno-erotic metonyms for masculine anxieties about gender, sexuality and the fate of the autonomous human in an increasingly technological world (see Springer 1996).

Gibson is not the only cyberpunk writer to explore the cyborg fusion of human and machine, and cyborgs are a key facet of the cyberpunk worlds of Neal Stephenson (*Snow Crash*, 1992), Rudy Rucker (the *Ware Tetralogy*, 1982–2000), Pat Cadigan (*Mindplayers* 1987' *Synners* 1991), and Laura J. Mixon (*Glass Houses*, 1992). These texts illustrate how cyberpunk writing is acutely concerned with the body as both the site of intense cultural inscription and as a potential encumbrance in a world of digital informatics, with texts often imagining the reinscription or transformation of the body. As Bruce Sterling observes, cyberpunk repeatedly returns to the 'theme of body invasion: prosthetic limbs, implanted circuitry, genetic alteration' (1986: ix), and frequently there is an expressed desire to escape from the 'meat' realm of the body. In Gibson's *Neuromancer*, for example, Molly both is the male protagonist, Case's, love interest and functions as the cyborg body that Case's consciousness can inhabit through a Simstim link in order to complete his mission. The disembodiment of cyberspace is celebrated in the cyberculture magazine *Mondo 2000*, and in other masculinist techno-fantasies of transcending the 'meat' into a utopian realm of pure consciousness. The elision of the body in specific dreams of cyberspace transcendence or post-humanism[6] has been critiqued by many theorists attuned to the fact that Western culture has insistently denigrated immanence and the body: the gender politics of technology here take a disturbing new turn with the body, associated not only with gender but with racial and economic others, conceived as an encumbrance that can be discarded (see Balsamo 1995; Hayles 1999; Sobchack 1995; Stone 1991). Thus, in their presentations of the cyborg, women writers such Cadigan and Mixon seek to challenge stereotypes and conventional dualities, and refuse the denigration of the body. Cadigan's 'Deadpan' Allie in *Mindplayers* achieves an embodied fusing of male and female through the incorporation of the psyche of a dead man. In her virtual reality links with machines, the cyborg Ruby, Mixon's character in *Glass Houses*, experiences different genders and perspectives which multiply her subjectivity and enable her to experience a simultaneity of subjective and objective self-perception. In these cases, the individual does not transcend the body, but does become a technological subject who exceeds and undermines the boundaries of singular selfhood. Such cyborg texts emphasize physicality and diversity, offering the technological body as an opening out into other bodily possibilities, a techno-extension of the subject into a multiplicity of positions, experiences and processes.

SCREENS, BODIES AND LATE TWENTIETH-CENTURY CULTURE

In the last decade of the twentieth century, technology contributed to a reassessment of human identity that extended beyond the pages of science fiction. Humanism, and the basic assumptions about subjectivity that had underpinned a reasonably stable conception of the human, were challenged by speculations about a possible posthuman future. Variations of what we could term cyborg subjects, no longer the discrete Cartesian ego but a subject situated at an interface of communication, media and medical technology, who was constructed in and through these technologies, appeared to be a very real prospect. And posthumanism theorized this subject far beyond the contingent self of postmodernity, conceiving human biological embodiment and consciousness as conditional and incidental and the body as fundamentally continuous with the prosthetic possibilities of robotic extensions, cybernetic mechanisms and computer simulations (Hayles 1999: 2–3).

Fiction and film of the 1980s and 1990s had already imagined an extended, reconstituted, technologized cyborg subject, who then emerged in theory as a challenge to a world view that had placed primacy on the unified, organic human being. As Scott Bukatman puts it, in posthumanism, 'the body is no longer the repository of the soul' and it is 'technologies that now construct our experiences and therefore our *selves*' (2000: 98, 111). However, it is in late twentieth-century performance art that the posthuman self emerges into full realization, enacted and experienced rather than being discursively constructed in philosophical or fictional speculation. Modifying, extending or converting their bodies through technologies, the French artist ORLAN and the Australian Stelarc present a visceral posthumanism. ORLAN, in her 'Carnal Art' performances in the 1990s, underwent a series of plastic-surgery operations that recreated and distorted her body through the lens of Western art, having cheek implants grafted on to her forehead, for example, in an exaggeration of the *Mona Lisa's* brow. In these videoed and broadcasted performances, ORLAN recited poetry and theory while the medical and media technologies exposed and extended the boundaries of her physical self (see <www.ORLAN.net>). Stelarc's performances engage with prosthetic extensions and enhancements, such as a robot 'Third Hand', an exoskelton, an extra ear (grafted on his arm) and the remote stimulation and movement of his body via the Internet (<www.stelarc.va.com.au>). His work extends and challenges his physical body, but also shifts its agency and locus of consciousness by enabling other users to move his arm or listen to the 'third ear' via computer connections.

For Stelarc, and particularly for ORLAN, the screens that disseminate their performances are fundamental rather than incidental technologies. Their enactments of the posthuman are facilitated through the electronic technology of the screen which plays a role in breeching the closed boundaries of the physical self and communicating the subsequently reconfigured subjectivity. In their forms of screen identity, these artists are recasting, rather than inventing, a version of the technological subject that is also the concern of earlier artists and writers: Duchamp in his *Large Glass* or Beckett in *Krapp's Last Tape*, for example. But the omnipresence of the screen, in its form as the television screen, in the second half of the twentieth century accelerated the interest in the technological mediation of identity. From the advent of mass TV broadcasting in the 1950s, the potential for offering not just a window to the world, but a 'kind of *hypperrealism*', was, as Spigel notes, the promise of early television for its audience (1992: 133). And, as TV became ubiquitous in Western homes, so too did the possibility of understanding the self through the hyperreality of the television screen. TV thus exemplified, expanded and reinforced the notion of a screen life and its central place in a postmodern mediascape, where reality is an extension of the mass media. Debord's society of the spectacle, in which 'everything that was directly lived has receded into a representation' (1967: 7), is one that has the television screen, and the screen lives produced by it, at its heart. For a postmodern theorist such as Baudrillard, screens – television, film or computer screens – have usurped the place of reality, bringing us to a space where we exist only in and through the technologized image. And it is the new possibilities created by media and communication forms that have made screen identity much more than a theoretical postulation.

Although unscripted television shows featuring members of the public had been part of broadcast entertainment since the 1950s, 'reality TV' as an acknowledged television genre really emerged in the 1990s, with docu-soaps such as *Sylvania Waters*, emergency services series such as *Cops*, and culminating in the game shows *Survivor* and *Big Brother* (see Brenton and Cohen 2003). Reality TV belies the distinction between the audience and TV participants, bringing this audience into the televisual hyperreal as actual or potential participants. The ostensible pretext of reality TV, of objective reality observed dispassionately and impartially, is completely undercut by the spectacularity that it produces and requires. Instead of a camera-eye view of authentic selfhood, it manufactures a selfhood that is only understandable through the grammar of reality TV and its screen images. This inverse relationship, where the hyperreal replaces the real, makes reality TV the perfect metaphor for the postmodern age because it represents the self-conscious spectacularization of the self and the projection of the spectacle of self on to screen – purporting to be reality. But, more than this, the selves manufactured by the TV screen are intimately technological selves, posthuman selves who are unreadable and impossible without the expectations and forms of visual technology. The omnipresence of surveillance cameras in everyday life – which themselves produced the material for additional reality TV shows, news footage and visual diaries – further embedded screen presence as an inevitable factor of late twentieth-century living. Alongside this were the opportunities offered by the Internet for immersing in a virtual screen life, the psychological effects of which are examined by Sherry Turkle in her 1995 *Life on the Screen: Identity in the Age of the Internet*. The ubiquity of screen identity in Western culture has only been reinforced since Turkle's study by the presentation of screen selves on the World Wide Web. Bulletin board services in the 1980s, and online communities with chat rooms in the 1990s, were the precursors for the social-networking services that emerged with the launch of Friendster in 2002. Displaying a profile, visual images and enabling interaction between users through written conversations, comments, live feeds, video streaming, groups, online activities and so on, these networks provide the architecture through which a screen identity can be fully realized, and are increasingly a key forum for individuals to represent themselves and interrelate with others; launched as a university site by a student at Harvard in 2004, by 2010 the Facebook social network had over 400 million users.

Social-networking is not the extreme technological performances of Stelarc or ORLAN, or the 'jacking in' to cyberspace imagined in cyberpunk fiction, but it does exemplify a shift in human existence where a technological elsewhere accessed through a personal screen appears to transport us beyond the boundaries of our embodied selves. This, in turn, points to the dangers of a posthuman technophilia which rejects the materiality of the world and embodied politics, thereby negating the substantial inequities which continue to define human life on our planet. The technological transformation and extension of the self means we are no longer a bounded, biological unit; instead, we are inevitably part of an intelligent system that comprises information, machines and bodies. But this system remains part of a densely complex material world in which economic, social, political and corporeal forces continue to matter. Digital code and language, flesh and machines, biological and artificial interpenetrate and interconnect but do not collapse into one another; as Hayles points out, 'boundaries are *both* permeable and meaningful, humans are distinct from intelligent machines even while the two are become increasingly entwined' (2005: 242). For Hayles, the concept of 'intermediation', the complex transactions between the medium of the human body and other media (see Hayles 2005, 2008) is what constitutes the 'cognisphere', the 'globally interconnected cognitive systems in which humans are increasingly embedded' (2006: 161). Any possible posthuman future is one in which interconnectedness should be paramount and where the politics of transactions continue to matter.

In her 1995 hypertext *Patchwork Girl*, Shelley Jackson explores the gendered body as the site of complex transactions and intermediation, considering how a specific medium – digital, literary, theoretical or somatic – is transformed in a dynamic interrelation with the others. As a hypertext, *Patchwork Girl* requires the reader actively to participate in this interrelation, becoming a wreader at the screen who has their own cognitive and physical actions foregrounded by the text's actions. Jackson takes her title from L. Frank Baum's *The Patchwork Girl of Oz* (1913), the seventh of his Oz novels, and so her cyborg protagonist evokes Baum's other artificial humanoids like the Tin Woodman or Tik-Tok, the clockwork robot. But the Patchwork Girl 'Scraps' and her genesis is very particular: she has been stitched together by a magician's wife to be a docile servant, but is accidentally given too much Brain Furniture (including an overdose of 'Cleverness' – the magician's 'substitute for "Intelligence"' – and a quantity of 'Poesy') before she is magically animated by the Crooked Magician. Scraps is thus a boundary figure who is in excess of her proscribed role and throughout Baum's text she displays resilience, joy and a sense of self-worth, coupled with repeated poetic outbursts.

Jackson takes Baum's sewn Patchwork Girl and crosses her with the stitched body on Dr Frankenstein's surgeon's table to create a text that takes seriously both embodiment and the constructed nature of that embodiment. On the first screen of the text, the wreader encounters an image of the patchwork girl, a naked woman pieced together from body fragments, the sutures and scars marking her body like em-dashes on a page. With this image of the 'modern monster' (as the sub-title refers), Jackson points to the absolute alterity of technology, its radical disjunction of the human wreading subject, but also to the somatic ground of our interfaces with technology. Jackson's monster is taken from the (textual) remnants of Mary Shelley's *Frankenstein* and Baum's *The Patchwork Girl of Oz*; she is the female (and the feminine) pieces that Victor Frankenstein discards and the renegade 'cleverness' that makes Scraps more than a mechanical servant. Jackson's Patchwork Girl is held together in the electronic text by lines/links, she is stitched together by symbols (language) that are hardwired into the structure of the machine – computer code that produces and interacts with the language and images on the screen but is never simply reducible to this shifting surface manifestation. Thus, she is characterized by hybridity and monstrousness, refusing to conform to fixed and neutral categories. Stitched into her body the Patchwork Girl has 'fallen angels', 'hybrids, monsters'; '[h]aving no identity' she is 'mosaic, cobbled-together of unmatched parts, crazy-quilted', 'cross-bred, cross-dressed, cross-referenced' [*bad dreams*]. This stitched-together woman is revisited and re-membered in different ways at the opening images of each of the five sections that can be accessed through the title page of *Patchwork Girl*. Throughout the hypertext, the wreader fulfils the role of a Dr Frankenstein, collating fragments to construct a textual body: 'You can resurrect me, but only piecemeal. If you want to see the whole you will have to sew me together yourself' [*graveyard*].

The title page of *Patchwork Girl* articulates the 'distributed authorship' that is central to the politics and aesthetics of this electronic text: the author is given as 'Mary/Shelley, & Herself' [*title page*], in what Hayles decribes as a 'performative gesture indicating that the authorial function is distributed across both names' (Hayles 2000: 38). A disruption of origin here is matched by the different structures of the text, which can be viewed either through text windows or Storyspace map windows. Within this textual-visual matrix, different link structures function. Much of *Patchwork Girl* is classically hypertextual, with different pathways intersecting in lexias, but some sections are chronological ('story'), while another section, 'crazy quilt', has a grid-like layout with each lexia presented in two forms, one that identifies and references the source texts that are quoted and one that doesn't. At this structural level, then, *Patchwork Girl* displays its difference from the complex, Chinese Box, structure of *Frankenstein*. According to Carazo and Jiménez, in the

absence of the ordered narrative levels of Shelley's text, the 'different ontological levels (author, character, reader)' of *Patchwork Girl* 'mingle mon-
strously' (2000: 122). Bodily mingling is the paramount concern of the
'graveyard' lexias, which offer the stories of each of the monster's body parts,
bringing the trace selves into the text/body of what might, tentatively, be
called the protagonist. Such mingling also occurs between her and her creator
Mary, in the lexias which describe the grafting skin exchange between them
([*mary*], [*surgery*], [*join*], [*us*]). That this metonymically enacts the grafting and
mingling of the hypertext wreader, who leaves the trace of her path on the
text as she traces a path in her action of wreading, is made explicit in [*hazy
whole*]: 'if you touch me, your flesh is mixed with mine, and if you pull
away, you may take some of me with you, and leave a token behind'. The
mingling of texts, readers, writers and bodies also guides the section 'crazy
quilt', in which lexias stitch together quotes from *The Patchwork Girl of Oz*,
Frankenstein, Hélène Cixous's 'Coming to Writing', Klaus Theweleit's *Male
Fantasies vol. 1: Women, Floods and Bodies*, Bolter, Joyce, Smith and Bernstein's
Getting Started in Storyspace, Deleuze and Guattari's *A Thousand Plateaus*, and
Elle magazine.

The mingling of texts occurs at a semantic level within lexia, as in [*a single
space*], part of the crazy quilt section, where Bolter et al.'s manual and Baum's
novel are interspliced:

I cut up the quilt, creating a new copy of each paragraph in its own writing space,
a very well shaped-shaped girl which I stuffed with cotton-wadding.

At the textual level, the fabrication of Scraps, as related by the magician's
wife, interacts with Bolter et al.'s directions for the construction of a
Storyspace hypertext, making apparent the actual different levels of this text
– the material computer-coding and programming that produces the linguistic symbols the wreader uses – and the interactivity, or intermediation, that
occurs between and within these different levels. The intertextual feedback
in this lexia offers us the textuality of femininity and our own meaning-
making (Scraps's production as 'girl', our reading of this text in the light of
Mary Shelley, Cixous, Deleuze and Guattarri and so on), and the materiality
of those very activities whereby we constitute the embodied, active site at
which meaning happens; we have after all been clicking links to get to this
lexia along the singular pathway we have traced in *Patchwork Girl*. The sense
of embodied speech, and poetry itself as a body, is reiterated in the lexia
[*write?*] in which the voices of Scraps, the monster and Cixous's 'Coming to
Writing' merge.

What clearly emerges from *Patchwork Girl* is the material scene of the
machine–human interaction of hypertext writing, a sense of the materiality
of writing, of writing as stitching. As Mary Shelley writes in the 'journal'
section, 'I had made her, writing deep into the night by candle light until
the tiny black letters blurred into stitches' ([*written*]; the same sentence appears
in' [*sewn*]). The text is stitched together in the links followed on a reading

path by the wreader, the 'dotted line' that is followed to produce 'a discontinuous trace' [*hop*] that serves to intermingle elements, the line as 'permeable membrane', 'potential', 'fold' [*dotted line*]. The bodily vocabulary is deliberate here and features also as stitching and linking are brought together with examinations of scars and sutures, surgery and quilting (see [*cut*] and [*seam'd*], for example). The acute self-consciousness of this text emerges particularly in the 'body of text' section, in [*this writing*], for example, which describes the unlocated space of hypertext: 'assembling these patched words in electronic space . . . I can see only that part immediately before me'. Compared to the 'spatial and even volumetric' experience of book reading, hypertext forces the question 'where am I now?' [*this writing*], highlighting the cyborg effects on the hypertext wreader and writer who must become intimate with the functioning of this machine text and is thereby displaced by and in it.

Patchwork Girl highlights the breaching of the boundaries of the discrete, organic human subject in its choice of protagonist(s), its textual strategies and its material, technological form. It emphasizes the pattern of information that cybernetics revealed, but also the formation of agency and identity through patterns in the act of interpellation, the hailing of us into a subject position:

I am made up of a multiplicity of anonymous particles, and have no absolute boundaries. I am a swarm. "Scraps? Did you call me Scraps? Is that my name?" [*self swarm*]

Scraps is literally pieced together, animated and named in Baum's *The Patchwork Girl of Oz*, but this process does not differ substantially from the formation of a discrete identity out of the flows of information that are embodied in our material selves: we too are interpellated into language and identity and, in our interactions with intelligent machines, we are brought to recognize the 'anonymous particles' that actually constitute our individuality. In Jackson's text, this is not a revelation to be mourned; but nor is it a signal of an imminent shift from temporally bound analogue particles to a transcendence in digital codes. The corporeality of language, of reading and writing, of knowledge, of experience, is repeatedly emphasized in *Patchwork Girl*, and this is an intimate corporeality that places us within bodies but also opens those bodies up to others: 'We are inevitably annexed to other bodies: human bodies and bodies of knowledge' [*bodies too*].

The ubiquity of computers and screen identities in the Western world at the end of the twentieth century does not herald a transition where we leave our bodies and become transcendent techno-subjects. As *Patchwork Girl* articulates, computing technology and the cyborgs created by it are inextricably interwoven into the media that constitute them and emerge from a dynamic interaction between materialities. Screen selves, reliant on computers which are made somewhere by someone and used by some people in some places, return us to the embodied and situated politics of technology. Literature of the twentieth century is a prime site for examining these politics, and for understanding what technology has meant for challenging traditional definitions of the literary, the text and the reading subject. What I would emphasize at the close of this study is the importance of demystifying technology, of understanding where it comes from and why, who makes it, how it leads to or underpins the distribution of power, or constructs particular opportunities of human possibility while negating others. It is crucial to acknowledge the class, race and gender patterns of technology and its relation to the planet we inhabit: technology is never and was never neutral; it is political and substantial, a material effect and force rather than a disembodied concept, that fundamentally changes how we understand ourselves as human subjects. What the technologies of the twentieth century show, and what the literature and culture of the century negotiates in different ways, is that the meaning and use of those technologies is always open to reinterpretation and re-presentation.

The great fear as the twentieth century came to a close was the millennium bug, Y2K. The millennium bug stemmed from a programming problem within mainframe application codes that stored dates as yymmdd: as the year turned from 1999 to 2000, the truncated date form would mean that stored dates would not sort correctly. The fear was that this would result in the malfunction of computer mainframes and so to the collapse of networks, infrastructure and utilities, leading to global catastrophe and collapse. Millions of dollars were spent on reprogramming and code patching and, as the end of December 1999 approached, people panic-bought tinned goods, bottled water, batteries and first-aid kits. As the millennium turned and, around the world, clocks registered the time 00:00:01 on 01.01.00, nothing spectacular really happened; the computing technology of the twentieth century persisted practically seamlessly into the twenty-first. This technology has a profoundly mixed heritage; with links to military technology and countercultural energies, it has affected writing and conceptions of the human subject, produced new media spaces for experimentation and reinvention, and reprised the networked communication that the nineteenth-century telegraph offered. It is the computer that connects us most directly to the technology, literature and culture of our twentieth-century forebears and points us towards the futures selves we need to actively negotiate.

Notes

Chapter 1 Introduction: The Twentieth-Century
Technological Imaginary

1   Ada Lovelace makes this comment in Note A to her translation of L. F.
    Menabrae's 'Sketch of the Analytical Engine Invented by Charles Babbage',
    1842. The full text is available at <http://www.fourmilab.ch/babbage/
    sketch.html>.
2   The crash is described in detail in L. T. C. Rolt, 1955. *Red for Danger: A
    History of Railway Accidents and Railway Safety* (London: The Bodley Head;
    3rd edn, Newton Abbot: David & Charles, 1976), 181–4.
3   Erichsen's *On Railway and Other Injuries of the Nervous System* was published
    in 1866, with an expanded and rewritten edition in appearing in 1875 as *On
    Concussion of the Spine, Nervous Shock, and Other Obscure Injuries of the Nervous
    System in their Clinical and Medico-Legal Aspects.*
4   See John Clute's 'Edisonade' for an account of the SF representations of
    Edison in Clute and Nicholls 1999: 368–70.
5   For an account of how Pound's radio speeches were written, recorded, and
    broadcast, see Introduction to Leonard Doob (ed.), *"Ezra Pound Speaking":
    Radio Speeches of World War II* (Westport, CT: Greenwood, 1978). For his
    radio operas, see Margaret Fisher, *Ezra Pound's Radio Operas: The BBC
    Experiments, 1931–1933* (Cambridge, MA: MIT Press, 2002).

Chapter 2 Writing Technology: Literature and Theory

1   The German cultural critic Siegfried Kracauer had already discussed the
    'distraction' experienced in 1920s Berlin picture houses in his 1926 essay
    'Kult der Zerstreuung: Über die Berliner Lichtspielhäuser' ('Cult of
    Distraction': published in English in *New German Critique* 14/40 (winter
    1987): 91–6).
2   This is discussed at length in McLuhan's *The Gutenberg Galaxy* (1962).

Chapter 3 Media Technologies and Modern Culture

1   The place of the chess-playing 'Turk' automaton in the pre-history of
    robots is discussed in chapter 6. This Ajeeb was made by Charles Hooper,
    a Bristol cabinet maker, in 1868. Like the Kempelen original, Hooper's
    Ajeeb was worked from inside by an experienced chess player. Ajeeb was

exhibited in the Eden Museum, New York City, in 1868 before transferring to Coney Island in 1915. It was destroyed by one of the many Coney Island fires in 1929.

2 See Kathy Peiss, 1986. *Cheap Amusements: Working Women and Leisure in Turn-of-the-Century New York*, Philadelphia, PA: Temple University Press, for further discussion of the different leisure cultures and styles of working-class women.

3 For a discussion of H.D.'s relationship to radio, see Adalaide Morris, 'Sound Technologies and the Modernist Epic: H.D. on the Air', in *Sound States: Innovative Poetics and Acoustical Technologies*, ed. Adalaide Morris (Chapel Hill, NC, and London: University of North Carolina Press, 1997), 32–55.

4 The *Kansas City Star* style sheet details, in a strange echo of Pound and Marineti's modernist manifestos: 'Eliminate every superfluous word'. The style sheet *c.*1915 can be accessed at <http://lostgeneration.com/includes/Hemingwaystylesheet.pdf> or obtained via email from <starinfo@kcstar.com>.

5 Although Marconi is credited with inventing the radio, Nikola Tesla was the first person to patent radio technology; the USA Supreme Court verified this in 1943 by overturning Marconi's patent.

Chapter 4   Cold War Technologies

1 Daniel Tiffany offers an astounding example of the US atom bomb as spectacle: in October 1945, the LA Coliseum hosted a huge-scale show enacting the detonation of the bomb (see Tiffany, *Toy Medium: Materialism and Modern Lyric*, Berkeley, CA: California University Press, 2000, 221).

Chapter 5   Technological Texts: from Typewriters to Hypermedia

1 There are many patents and prototypes that pre-date Sholes, and the actual invention of the typewriter is debated by the numerous sources on the subject: one of the earliest patents was obtained in England by Henry Mill in 1714.

2 In her subsequent literary career, Stein would have Alice B. Toklas as her partner and type-writer, writing her autobiography through the perspective of the woman who typed it with *The Autobiography of Alice B. Toklas* (1933).

3 For the argument that the typewriter is not inevitably a female technology, see Margery W. Davies, *Woman's Place is at the Typewriter: Office Work and Office Workers 1870–1930* (Philadelphia, PA: Temple University Press, 1982).

Chapter 6   Robots, Cyborgs and the Technological Body

1 Donna Haraway, 'A Cyborg Manifesto: Science, Technology, and Socialist-Feminism in the Late Twentieth-Century', in *Simians, Cyborgs, and Women: The Reinvention of Nature* (London and New York: Routledge, 1991), 181.

2 See, for example, the case of Judge Schreber (*Memoirs of My Nervous Illness*, Daniel Paul Schreber, 1903, New York: New York Review of Books, 2000), Joey ('Joey: A "Mechanical Boy"', Bruno Bettelheim, *Scientific America* 200/3: 116–27, and Victor Tausk's influential 1919 essay, 'On the Origin of

the "Influencing Machine" in Schizophrenia', published in translation in *The Psychoanalytic Quarterly* 2 (1933): 519–56.

3   Paul Selver's 1922 translation of *R.U.R.* into English cuts speeches and dispenses with a key character, Damon, the other robot leader who believes in sacrifice for the good of the group. Claudia Novack-Jones's 1989 translation restores the character of Damon and the missing lines throughout, but there are still issues with her translation; see Merritt Abrash, '*R.U.R.* Restored and Reconsidered', *Extrapolation* 32 (1991): 185–92, and Kamila Kinyon, 'The Phenomenology of Robots: Confrontation with Death in Karel Čapek's "R. U. R." ', *Science Fiction Studies* 26/3 (November 1999): 379–400.

4   Asimov's Three Laws of Robotics, introduced in his 1942 short story 'Runaround', are as follows: 'A robot may not injure a human being or, through inaction, allow a human being to come to harm; A robot must obey any orders given to it by human beings, except where such orders would conflict with the First Law; A robot must protect its own existence as long as such protection does not conflict with the First or Second Law.'

5   A list of the sexualized, dangerous female robots and cyborgs of the late twentieth century would include Eve8 from *Eve of Destruction* and the 'Terminatrix' from *Terminator 3* (2003).

6   In the following discussion, I use the terms posthuman/posthumanism to indicate the philosophical and cultural speculations about moving beyond the limits of humanism rather than the terms transhuman/transhumanism, from the phrase *transitional humans*, which relates very specifically to the futurist techno-visions of Extropians, Transtopians and Singularitarians (see Hook 2003).

Select Bibliography

Aarseth, Espen J., 1997. *Cybertext: Perspectives on Ergodic Literature*. Baltimore, NJ: Johns Hopkins University Press.

Acker, Kathy, 1988. *Empire of the Senseless*. New York: Grove Press.

Adams, Henry, [1907] 1973. *The Education of Henry Adams*, ed. Erenest Samuels. Boston, MA: Houghton Mifflin.

Aldiss, Brian, 1986. *Trillion Year Spree: The History of Science Fiction*. London: Gollancz.

Allen, Grant (writing as Olive Pratt Rayner), [1897] 2004. *The Type-Writer Girl*, intro. and ed. Clarissa J. Suranyi. Peterborough, ON: Broadview.

Almon, Bert, 1997. 'Les Murray's Critique of the Enlightenment', in *Counter Balancing Light: Essays on the Poetry of Les Murray*. Armidale, NSW: Kardoorair Press, 1–19.

Amerika, Mark, 1997. *Grammatron*, <http://www.grammatron.com/index2.html>.

Apollonio, Umbro, ed. 1973. *Futurist Manifestos*. London: Thames and Hudson.

Armitage, John and Friedrich Kittler, 2006. 'From Discourse Networks to Cultural Mathematics: An Interview with Friedrich Kittler', *Theory, Culture & Society* 23/7–8: 17–38.

Armstrong, Tim, 1998. *Modernism, Technology and the Body: A Culture Study*. Cambridge: Cambridge University Press.

Arnheim, Rudolf, 1936. *Radio*, trans. Margaret Ludwig and Herbert Read. London: Faber and Faber.

Auden, W. H., 1979. *Selected Poems* London: Faber and Faber.

——— 1986. *The English Auden: Poems, Essays and Dramatic Writings 1927–1939*. London: Faber and Faber.

Avery, Todd, 2006. *Radio Modernism: Literature, Ethics and the BBC 1922–1938*, Farnham, UK: Ashgate.

Baily, Kenneth, 1950. *Here's Television*. London: Vox Mundi.

Ballard, J. G., [1973] 1995. *Crash*. London: Vintage.

Balsamo, Anne, 1995. 'Forms of Technological Embodiment: Reading the Body in Contemporary Culture', in *Cyberspace/Cyberbodies/Cyberpunk: Cultures of Technological Embodiment*, ed. Mike Featherstone and Roger Burrows. London: Sage, 215–38.

Barth, John, 1968. 'Lost in the Funhouse', in *Lost in the Funhouse: Fiction for Print, Tape, Live Voice*. New York: Doubleday, 72–97.

——— 1997. 'Click', *Atlantic Monthly* (December): 81–96.

Bathrick, David, 1997. 'Making a National Family with the Radio: The Nazi *Wunschkonzert*', *Modernism/Modernity* 4/1: 115–27.

Baudrillard, Jean, [1983] 1985. 'The Ecstasy of Communication', trans. John Johnston, in *Postmodern Culture*, ed. Hal Foster. London: Pluto Press, 126–34.

—— [1988] 1993. 'Interview (The Work of Art in the Electronic Age)', trans. Lucy Forsyth, in *Baudrillard Live: Selected Interviews*, ed. Mike Gane. London and New York: Routledge, 145–51.

—— [1991] 2006. *The Gulf War Did Not Take Place*, trans. Paul Patton. Sydney: Power Publications.

Baum, L. Frank, [1913] 1990. *The Patchwork Girl of Oz*. Mineola, NY: Dover Publications.

Beckett, Samuel, 1984. *Collected Shorter Plays*. London: Faber and Faber.

Bell, Alice, 2007. '"Do You Want to Hear about It?" Exploring Possible Worlds in Michael Joyce's Hyperfiction, *afternoon, a story*', in *Contemporary Stylistics*, ed. Marina Lambrou and Peter Stockwell. London and New York: Continuum, 43–55.

Bell, David and Barbara Kennedy, 2000. *The Cybercultures Reader*. London and New York: Routledge.

Bell, Ian F. A., 1981. *Critic as Scientist: The Modernist Poetics of Ezra Pound*. London: Methuen.

Benjamin, Walter, 1999. *Illuminations,* ed. Hannah Arendt, trans. Harry Zorn. London: Pimlico.

Berners-Lee, Tim and Mark Fischetti, 1999. *Weaving the Web: The Past, Present and Future of the World Wide Web by Its Inventor*. London: Orion Business Books.

Berry, Eleanor, 1988. 'Machine Technology and Technique in the Poetry of Marianne Moore and William Carlos Williams', *William Carlos Williams Review* 14/1: 50–68.

Birkerts, Sven, 1994. *The Gutenberg Elegies: The Fate of Reading in an Electronic Age*. London: Faber & Faber.

BLAST: Review of the Great English Vortex 1 (29 June) 1914; 2 (July) 1915, ed. Wyndham Lewis. New York: Kraus Reprint Corporation, 1967.

Bliven Jr., Bruce, 1954. *The Wonderful Writing Machine*. New York: Random House.

Boddy, William, 1990. *Fifties Television: The Industry and Its Critics*. Urbana and Chicago, IL: University of Illinois Press

Bolter, Jay David, 1991. *Writing Space: The Computer, Hypertext and the History of Writing*. Hillsdale, NJ: Lawrence Erlbaum.

Borgs, Jorge Luis, [1941] 1964. 'The Garden of Forking Paths', trans. Donald A. Yates, in *Labyrinths: Selected Stories and Other Writings*. New York: New Directions, 19–29.

Boyd, James, ed., 1941. *The Free Company Presents . . . A Collection of Plays about the Meaning of America*. New York: Dodd, Mead & Company.

Braidotti, Rosi, 2002. *Metamorphosis: Towards a Materialist Theory of Becoming*. Cambridge: Polity.

—— 2006. 'Posthuman, All Too Human: Towards a New Process Ontology', *Theory, Culture & Society* 23/7–8: 197–208.

Brenton, Sam and Reuben Cohen, 2003. *Shooting People: Adventures in Reality TV*. London: Verso.

Brown, Robert Carlton, ed., 1931. *Readies for Bob Brown's Machine*. Cagnes-Sur-Mer: Roving Eye Press.

Brown, Robert J., 1998. *Manipulating the Ether: The Power of Broadcast Radio in Thirties America*. Jefferson, NC: McFarland and Company.

Brunner, Edward, 2001. *Cold War Poetry*. Urbana, IL: University of Illinois Press.

Bukatman, Scott, 1993. *Terminal Identity: The Virtual Subject in Post-Modern Science Fiction*. Durham, NC, and London: Duke University Press.

—— 2000. 'Postcards from the Posthuman Solar System', in *Posthumanism*, ed. Neil Badmington. Houndmills: Palgrave, 98–111.

Bunch, David R., [1961] 1989. 'The Problem Was Lubrication', in *Robots*, ed. Isaac Asimov, Charles G. Waugh and Martin H. Greenberg. London: Robinson, 223–6.

Burroughs, William, 1959. *Naked Lunch*. New York: Ballantyne.

—— [1962] 2001. *The Ticket That Exploded*. London: HarperCollins.

—— [1964] 1999. *Nova Express*. New York: Grove Press.

Bush, Vannevar, [1945] 1991. 'As We May Think', in *From Memex to Hypertext: Vannevar Bush and the Mind's Machine*, ed. Paul Kahn. Boston, MA, and London: Academic Press, 85–110.

Cadigan, Pat, [1987] 2000. *Mindplayers*. London: Gollancz.

Campbell, Timothy C., 2006. *Wireless Writing in the Age of Marconi*. Minneapolis, MN, and London: University of Minnesota Press.

Čapek, Karel, [1921] 1923. *R.U.R. (Rossum's Universal Robots)*, trans. Paul Selver. New York: Doubleday.

Carazo, Carolina Sánchez-Palencia and Manuel Almagro Jiménez, 2006. 'Gathering the Limbs of the Text in Shelley Jackson's Patchwork Girl', *Atlantis: Revista de la Asociación Española de Estudios Ingleses y Norteamericanos* 28/1 (June): 115–29

Cavallaro, Dani, 2000. *Cyberpunk and Cyberculture: Science Fiction and the Work of William Gibson*. London: Athlone Press.

Cayley, John, 1994. *Golden Lion*, diskette. London: Wellsweep Press.

—— 1995. *Book Unbound*, diskette. London: Wellsweep Press.

—— 1996. 'Beyond Codexspace: Potentialities of Literary Cybertext', *Visible Langauge* 30/3: 165–83.

Chase, Stuart, 1929. *Men and Machines*. New York: Macmillan.

Christie, Ian, 1994. *The Last Machine: Early Cinema and the Birth of the Modern World*. London: BFI.

Clute, John and Peter Nicholls, eds, 1999. *The Encyclopedia of Science Fiction*. London: Orbit.

Clynes, Manfred E. and Nathan S. Kline, [1960] 1995. 'Cyborgs and Space', *Astronautics* (September), reprinted in *The Cyborg Handbook*, ed. Chris Hables Gray. New York: Routledge, 29–33.

Cohen, Debra Rae, Michael Coyle and Jane Lewty, eds, 2009. *Broadcasting Modernism*. Gainesville, FL: University of Florida Press.

Coupland, Douglas, 1995. *Microserfs*. London: HarperCollins.

Coyle, Michael, 2001a. 'T. S. Eliot on the Air: 'Culture' and the Challenges of Mass Communication', in *T. S. Eliot and Our Turning World*, ed. Jewel Spears Brooker. New York: St Martin's Press, 141–54.

—— 2001b. 'T. S. Eliot's Radio Broadcasts, 1929–63: A Chronological Checklist', in *T. S. Eliot and Our Turning World*, ed. Jewel Spears Brooker. New York: St Martin's Press, 205–13.

Crary, Jonathan, 1990. *Techniques of the Observer: On Vision and Modernity in the Nineteenth Century*. Cambridge, MA: MIT Press.

Crook, Tim, 1998. *International Radio Journalism: History, Theory and Practice*. London and New York: Routledge.

—— 1999. *Radio Drama: Theory and Practice*. London and New York: Routledge.

cummings, e e, 1991. *Complete Poems 1904–1962*, ed. George J. Firmage. New York: Liveright.

Cunnell, Howard, 2007. 'Fast This Time: Jack Kerouac and the Writing of *On The Road*', in Jack Kerouac, *On the Road: The Original Scroll*. London: Penguin, 1–52.

Dadley, Portia, 1996. 'The Garden of Edison: Invention and the American Imagination', in *Cultural Babbage: Technology, Time and Invention*, ed. Francis Spufford and Jenny Uglow. London: Faber & Faber, 81–98.

Daly, Nicholas, 2004. *Literature, Technology, and Modernity 1860–2000*. Cambridge: Cambridge University Press.

Danielewski, Mark Z., 2000. *House of Leaves*. New York and London: Doubleday.

Danius, Sarah, 2002. *The Senses of Modernism: Technology, Perception and Aesthetics*. Ithaca, NY, and London: Cornell University Press.

Debord, Guy, [1967] 1983. *Society of the Spectacle*, trans. Ken Knabb. London: Rebel Press.

Deleuze, Gilles, 1987. 'Dead Psychoanalysis: Analyse', in *Dialogues*, Gilles Deleuze and Claire Parnet, trans. Hugh Tomlinson and Barbara Habberjam. London: Athlone Press, 77–123.

Deleuze, Gilles and Félix Guattari, 1984. *Anti-Oedipus: Capitalism and Schizophrenia*, trans. Robert Hurley, Mark Seem and Helen R. Lane. London and New York: Continuum.

—— 1988. *A Thousand Plateaus: Capitalism and Schizophrenia*, trans. Brian Massumi. London: Athlone Press, 1988.

DeLillo, Don, [1972] 2004. *End Zone*. London: Picador.

—— 1985. *White Noise*. Harmondsworth: Penguin.

—— [1997a] 1998. *Underworld*. London: Macmillan.

—— 1997b. 'The Power of History', *New York Times Magazine*, 7 September: 60–3.

—— [2003] 2004. *Cosmopolis*. London: Macmillan.

Denning, Michael, 1987. *Cover Stories: Narrative and Ideology in the British Spy Thriller*. London: Routledge.

DePietro, Thomas, 2005. *Conversations with Don DeLillo*. Jackson, MS: University Press of Mississippi.

Donald, James, Anne Friedberg and Laura Marcus, eds, 1998. *Close-up 1927–33: Cinema and Modernism*. New York: Continuum.

Dick, Philip K., [1968] 1987. *Do Androids Dream of Electric Sheep?* London: Grafton.

Dos Passos, [1925] 1986. *Manhattan Transfer*. London: Penguin.

—— 1936. 'Grosz Comes to America', *Esquire* 6 (September): 105, 128, 131.

—— [1938] 2001. *U.S.A.* (*The 42nd Parallel*, 1930; *1919*, 1932; *The Big Money*, 1936). London: Penguin.

—— 1968. 'What Makes a Novelist', *National Review*, 16 January: 29–32.

Douglas, J. Yellowlees, 1994. '"How Do I Stop This Thing?": Closure and Indeterminacy in Interactive Narratives', in *Hyper/Text/Theory*, ed. George P. Landow. Baltimore, NJ: Johns Hopkins University Press, 159–88.

Douglas, Keith, [1946] 2008. *Alamein to Zem Zem*. London: Faber & Faber, 2008.

—— 1979. *Complete Poems*, ed. Desmond Graham. Oxford: Oxford University Press.

Drakakis, John, ed. 1981. *British Radio Drama*. Cambridge: Cambridge University Press.

Dworkin, Craig, 1999. 'Seeing Words Machinewise': Technology and Visual Prosody', *Sagetrieb: A Journal Devoted to Poets in the Imagist/Objectivist Tradition*, 18/1: 59–86.

Eliot, T. S., [1940] 1972. *The Waste Land and Other Poems*. London: Faber & Faber.

—— 1971. *The Waste Land: A Facsimile and Transcript of the Original Drafts Including the Annotations of Ezra Pound*, ed. Valerie Eliot. London: Faber & Faber.

Ellison, Harlan, [1967] 1984. 'I Have No Mouth, and I Must Scream', in *Machines That Think: The Best Science Fiction Stories about Robots and Computers*, ed. Isaac Asimov, Patricia S. Warrick and Martin H. Greenberg. London: Allen Lane, 233–50.

Ellison, Ralph, [1952] 1989. *Invisible Man*. New York: Vintage.

Ellman, Richard, 1987. 'Samuel Beckett: Nayman of Noland', in *Four Dubliners: Wilde, Yeats, Joyce and Becket.* New York: George Braziller, 89–119.

Ellul, Jacques, 1980. *The Technological System.* New York: Continuum.

Emden, Christian J., 2005. *Nietzsche on Language, Consciousness and the Body.* Urbana, IL: University of Illinois Press.

Ensslin, Astrid. 2007. *Canonizing Hypertext: Explorations and Constructions.* London: Continuum.

Epstein, Jacob, 1955. *An Autobiography.* London: Hulton Press.

Essig, Mark, 2003. *Edison and the Electric Chair: A Story of Light and Death.* Stroud, Glos: Sutton Publishing.

Feldman, Matt, 2006. *Beckett's Books: A Cultural History of Samuel Beckett's Interwar Notes.* London and New York: Continuum.

Filene, Edward A., 1932. *Successful Living in This Machine Age.* London and Toronto: Jonathan Cape.

Fleissner, Jennifer L., 2005. 'Dictation Anxiety: The Stenographer's Stake in *Dracula*', in *Literary Secretaries/Secretarial Culture*, ed. Leah Price and Pamela Thurschwell. Aldershot, UK: Ashgate, 63–90.

Fleming, Ian, [1958] 2004. *Dr No.* London: Penguin.

—— [1959] 2002. *Goldfinger.* London: Penguin.

—— 1961. *Thunderball.* London: Penguin.

—— [1965] 2004. *The Man with the Golden Gun.* London: Penguin.

—— 2003. *Casino Royale, Live and Let Die, Moonraker.* London: Penguin.

Flint, R. W., ed. 1972. *Marinetti: Selected Writings.* London: Secker & Warburg.

Foster, Hal, 1997. 'Prosthetic Gods', *Modernism/Modernity* 4/2: 5–38.

Frank, Adam, 2005. 'Valdemar's Tongue, Poe's Telegraphy', *English Literary History* 72/3: 635–66.

Freud, Sigmund, [1929] 1989. *Civilisation and Its Discontents*, trans. and ed. James Strachey. New York: W. W. Norton.

Funkhouser, Christopher T., 2005–6. 'Irregular Solid: John Cayley's Cybertextually Engineered Digital Poetry – an Essay', *EnterText* 5/4 (winter): 108–32.

—— 2007. *Prehistoric Digital Poetry: An Archaeology of Forms, 1959–1995.* Tuscaloosa, AL: University of Alabama Press.

Gane, Nicholas, 2005. 'Radical Post-humanism: Friedrich Kittler and the Primacy of Technology', *Theory, Culture & Society* 22/3: 25–41.

Gane, Nicholas and Donna Haraway, 2006. 'When We Have Never Been Human, What Is to Be Done?: Interview with Donna Haraway', *Theory, Culture & Society* 23/7–8: 135–58.

Garrett, Stewart, 2000. *Between Film and Screen; Modernisms's Photo Synthesis.* Chicago, IL: University of Chicago Press.

Geddes, Keith and Gordon Bussey, 1991. *The Setmakers: A History of the Radio and Television Industry.* London: BREMA.

Gersh, Louis H. and Robert Weinberg, 2006. *The Science of James Bond: From Bullets to Bowler Hats to Boat Jumps, the Real Technology behind 007's Fabulous Films.* Hoboken, NJ: John Wiley.

Gibson, William, 1984. *Neuromancer.* London: Victor Gollancz.

—— [1986] 2006. *Count Zero.* New York: Ace Books.

—— [1988] 2000. *Mona Lisa Overdrive.* London: Voyager.

—— 1995. *Burning Chrome.* London: Victor Gollancz.

Ginsberg, Allen, 1984. *Collected Poems 1947–1980.* New York: Harper & Row.

—— 2000. *Deliberate Prose: Selected Essays, 1952–1995*, ed. Bill Morgan. New York: Harper.

Gitelman, Lisa, 1999. *Scripts, Grooves, and Writing Machines: Representing Technology in the Edison Era.* Stanford, CA.: Stanford University Press.

—— 2006. *Always Already New: Media, History and the Data of Culture.* Cambridge, MA: MIT Press.

Gitelman, Lisa and N. Katherine Hayles, 2002. 'Materiality Has Always Been in Play', an interview with N. Katherine Hayles, *The Iowa Review Web*, <http://iowareview. uiowa.edu/TIRW/TIRW_Archive/tirweb/feature/hayles/hayles.htm>.

Glazier, Loss Pequeño, 2001. *Digital Poetics: The Making of E-Poetries.* Tuscaloosa, AL: University of Alabama Press.

Gourmont, Rémy de, [1903] 1992. *The Natural Philosophy of Love*, trans. Ezra Pound 1922. London: Quartet Books.

Graham, Elaine L., 2003. *Representations of the Post/Human: Monsters, Aliens and Others in Popular Culture.* New Brunswick, NJ: Rutgers University Press.

Gray, Chris Hables, 1995. *The Cyborg Handbook.* New York and London: Routledge.

Greenberg, Mark L. and Lance Schachterle, eds, 1992. *Literature and Technology.* London and Toronto: Associated University Presses.

Greenlaw, Lavinia, 1993. *Night Photograph.* London: Faber & Faber.

—— 1997. *A World Where News Travelled Slowly.* London: Faber & Faber

Guertin, Carolyn. 1999. 'Gesturing toward the Visual: Virtual Reality, Hypertext and Embodied Feminist Criticism', *Surfaces* 8/1: 3–18.

Gunning, Tom, 1986. 'The Cinema of Attractions: Early Cinema, Its Spectators, and the Avant-Garde', *Wide Angle* 8/3&4 (fall): 63–70.

—— 1989a. 'Primitive Cinema – A Frame-up? Or the Trick's on Us', *Cinema Journal* 28/2 (winter): 3–12.

—— 1989b. 'An Aesthetic of Astonishment: Early Film and The Incredulous Spectator', *Art and Text* 34 (spring): 31–45.

—— 2001. 'Doing for the Eye What the Phonograph Does for the Ear', in *The Sounds of Early Cinema*, ed. Richard Abel and Rick Altman. Bloomington, IN: Indiana University Press, 13–31.

Guralnick, Elissa S., 1996. *Sight Unseen: Beckett, Pinter, Stoppard, and Other Contemporary Dramatists on Radio.* Athens, OH: Ohio University Press.

Guyer, Carolyn, 1993. *Quibbling*, CD Rom, Watertown, MA: Eastgate Systems.

Hamill, John, 1999. 'Confronting the Monolith: Authority and the Cold War in "Gravity's Rainbow"', *Journal of American Studies* 33/3: 417–36.

Haraway, Donna, 1985. 'Manifesto for Cyborgs: Science, Technology and Socialist Feminism in the 1980s', *Socialist Review* 15/2: 65–107. Reprinted in revised form as 'A Cyborg Manifesto: Science, Technology, and Socialist-Feminism in the Late Twentieth-Century', in *Simians, Cyborgs, and Women: The Reinvention of Nature.* London and New York: Routledge, 1991, 149–81.

—— 1991. 'Reading Buchi Emecheta: Contests for "Women's Experience" in Women's Studies', in *Simians, Cyborgs, and Women: The Reinvention of Nature.* London and New York: Routledge, 109–24.

Harrington, Ralph, 2003. 'The Railway Accident: Trains, Trauma and Technological Crisis in Nineteenth-century Britain', *University of York Institute of Railway Studies and Transport History*, <http://www.york.ac.uk/inst/irs/irshome/papers/rlyacc.htm> n.p.

Hayles, N. Katherine, 1997. 'Voices Out of Bodies, Bodies Out of Voices: Audiotape and the Production of Subjectivity', in *Sound States: Innovative Poetics and Acoustical*

Technologies, ed. Adalaide Morris. Chapell Hill, NC, and London: University of North Carolina Press, 74–96.

—— 1999. *How We Became Posthuman: Virtual Bodies in Cybernetics, Literature and Informatics*. Chicago, IL, and London: University of Chicago Press.

—— 2000. 'Flickering Connectives in Shelley Jackson's *Patchwork Girl*: The Importance of Media-Specific Analysis', *Postmodern Culture* 10/2 (January): np.

—— 2002. *Writing Machines*. Cambridge, MA: MIT Press.

—— 2005. *My Mother Was a Computer: Digital Subjects and Literary Texts*. Chicago, IL, and London: University of Chicago Press.

—— 2006. 'Unfinished Work: From Cyborgs to Cognisphere', *Theory, Culture & Society* 23/7–8: 159–66.

—— 2008. *Electronic Literature: New Horizons for the Literary*. Notre Dame: University of Notre Dame Press.

H.D., 1974. *Tribute to Freud*. New York: New Directions.

—— 1984. *Collected Poems: 1912–1944*. New York: New Directions.

Heidegger, Martin, [1942–3] 1992. *Parmenides*. Bloomington, IN: Indiana University Press.

—— [1955] 1977. *The Question Concerning Technology and Other Essays*, trans. William Lovitt. New York: Harper & Row.

—— [1959] 1966. *Discourse on Thinking*, trans John M. Anderson and E. Hans Freund. New York: Harper & Row.

Hersey, John, 1946. *Hiroshima*. New York: Knopf.

Hilmes, Michele, 1997. *Radio Voices: American Broadcasting, 1922–1952*. Minneapolis, MN: University of Minnesota Press.

Holme, Christopher, 1981. 'The Radio Drama of Louis MacNeice', in *British Radio Drama*, ed. John Drakakis. Cambridge: Cambridge University Press, 37–71.

Hook, C. Christopher, 2003. 'Transhumanism and Posthumanism', in *Encyclopaedia of BioEthics*, 3rd edn, ed. Stephen Garrad Post. Farmington Hills, MI: Gale, 2517–20.

Horkheimer Max and Theodore W. Adorno, [1947] 1982. *Dialectic of Enlightenment*, trans. John Cumming. New York: Continuum.

Hubbell, Richard, 1956. *Television Programming and Production* 3rd edn. New York: Rinehart.

Hutchinson, Thomas H., 1948. *Here Is Television, Your Window on the World*. New York: Hastings House.

Huxley, Aldous, [1932] 1969. *Brave New World*. Harmondsworth: Penguin.

Huyssen, Andreas, 1986. 'The Vamp and the Machine: Fritz Lang's *Metropolis*', in *After the Great Divide: Modernism, Mass Culture, Postmodernism*. Bloomington and Indianapolis, IN: Indiana University Press, 65–81.

International Telecommunication Union, 2009. 'The World in 2009: ICT Facts and Figures', <http://www.itu.int/ITU-D/ict/material/Telecom09_flyer.pdf>.

Jackson, Shelley, 1995. *Patchwork Girl*, CD Rom. Watertown, MA: Eastgate Systems.

James, Edward, 1995. 'Science Fiction by Gaslight: An Introduction to English-Language Science Fiction in the Nineteenth Century', in *Anticipations: Essays on Early Science Fiction and Its Precursors*, ed. David Seed. Liverpool: Liverpool University Press, 26–45.

James, Henry, [1898] 2002. *In the Cage*. London: Hesperus Press.

Jameson, Fredric, 1991. *Postmodernism, or the Cultural Logic of Late Capitalism*. Durham, NC: Duke University Press.

Jones, Amelia, 2004. *Irrational Modernism: A Neurasthenic History of New York Dada*. Cambridge, MA: MIT Press.

Joyce, Michael, 1990. *afternoon, a story*, CD Rom. Watertown, MA: Eastgate Systems.

—— 1995. *Of two minds: hypertext pedagogy and poetics*. Ann Arbor, MI: University of Michigan Press.

—— 1996a. *Twilight, a Symphony*, CD Rom. Watertown, MA: Eastgate Systems.

—— 1996b. *Twelve Blue*, <http://collection.eliterature.org/1/works/ joyce__twelve_ blue.html>.

Juncker, Clara, 1990. 'Dos Passos Movie Star: Hollywood Success and American Failure', *American Studies in Scandinavia* 22/1: 1–14.

Kahn, Douglas, 1992. 'Death in Light of the Phonograph: Raymond Roussel's Locus Solus', in *Wireless Imagination: Sound, Radio, and the Avant-Garde*, ed. Kahn, Douglas and Gregory Whitehead. Cambridge, MA: MIT Press, 69–103

Kahn, Douglas and Gregory Whitehead, eds, 1992. *Wireless Imagination: Sound, Radio, and the Avant-Garde*. Cambridge, MA: MIT Press.

Kane, Paul, 1996. *Australian Poetry: Romanticism and Negativity*. Melbourne: Cambridge University Press.

Kauer, Ute. 2005. 'Literature as Virtual Reality: Jeanette Winterson's *The Powerbook*', *Anglia: Zeitschrift für Englische Philologie* 123/1: 90–103.

Keep, Christopher, 1997. 'The Cultural Work of the Type-Writer Girl', *Victorian Studies* 40/3: 401–27.

—— 2001. 'Blinded by the Type: Gender and Information Technology at the Turn of the Century', *Nineteenth-Century Contexts* 23: 149–73.

Kenner, Hugh, 1971. *The Pound Era*. Berkeley and Los Angeles, CA: University of California Press.

—— 1987. *The Mechanic Muse*. New York: Oxford University Press.

Kent, Steve L., 2001. *The Ultimate History of Video Games: From Pong to Pokemon – The Story Behind the Craze That Touched Our Lives and Changed the World*. New York: Three Rivers Press.

Kerouac, Jack, [1951] 2007. *On The Road: The Original Scroll*, ed. Howard Cunnell. London: Penguin.

—— [1958] 1992. 'Essentials of Spontaneous Prose', in *The Portable Beat Reader*, ed. Ann Charters. London: Penguin, 57–8.

Kerr, Douglas, 2002. 'Orwell's BBC Broadcasts: Colonial Discourse and the Rhetoric of Propaganda', *Textual Practice* 16/3: 473–90.

Ketabgian, Tamara, 1997. 'The Human Prosthesis: Workers and Machines in the Victorian Industrial Scene'. *Critical Matrix* 11/1: 4–32.

Kipling, Rudyard, [1904] 1987. *Traffics and Discoveries*. Harmondsworth: Penguin.

Kirby, Lynne, 1997. *Parallel Tracks: The Railroad and Silent Cinema*. Exeter: University of Exeter Press.

Kittler, Friedrich A., 1990. *Discourse Networks 1800/1900*, trans. Michael Metteer with Chris Cullens. Stanford, CA: Stanford University Press.

—— 1997. 'Media and Drugs in Pynchon's Second World War', trans. Michael Wutz and Geoffrey Winthrop-Young, in *Reading Matters: Narratives in the New Media Ecology*, ed. Joseph Tabbi and Michael Wutz. Ithaca, NY, and London: Cornell University Press, 157–72.

—— 1999. *Gramophone, Film, Typewriter*, trans. Geoffrey Winthorp-Young and Michael Wutz. Stanford, CA: Stanford University Press.

—— 2010. *Optical Media*, trans. Anthony Enns. Cambridge: Polity.

Kline, S. J., 1985. 'What Is Technology?', *Bulletin of Science, Technology and Society* 1: 215–18.

Knowlson, James, 1976. '*Krapp's Last* Tape: The Evolution of a Play, 1958-1975.' *Journal of Beckett Studies* 1 (Winter): n.p. <http://www.english.fsu.edu.jobs/num01/jobs01.htm>.

Koolhaas, Rem, 1994. *Delirious New York: A Retroactive Manifesto for Manhattan*. New York: The Monacelli Press.

Kracauer, Seigfried, 1995. *The Mass Ornament: Weimar Essays*, trans. Thomas Y. Levin. Cambridge, MA, and London: Harvard University Press.

Krakauer, Eric L., 1998. *The Disposition of the Subject: Reading Adorno's Dialectic of Technology*. Evanston, IL: Northwestern University Press.

Landow, George P., 2006. *Hypertext 3.0: Critical Theory and New Media in a Global Era*. Baltimore, NJ: Johns Hopkins University Press.

Larsen, Deena, 1993. *Marble Springs*, CD Rom (Hypercard). Watertown, MA: Eastgate Systems.

Lawrence, D. H., [1913] 1994. *Sons and Lovers*. London: Penguin.

—— [1915] 1970. *The Rainbow*. London: Penguin.

—— [1920] 1960. *Women in Love*. London: Penguin.

—— [1923] 1977. *Studies in Classic American Literature*. London: Penguin.

—— [1928] 1960. *Lady Chatterley's Lover*. London: Penguin.

Lawrence, Karen, 1981. *The Odyssey of Style in 'Ulysses'*. Princeton, NJ: Princeton University Press.

Lea, Daniel, 2001. *Animal Farm and Nineteen Eighty-Four: A Reader's Guide to Essential Criticism*. Basingstoke: Palgrave.

—— 2010. 'Horror Comics and High-Brow Sadism: Dramatising George Orwell in the 1950s', *Literature and History* 19/1: 65–79.

Le Carré, John, [1963] 1999. *The Spy Who Came in from the Cold*. London: Pan.

—— [1965] 1967. *The Looking-Glass War*. London: Pan.

—— [1968] 1971. *A Small Town in Germany*. London: Pan.

Lenthall, Bruce, 2007. *Radio's America: The Great Depression and the Rise of Modern Mass Culture*. Chicago, IL: University of Chicago Press.

Lifton, Robert Jay, 1967. *Death in Life: Survivors of Hiroshima*. New York: Basic Books.

Linder, Christopher, 2003. 'Criminal Vision and the Ideology of Detection in Fleming's 007 Series', *The James Bond Phenomenon: A Critical Reader*, ed. Christopher Linder. Manchester: Manchester University Press, 76–88.

Loy, Mina, 1996. *The Lost Lunar Baedeker*, ed. Roger Connover. New York: Farrar, Straus & Giroux.

Luckhurst, Roger and Josephine McDonagh, 2002. *Transactions and Encounters: Science and Culture in the Nineteenth Century*. Manchester: Manchester University Press.

McCabe, Susan, 2005. *Cinematic Modernism: Modernist Poetry and Film*. Cambridge: Cambridge University Press.

McCaffery, Larry, 1992. *Storming the Reality Studio: A Case Book of Cyberpunk and Postmodern Science Fiction*. Durham, NC: Duke University Press.

McCarron, Kevin, 1995. 'Corpses, Animals, Machines and Mannequins: The Body and Cyberpunk', in *Cyberpace/Cyberbodies/Cyberpink: Cultures of Technological Enbodiment*, ed. Mike Featherstone and Roger Burrows. London: Sage, 261–73.

McDaid, John, 1992. *Uncle Buddy's Phantom Funhouse*, CD Rom. Watertown, MA: Eastgate Systems.

MacLeish, Archibald, 1937. *The Fall of the City*. London: Boriswood.

—— 1939. *Air Raid*. London: Bodley Head.

McLuhan, Marshall, 1962. *The Gutenberg Galaxy: The Making of Typographic Man*. Toronto, ON: Toronto University Press.
—— [1964a] 2001. *Understanding Media*. New York: Routledge.
—— 1964b. 'Notes on Burroughs', *Nation* (28 December): 517–19.
MacNeice, Louis, 1939. *Autumn Journal*. London: Faber and Faber.
—— 1944. *Christopher Columbus: A Radio Play*. London: Faber and Faber.
—— 1947. *The Dark Tower and Other Radio Scripts*. London: Faber and Faber.
—— 1954. *Autumn Sequel*. London: Faber and Faber.
Marcus, Laura, 2007. *The Tenth Muse: Writing about Cinema in the Modernist Period*. Oxford: Oxford University Press.
Marcuse, Herbert, 1998. *Technology, War and Facism*. London: Routledge.
—— 1964. *One Dimensional Man*. Boston, MA: Beacon.
Mares, Geo Carl, 1909. *The History of the Typewriter: Being an Illustrated Account of the Origin, Rise and Development of the Writing Machine*. London: Guilbert Pitman.
Marvin, Carolyn, 1988. *When Old Technologies Were New: Thinking About Electric Communication in the Late Nineteenth Century*. New York and Oxford: Oxford University Press.
Marx, Leo, 1964. *The Machine in the Garden: Technology and the Pastoral Ideal in America*. Oxford: Oxford University Press.
Matheson, Hilda, 1933. *Broadcasting*. London: Thornton Butterworth Limited.
Matthews, Steven, 2001. *Les Murray*. Manchester and New York: Manchester University Press.
Maude, Ulrike, 2009. *Beckett, Technology and the Body*. Cambridge: Cambridge University Press.
Memmot, Talan, 2000. *Lexia to Perplexia*, <http://www.uiowa.edu/~iareview /tirweb/ hypermedia/talan_memmott/index.html>.
Menke, Richard, 2000. 'Telegraphic Realism: Henry James's *In the Cage*', *PMLA* 115/5 (October): 975–90
Miki, Roy, 1983. 'Driving and Writing', in *William Carlos Williams: Man and Poet*, ed. Carroll F. Terrell. Orono, ME: National Poetry Foundation: 111–28.
Miller, Toby, 1992. 'Editorial Introduction for Radio', *Continuum: The Australian Journal of Media and Culture* 6/1, "Radio – Sound" issue, n.p.: <http:// wwwmcc.murdoch. edu.au/ReadingRoom/6.1/Miller.html>.
Mixon, Laura J., 1992. *Glass Houses*. New York: Tom Doherty Assoc.
Moore, Marianne, 1984. *Complete Poems*. London: Faber & Faber.
Moravec, Hans, 1988. *Mind Children: The Future of Robot and Human Intelligence*. Cambridge, MA: Harvard University Press.
Morley, Catherine, 2008. 'Writing in the Wake of 9/11', in *American Thought and Culture in the Twenty-First Century*, ed. Martin Halliwell and Catherine Morley. Edinburgh: Edinburgh University Press, 245–58.
Moulthrop, Stuart, 1991a. *Victory Garden*, CD Rom. Watertown, MA: Eastgate Systems.
—— 1991b. 'You Say You Want a Revolution? Hypertext and the Laws of Media', *Postmodern Culture: An Electronic Journal of Interdisciplinary Criticism* 1/3 (May): n.p.
—— 1995. 'Traveling in the Breakdown Lane: A Principle of Resistance for Hypertext', *Mosaic: A Journal for the Interdisciplinary Study of Literature* 28/4 (December): 55–77.
—— 1999. *Reagan Library*: <http://iat.ubalt.edu/moulthrop/rl/pages>.
Mumford, Lewis, 1967. *The Myth of the Machine: Technics and Human Development*. New York: Harcourt, Brace & World.

Murphet, Julian and Lydia Rainford, eds, 2003. *Literature and Visual Technologies: Writing After Cinema*. Basingstoke: Palgrave Macmillan.

Murray, Les, 1998. *Collected Poems*. Manchester: Carcanet.

Myers, Tony, 2001. 'The Postmodern Imaginary in William Gibson's *Neuromancer*', *Modern Fiction Studies* 47/4: 887–909.

Nadel, Alan, 2005. *Television in Black and White: Race and National Identity*. Lawrence, KS: University Press of Kansas.

Nänny, Max, 1973. *Ezra Pound: Poetics for an Electric Age*. Switzerland: Francke Verlag Bern.

Nead, Lynda, 2007. *The Haunted Gallery: Painting, Photography and Film Around 1900*. Cambridge: Cambridge University Press.

Nelson, Ted, 1981. *Literary Machines*. Swarthmore, PA: self-published.

Noakes, Richard, 2002. '"Instruments to Lay Hold of Spirits": Technologizing the Bodies of Victorian Spiritualism', in *Bodies / Machines*, ed. Iwan Rhys Morus. Oxford and New York: Berg: 125–64.

North, Michael, 2004. *Camera Works: Photography and the Twentieth-Century Word*. Oxford: Oxford University Press.

Nye, David, 1996. *American Technological Sublime*. Cambridge, MA: MIT Press.

O'Donnell, Patrick, 2005. 'James Bond, Cyborg-Aristocrat', in *Ian Flemming & James Bond: The Cultural Politics of 007*, ed. Edward P. Commentale, Stephen Watt, and Skip Willman. Bloomington and Indianapolis, IN: Indiana University Press, 55–68.

Olson, Charles, 1950. 'Projective Verse', in *Selected Writings of Charles Olson*, ed. Robert Creeley. New York: New Directions, 15–26.

—— 1993. *Selected Poems*, ed. Robert Creeley. Berkeley, CA: University of California Press.

Orwell, George, [1949] 1954. *Nineteen Eighty-Four*. Harmondsworth: Penguin.

Page, Barbara, 1998. 'Women Writers and the Restive Text: Feminism, Experimental Writing, and Hypertext', in *Cyberspace Textuality: Computer Technology and Literary Theory*, ed. Marie-Laure Ryan. Bloomington and Indianapolis, IN: Indiana University Press, 111–36.

Papanagou, Vaios, 2000. 'The Garden of Forking Paths': <http://www.geocities. com/papanagnou/cover.htm>.

Peel, Robin, 2002. *Writing Back: Sylvia Plath and Cold War Politics*. Madison, WI: Farleigh Dickinson University Press.

—— 2006. 'Body, Word, and Photograph: Sylvia Plath's Cold War Collage and the Thalidomide Scandal', *Journal of American Studies* 40/1: 71–95.

Perloff, Marjorie, 1983. '"To Give a Design": Williams and the Visualization of Poetry', *William Carlos Williams: Man and Poet*, ed. Carroll F. Terrell. Orono, ME: National Poetry Foundation: 159–86.

—— 1986. *The Futurist Moment: Avant-Garde, Avant Guerre, and the Language of Rupture*. Chicago, IL, and London: University of Chicago Press.

—— 1999. 'The Silence That Is Not Silence: Acoustic Art in Samuel Beckett's *Embers*', in *Samuel Beckett and the Arts: Music, Visual Arts and Non-Print Media*, ed. Lois Oppenheim. New York and London: Garland Publishing, 247–68.

Piette, Adam, 2009. 'War Poetry in Britain', in *The Cambridge Companion to the Literature of World War II*, ed. Marina Mackay. Cambridge: Cambridge University Press, 13–25.

Plant, Sadie, 1997. *Zeros + Ones: Digital Women and the New Techoculture*. London: Fourth Estate.

Poe, Edgar Allan, [1845] 1976. 'The Facts in the Case of M. Valdemar', in *The Science Fiction of Edgar Allan Poe*, ed. Harold Beaver. London: Penguin, 194–204.

Porter, Peter, 2003. 'Review of *New Collected Poems* by Les Murray', *Guardian*, Saturday 15 March: <http.//books.guardian.co.uk/review/story /0,12084,913649,00. html>.

Pound, Ezra, 1911. 'I Gather the Limbs of Osiris, II: A Rather Dull Introduction'', *New Age* 10/6 (7 December): 130.

—— 1912. 'I Gather The Limbs of Osiris, IX: On Technique', *New Age* 10/13 (25 January): 297–8.

—— 1928. 'Pound "Desideria"', *The Exile* 3 (spring): 108.

—— 1954. *Literary Essays of Ezra Pound*, ed. T. S. Eliot. London: Faber and Faber.

—— 1980. *Ezra Pound and the Visual Arts*, ed. Harriet Zinnes. New York: New Directions.

Pupin, Michael, 1930. *Romance of the Machine*. New York and London: Charles Scribner's Sons.

Pynchon, Thomas, [1973] 2000. *Gravity's Rainbow*. London: Vintage.

—— 1984. 'Is It O.K. to Be a Luddite?', *The New York Times Book Review* (28 October): 40–1.

Rabinbach, Anson, 1990, *The Human Motor: Energy, Fatigue, and the Origins of Modernity*. Berkeley, CA: University of California Press.

Roberts, Adam, 2000. *Science Fiction*. London and New York: Routledge.

—— 2006. *The History of Science Fiction*. New York: Palgrave Macmillan.

Rodker, John, 1996. *Poems & Adolphe 1920*, ed. Andrew Crozier. Manchester: Carcanet.

Ronell, Avital, 1989. *The Telephone Book*. Lincoln, NB: University of Nebraska Press.

Roszak, Theodore, 2000. 'A Taste for Industrial Light and Magic', in *From Satori to Silicon Valley*, <http://www-sul.stanford.edu/mac/primary/docs/satori/index.html> n.p.

Sauerberg, Lars Ole, 1984. *Secret Agents in Fiction: Ian Fleming, John le Carré and Len Deighton*. London: Macmillan.

Schivelbusch, Wolfgang, 1987. *The Railway Journey: The Industrialization and Perception of Time and Space*. Berkeley, CA: University of California Press.

Schnapp, Jeffrey T. 1994. 'Propeller Talk', *Modernism/modernity* 1/3: 153–78.

—— 1999. 'Crash (Speed as Engine of Individuation)', *Modernism/modernity* 6/1: 1–49.

Schneider, John F., 1998. 'The History of KQW/KCBS', <http://www.oldradio. com/ archives/stations/sf/articles.htm>.

Schroeder, Randy, 2002. 'Inheriting Chaos: Burroughs, Pynchon, Sterling, Rucker', *Extrapolation* 43/1: 89 97.

Sconce, Jeffrey, 2000. *Haunted Media: Electronic Presence from Telegraphy to Television*. Durham, NC: Duke University Press.

Seifer, Marc J., 1998. *Wizard: The Life and Times of Nikola Tesla: Biography of a Genius*. New York: Citadel Press.

Self, Will, 2002. *Dorian: An Imitation*. London: Penguin.

Selig, Robert L., 2000. 'The Endless Reading of Fiction: Stuart Moulthrop's Hypertext Novel Victory Garden', *Contemporary Literature* 41/4: 642–60.

Seltzer, Mark, 1992. *Bodies and Machines*. New York and London: Routledge.

—— 2000. 'The Postal Unconscious', *Henry James Review* 21/3: 197–206.

Shackleford, Laura, 2005. 'Narrative Subjects Meet Their Limits: John Barth's "Click" and the Remediation of Hypertext', *Contemporary Literature* 46/2: 275–310.

Shail, Andrew, 2006. '"She Looks Just Like One of We-all": British Cinema Culture and the Origins of Woolf's *Orlando*', *Critical Quarterly* 48/2 (summer): 45–76.

—— 2008. 'Time in Film 1908–1914 and the Emergence of High Literary Modernism', unpublished conference paper *Modernism and Visual Culture Conference*, Oxford, UK.

Shiach, Morag, 2000. 'Modernity, Labour and the Typewriter', in *Modernist Sexualities*, ed. Hugh Stevens and Caroline Howlett. Manchester: Manchester University Press, 115–29.

Silkin, Jon, ed., 1981. *The Penguin Book of First World War Poetry*. Harmondsworth: Penguin.

Slade, Joseph W., 1992. 'Technology and the Spy Novel', in *Literature and Technology*, eds Mark L. Greenberg and Lance Schachterle. London and Toronto: Associated University Presses, 225–52.

Sobchack, Vivian, 1995. 'Beating the Meat/Surviving the Text, or How to Get Out of This Century Alive', in *Cyberspace/Cyberbodies/Cyberpunk: Cultures of Technological Embodiment*, ed. Mike Featherstone and Roger Burrows. London: Sage, 205–14.

Soumerai, Eve Nussbaum and Carol D. Schulz, 1998. *Daily Life During the Holocaust*. Westport, CT: Greenwood Press.

Spencer, Nicholas, 2002. 'Beyond the Mutations of Media and Military Technologies in Don De Lillo's Underworld', *Arizona Quarterly: A Journal of American Literature, Culture, and Theory* 58/2: 89–112.

Spiegel, Alan, 1976. *Fiction and the Camera Eye: Visual Consciousness in Film and the Modern Novel*. Charlottesville, VA: University Press of Virginia.

Spigel, Lynn, 1992. *Make Room for TV: Television and the Family Ideal in Postwar America*. Chicago, IL, and London: University of Chicago Press.

Springer, Claudia, 1996. *Electronic Eros: Bodies and Desire in the Postindustrial Age*. Austin, TX: University of Texas Press.

Stefans, Brian Kim, 2003. *Fashionable Noise: On Digital Poetics*. Berkeley, CA: Atelos Press.

Steiner, George, 1988. 'The Long Life of Metaphor: An Approach to the "Shoah"', in *Writing and the Holocaust*, ed. Berel Lang. New York: Holmes & Meier, 154–71.

Steinman, Lisa M., 1984. 'Modern America, Modernism and Marianne Moore', *Twentieth Century Literature* 30/2–3: 210–30.

—— 1992. 'Modernism, Modernity, and Technology: Following the Engineers', in *Critical Essays on American Modernism*, ed. Michael J. Hoffman and Patrick D. Murphy. New York: G. K. Hall, 199–210.

Sterling, Bruce, ed., 1986. *Mirrorshades: The Cyberpunk Anthology*. London: Grafton.

Stokesbury, Leon, ed., 1990. *Articles of War: A Collection of American Poetry about World War II*. Fayetteville, AR: University of Arkansas Press.

Stone, Allucquere Rosanne, 1991. 'Will the Real Body Please Stand Up?: Boundary Stories about Virtual Cultures', *Cyberspace: First Steps*, ed. Michael Benedikt. Cambridge, MA, and London: MIT Press, 81–118.

Sussman, Herbert, 2000. 'Machine Dreams: The Culture of Technology', *Victorian Literature and Culture* 28/1: 197–204.

Suvin, Darko, 1979. *Metamorphoses of Science Fiction*. New Haven, CT: Yale University Press.

Tate, Trudi, 1997. 'The Culture of the Tank, 1916–1918', *Modernism/modernity* 4/1: 69–87.

Terrell, Carroll F., 1980. *A Companion to the Cantos of Ezra Pound*. Berkeley, CA: University of California Press.

Theall, Donald F., 1995. *Beyond the Word: Reconstructing Sense in the Joyce Era of Technology, Culture, and Comunication*. Toronto: University of Toronto Press.

—— 1997. *James Joyce's Techno-Poetics*. Toronto: University of Toronto Press.

Thurschwell, Pamela, 2001. *Literature, Technology and Magical Thinking 1880–1920*. Cambridge: Cambridge University Press.

Tichi, Cecelia, 1987. *Shifting Gears: Technology, Literature, Culture in Modernist America*. Chapel Hill, NC, and London: University of North Carolina Press.

—— 1991. *Electronic Hearth: Creating an American Television Culture*. Oxford: Oxford University Press.

Tiffany, Daniel, 1995. *Radio Corpse: Imagism and the Cryptaesthetic of Ezra Pound*. Cambridge, MA, and London: Harvard University Press.

Todd, Ellen Wiley, 1993. *The 'New Woman' Revised: Painting and Gender Politics on Fourteenth Street*. Berkeley, CA: University of California Press.

Treadwell, Sophie, [1928] 1993. *Machinal*. London: Nick Hern Books.

Trotter, David, 2007. *Cinema and Modernism*. Oxford: Blackwell.

Turing, Alan, 1950. 'Computing Machinery and Intelligence', *Mind* 50: 433–60.

Turkle, Sherry, [1995] 1996. *Life on the Screen: Identity in the Age of the Internet*. London: Wiedenfeld & Nicolson.

Twain, Mark, [1884] 1996. 'Mark Twain on Thought Transference', *Journal of the Society for Psychical Research* (October, 1884), reprinted in Jason Gary Horn, *Mark Twain and William James: Crafting a Free Self* (Columbia, MO: University of Missouri Press), 162–4.

—— 1891. 'Mental Telegraphy', *Harper's Magazine* 84/449 (December): 101.

Vice, Sue, 2000. *Holocaust Fiction*. London: Routledge.

Villiers de L'Isle Adam, Jean-Marie-Mathius-Philippe-Auguste, Comte de [1886] 1998. In *The Decadent Reader: Fiction, Fantasy, and Perversion from Fin-de-Siècle France*, ed. Asti Hustvedt. New York: Zone Books, 520–750.

Virilio, Paul, 1989. *War and Cinema: The Logistics of Perception*, trans. Patrick Camiller. London and New York: Verso.

Vonnegut, Kurt, [1952] 1990. *Player Piano* London: Grafton Books.

—— 1963 [2008]. *Cat's Cradle*. London: Penguin.

—— 1965. 'Speaking of Books: Science Fiction', *New York Times Book Review* (5 September): 2.

—— [1969] 2000. *Slaughterhouse Five*. London: Vintage.

Weber, Max, 1947. *The Theory of Social and Economic Organization*, trans. A. M. Henderson and Talcott Parsons. New York and Oxford: Oxford University Press.

Wershler-Henry, Darren, 2007. *The Iron Whim: A Fragmented History of Typewriting*. Ithaca, NY: Cornell University Press.

Whitehead, Kate, 1990. 'Broadcasting Bloomsbury', *Yearbook of English Studies* 20: *Literature in the Modern Media: Radio, Film, and Television Special*: 121–31.

Wicke, Jennifer, 1992. 'Vampiric Typewriting: *Dracula* and Its Media', *English Literary History* 59/2: 467–93.

Wiener, Norbert, [1948], 1965. *Cybernetics; or Control and Communication in the Animal and Machine*, 2nd edn. Cambridge, MA: MIT Press.

—— [1950] 1954. *The Human Use of Human Beings: Cybernetics and Society*. Boston, MA: Houghton Mifflin.

Wilcox, Johnnie, 2007. "Black Power: Minstrelsy and Electricity in Ralph Ellison's *Invisible Man*', *Callaloo* 30/4: 987–1009.

Willetts, Peter, 2009. 'Who Really Created the Internet', lecture at City University, London, UK (29 October): <http://www.city.ac.uk/whatson/2009/10_oct/291009_Peter_Willetts.html>.

Williams, Keith, 1996. *British Writers and the Media, 1930–45*. Houndmills: Macmillan.

—— 2003. 'Ulysses in Toontown: "Vision Animated to Bursting Point" in Joyce's "Circe"', in *Literature and Visual Technologies: Writing After Cinema*, ed. Julian Murphet and Lydia Rainford. Basingstoke: Palgrave Macmillan, 96–121.

—— 2007. *H. G. Wells, Modernity and the Movies*. Liverpool: Liverpool University Press.

Williams, Raymond, 1974. *Television: Technology and Cultural Form*. London: Fontana.

Williams, William Carlos, 1969. *Selected Essays of William Carlos Williams*. New York: New Directions.

—— 1974. *The Embodiment of Knowledge*, ed. Ron Loewinsohn. New York: New Directions.

—— 2000. *Collected Poems I: 1909–1939*. Manchester: Carcanet.

Winterson, Jeanette, 2000. *The.Powerbook*. London: Jonathan Cape.

Wollen, Peter, 1989. 'Cinema/Americanism/The Robot'. *New Formations* 8: 7–34.

Wood, Gaby, 2002. *Edison's Eve: A Magical History of the Quest for Mechanical Life*. New York: Alfred A. Knopf.

Woolf, Virginia, [1925] 1992. *Mrs Dalloway* ed. Elaine Showalter. Harmondsworth: Penguin.

—— [1926] 1993. 'The Cinema', in *The Crowded Dance of Modern Life: Selected Essays Volume Two*, ed. Rachel Bowlby. London: Penguin.

—— [1927] 1977. *To The Lighthouse*. London: Grafton.

—— [1928] 1977. *Orlando*. London: Grafton.

—— [1941] 1978. *Between the Acts*. London: Grafton.

Worth, Katherine, 1981. 'Beckett and the Radio Medium', in *British Radio Drama*, ed. John Drakakis. Cambridge: Cambridge University Press, 191–217.

Zilliacus, Clas, 1976. *Beckett and Broadcasting: A Study of the Works of Samuel Beckett for and in Radio and Television*, Acta Academiae Aboensis, Ser. A. Humaniora, 51/2 (Abo: Abo Akademi).

Žižek, Slavoj, 2002. *The Desert of the Real*. London and New York: Verso.

Index

Aarseth, Espen 123–4, 126, 127
Acker, Kathy, *Empire of the Senseless* 42–3
Adams, Henry 142
Adorno, Theodor 14, 23, 28, 29, 30, 33, 86
  and Max Horkheimer 20, 27–8, 60, 88, 98
aeroplane(s) 16, 28, 30, 32, 82, 144
AI (artifical intelligence) 39, 46, 96, 140, 152, 153, 154, 157
Aldiss, Brian 21
Allen, Grant, *The Type-Writer Girl* 113, 114
Amerika, Mark, *Grammatron* 130
Amos 'n' Andy 70, 77
Analytical Engine 3, 97
Apollo 11 86
Arendt, Hannah 27
Arnheim, Rudolf 61, 62, 63, 67, 71, 75
ARPANET 35, 95, 122
Asimov, Isaac 149
  Three Laws of Robotics 149, 157
atomic bomb 77, 86, 97
  see also nuclear bomb
atomic fictions 96
atomic weapons 31, 78, 96
  see also nuclear weapons
Auden, W. H. 65–6
Auschwitz 85, 86, 103
Auster, Paul 107
automata 137
automatic writing 3, 112, 114, 117

Babbage, Charles 3, 89
  see also Analytical Engine, Difference Engine
Baily, R. W., *Computer Poems* 122
Baird, John Logie 72
Bakhtin, Mikhail 123
Ballard, J. G., *Crash* 104–5
ballistics 8, 95
bananas 155
Barth, John, 'Click' 133–34, 135
  'Lost in the Funhouse' 128
Barthes, Roland 122, 123
Batman 94
Baudrillard, Jean 23, 37–8, 39, 40, 107–8, 162
Bauhaus 17
Baum, L. Frank 135, 163, 173
  see also The Patchwork Girl of Oz, The Wizard of Oz
BBC (British Broadcasting Corporation) 19, 61, 62, 63, 64, 65, 66, 69, 70, 71, 72, 73, 92, 155
Beat generation 87, 98, 100, 106, 119
Beckett, Samuel 52, 73–7
  All That Fall 73, 74–5
  Cascando 73, 75, 76
  Eh Joe 73, 76
  Embers 73, 74, 75, 76
  Ghost Trio 73, 76
  Krapp's Last Tape 76, 154–7, 161
  Rough for Radio I 73, 75
  Rough for Radio II 73, 76
  Waiting for Godot 76, 77
  What Where 76
  Words and Music 73, 75

Bellamy, Edward, *Looking Backward 2000–1887* 12
Benjamin, Walter 14, 23, 24–5, 26, 27, 37, 54, 78–9, 89, 137
  'On Some Motifs in Baudelaire' 54
  'The Storyteller' 78–9
  'The Work of Art in the Age of Mechanical Reproduction' 24, 26, 27
Berners-Lee, Tim 95
Bierce, Ambrose, 'Moxon's Master' 149
Big Brother 162
Binder, Eandoo, 'I, Robot' 149
Bladerunner 158–9
blogging 139
Bloomsbury group 64
body, the 5, 15–16, 40, 41, 45, 47, 76, 91, 113, 136–42, 153–7, 160–1, 163–6
Bond, James 90–3
Borges, Jorge Luis 124, 133
Bosanquet, Theodora 111, 112, 114, 116
Braidotti, Rosi 46, 47
Briggs, Raymond, *When the Wind Blows* 97
Brooklyn Bridge 14, 49
Brown, Robert Carlton 120
Bryher, Winnifred 51, 58
Bukatman, Scott 40, 161
Bunch, David R. 'The Problem Was Lubrication' 149
bureaucratic systems 90, 93, 100
Burroughs, William 98–9, 127, 129, 130
  Naked Lunch 99, 119
  Nova Express 119
  The Ticket That Exploded 119
Bush, Vannevar 121

Cabinet of Dr Caligari, The 54
Cadigan, Pat 35
  Mindplayers 160
Call of Duty 108
Cantril, Hadley, *The Invasion from Mars: A Study in the Pyschology of Panic* 69

Čapek, Karel, *R.U.R.* (*Rossum's Universal Robots*) 15, 148–9
capitalism 28, 38, 39, 40, 42, 60, 101, 104
Capote, Truman 117
car(s) 12, 16, 26, 29, 30, 33, 34, 52, 55, 87, 94, 100, 144
  car crash 16, 104–5, 124, 125, 128
Carré', John le 92–4, 102
  A Small Town in Germany 93
  The Looking-Glass War 93
  The Spy Who Came in From the Cold 93–4
Carter, Angela 40
Cartesian dualism 154, 156
Cayley, John 129, 130
CBS (Columbia Broadcasting System) 62, 66, 70
cell phone 106
Chaplin, Charlie 36, 51, 149
Chase, Stuart, *Men and Machines* 142–3, 149–50
Chesney, George Tomkyns, *The Battle of Dorking* 13
Ciardi, John 84
cinema 6, 18, 19, 20, 23, 28–9, 33, 40, 50–60, 72, 83–4, 103, 107
cinematograph(e) 2, 6, 7
Cixous, Hélène 165
Close Up 51, 57
Clynes, Manfred and Nathan Kline 139
CND (Campaign for Nuclear Disarmament) 97
cognisphere 163
Cole, Robert W., *The Struggle for Empire: A Story of the Year 2236* 12
Columbia Workshops 67
command control communication (C3) system 89, 90, 92
computer(s) 19, 20, 35, 38, 39, 42, 46, 89, 94–6, 100–1, 105, 108–9, 120–4, 131–4, 135, 151–4, 157, 161, 162, 165–7
  Apple Computers 122, 132
  Colossus 89, 94, 120
  EDSAC 94
  ENIAC 94
  IBM 94, 114, 152

computer(s) (cont.)
    Rockefeller Differential Analyser
      121
    UNIVAC 154
    see also Analytical Engine, Difference
      Engine
Coney Island 48–50, 59, 80
Constructivism 17
Cops 163
Corelli, Marie 13
Corwin, Norman 66
counter-culture 87, 98, 100, 102–3
Coupland, Douglas 96, 131–2
    Microserfs 131–2
Crane, Hart 14, 51
cremation 79–80
cummings, e e 19, 26, 114–15, 117
cyberculture 40, 45
cybernetics 46, 79, 102, 139, 153, 166
cyberpoetry 19, 129
cyberpunk 39–40, 160, 163
cybertext 96, 123–4, 130, 135
cyborg 2, 15, 45, 91, 92, 135, 136,
    138–40, 157–60, 161, 163, 166
Czolgosz, Leon 80

Daly, Nicholas 4, 52
Danielewski, Mark, *House of Leaves* 134
Death Race 108
Debord, Guy 20
Deep Blue 152
Deleuze, Gilles and Felix Guattari 23,
    41–2, 123, 165
Denning, Michael 90
Derrida, Jacques 123, 128
Descartes, Rene 137, 141, 154
desiring machine(s) 41
Dick, Philip K. 15, 57–9
    Do Androids Dream of Electric Sheep?
      57–9
Dickens, Charles 4, 5, 51
Dickey, James 84
Difference Engine 3
digital poetry 122, 129
Doom 108
Dos Passos, John 7, 14, 59–60, 120,
    146–8
    The Big Money 60, 146–7
    Manhattan Transfer 59, 147–8

Douglas, Keith 84, 85
    Alamein to Zem Zem 85
*Dr Strangelove, or How I Learned To Stop
    Worrying and Love the Bomb* 97–8
Drakakis, John 63, 71
Dresden 101
drugs: amphetamines 15, 104
    benny 118
    Prozac 132
    smart drugs 139
Duchamp, Marcel 143
    *The Bride Stripped Bare by Her
    Bachelors, Even* (*The Large Glass*)
    143, 161

Eberhardt, Richard 84
écriture féminine 128
ECT (Electroconvulsive Therapy) 88
Edison, Thomas 7, 8, 11, 50, 80–1,
    138, 147, 150
Eisenstein, Serge 51, 52, 54, 56, 58, 60
    70
electric chair 12, 80–1
electrocution 80–1, 88
Eliot, T. S. 14, 52, 56, 64–5, 115, 116,
    146
    The Waste Land 52, 65, 116, 146
Ellison, Harlan, 'I Have No Mouth,
    and I Must Scream' 96, 131
Ellison, Ralph, *Invisible Man* 158
Ellul, Jacques 23, 27
Enigma code 89, 153
Enigma machine 89
Epic of Gilgamesh 11
Epstein, Jacob 141
ergodic literature 123
eroticism 104, 138, 159–60

Facebook 163,
fascism 24, 27, 28, 30, 65, 69
Faulkner, William 52
feedback 116, 131, 135, 139,
    153, 165
feminism 15, 46, 81, 128–9, 139–40,
    144
Filene, Edward, *Successful Living in this
    Machine Age* 142, 143
film 3, 6, 24, 27, 35, 50–60, 85, 90,
    134, 158, 161

Fitzgerald, F. Scott 52
Fleming, Ian 90–3, 94, 98
 Casino Royale 91
 Diamonds Are Forever 91
 Dr No 90–1
 Goldfinger 91
 The Man With The Golden Gun 91
 Moonraker 90, 91–2
 Thunderball 90
Ford, Ford Maddox 83
Ford, Henry 15, 142, 146–7
Fordism 1, 15, 141
Forster, E. M. 64, 70
Foucauld, Pière 110
Foucault, Michel 43, 124
Frankenstein see Shelley, Mary,
  Frankenstein
French Lieutenant's Woman, The 127
Freud, Sigmund 1, 126
Freytag-Loringhoven, Baroness Elsa
  von 144
Fussell, Paul 82, 83
Future Eve, The (L'Eve Future) 7, 138,
  159

Gagarin, Yuri 94
Garbo, Greta 57
Geilgud, Val 69
George, Peter, *Red Alert* 97
Gibson, William 3, 15–16, 35, 39–40,
  51, 159, 160
 Neuromancer 15–16, 39, 51, 160
Ginsberg, Allen 98, 99, 118
Gitelman, Lisa 45, 46, 112
golem 137
Gourmont, Remy de 142, 144, 145
gramophone 3, 29–30
 see also phonograph
Graves, Robert 82
Greene, Graham 65, 90
Greenlaw, Lavinia 36–7
GreenNet 95
Griffith, D. W. 51, 55, 60, 84
gun(s) 85, 92, 99
 hand gun 91
 machine gun 82, 83
 shotgun 109
Gunning, Tom 50
Guthrie, Tyrone 63

Guyer, Carolyn, *Quibbling* 128
Gyson, Brion 119, 122, 129

Haraway, Donna 15, 45–6, 47, 135,
  139–40, 157
Hayles, N. Katherine 46–7, 124, 127,
  130, 131, 134, 135, 153, 155,
  161, 163, 164
H.D. 51, 56, 57–8
Heidegger, Martin 23, 27, 31–2, 33,
  34, 46, 88, 102, 110–11
Hemingway, Ernest 59, 67
Hersey, John, *Hiroshima* 96–7
heterarchy 126, 132, 134
Hiroshima 78, 96–7
Hoffman, E. T. A. 137
Hollywood 20, 24, 52, 59, 60, 107
Holocaust, the 32, 85–6
Hoover, J. Edgar 105
Horkheimer, Max *see* Adorno,
  Theodor and Max Horkheimer
Houédard, Dom Sylvester 115
How To Become a Successful Stenographer,
  For the Young Woman Who Wants
  to Makes Good 112
Hughes, Richard, *A Comedy of*
  Danger 63
Huxley, Aldous 52, 65
Huyssen, Andreas 148
hyperlink(s) 106, 122, 130
hypermedia text(s) 96, 122, 127, 130
hyperreal 37, 38, 39, 73, 107, 162
hypertext 19, 121–31, 132, 133–4,
  135, 163–6

influencing machine 146
Information Age 3, 89–90
Information Superhighway 96
information theory 43
Internet, the 1, 35, 44, 64, 95–6, 101,
  122, 131, 132, 162
Isherwood, Christopher 65
Italian Futurism 16–17, 144

Jackson, Shelley, *Patchwork Girl* 128,
  133, 135, 163–6
James, Henry 10, 62, 111, 112, 116
 In the Cage 10–11
James, William 112

Jameson, Frederic 23, 38–9, 40
Jarrell, Randall 84
Jazzercise 15
Jones, Amelia 15, 143, 144
Jones, D. F., *Colossus* 96
Jones, David 82
Joyce, James 20, 24, 52, 54, 55, 56,
    57, 60
   Finnegan's Wake 59
   Ulysses 14, 58–9
Joyce, Michael 124, 130, 165
   afternoon, a story 124–7

Keep, Christopher 112
Kempelen, Baron Wolfgang
    von 137
   Kempelen's Turk 149, 152
Kendry, J. F. 84
Kennedy, John F. 90
Kerouac, Jack 19, 100, 104, 117–19
   On The Road 100, 118–19
Kesey, Ken 100
Keyes, Sidney 84, 52
Kipling, Rudyard 21, 52–3, 62
   'Mrs Bathurst' 52–3, 56
   'Wireless' 10, 61
Kittler, Friedrich 3, 18, 43–5, 103,
    104, 105, 109, 110, 116, 120
Kline, Nathan *see* Clynes, Manfred and
    Nathan Kline
Kline, S. J. 23
Koolhaas, Rem 49
Kracauer, Siegfried 148
Kreemo Toffee 30
Kubrik, Stanley *see 2001: A Space
   Odyssey, Dr Strangelove*

Lacan, Jacques 43
La Mettrie, Julien Offray de 141
Landow, George 123
Larsen, Deena, *Marble Springs* 129
Lawrence, D. H. 14, 32–4, 52,
    116, 146
   Lady Chatterley's Lover 33
   The Rainbow 32
   Sons and Lovers 32
   Women in Love 32, 33
Leibniz, Gottfried 141
Lenthall, Bruce 66, 69

Levy, Amy, 'Ballade of a Special
    Edition' 5
Lewis, Alun 84
Lewis, Wyndham 19, 141
lexia 122
Loach, Ken 72
Lovelace, Ada 3
Loy, Mina 144–6
   'Crab Angel' 146
   'Der Blinde Junge' 146
   'Feminist Manifesto' 144
   'Human Cylinders' 144–5
   Love Songs 145–6
   'Sketch of a Man on a
    Platform' 144
   'The Costa San Giorgio' 144
   'Virgins Plus Curtains Minus
    Dots' 146
Lumière brothers 6, 50, 61, 69
Lutz, Theo 122

McCabe, Susan 51, 55
McDaid, John, *Uncle Buddy's Funhouse*
    127–8
MacLeish, Archibald 66, 67–8, 69,
    71, 76
   Air Raid 67–8, 75
   Fall of the City 67, 70, 71
McLuhan, Marshall 7–8, 23, 34–5,
    36, 37, 40, 43–4, 48, 64, 99,
    116–17
MacNeice, Louis 20, 65, 70–1
   Christopher Columbus 70–1
Macpherson, Kenneth 51, 57
manga 159
Manhattan 25, 50, 67
Mansfield, Katherine 51, 56
Marconi, Guglielmo 19, 60, 62
Marcus, Laura 54, 57, 58
Marcuse, Herbert 23, 27, 98
Mares, Geo Carl 110, 111,
    112, 116
Marey, Étienne-Jules 83
Marinetti, Filippo Tommaso 16–19,
    62, 82, 100, 142, 144, 150
Martineau, Harriet 138
Marvin, Carolyn 8
Matheson, Hilda 61, 63
Maude, Ulrika 76, 155, 156

mechanosphere 41, 42
media ecology 46
Melba, Dame Nellie 62
Méliès, George 50
memex 121
Memmott, Talan, *Lexia to Perplexia* 130
Metropolis 148, 159
microchip 94
military-industrial complex 44, 86, 92, 94, 95, 99, 101, 102
millennium bug 167
Miller, Arthur 67
Mixon, Laura J., *Glass Houses* 160
Modern Times 149
modernism 50–73, 14, 24, 116 140
Moholy-Nagy, Laszlo 17
Molly Millions 39, 160
montage 20, 51, 54–5, 58, 59–60
Moore, C. L., 'No Woman Born' 159
Moore, Marianne 56, 114, 115–16
Moore's Law 94
Moravec, Hans 153
Moulthrop, Stuart 123, 125, 130
Mumford, Lewis 23, 27
Murray, Les 35–6
Mussolini, Benito 65
Muybridge, Eadweard 6, 143

natureculture 45–6
NBC (National Broadcasting Company) 62
Nead, Linda 6
Nelson, Ted 121–2
New York Dada 15, 114, 143–4
nickelodeon 49, 51, 59
Nietzsche, Friedrich 111
nuclear bomb 105–6
    see also atomic bomb
nuclear weapons 17, 78, 96, 97

Oboler, Arch 66
Olson, Charles 19, 26, 117
ORLAN 161, 163
Orwell, George 20, 65, 66, 87–9
    Nineteen Eighty-Four 87–9, 96
Owen, Wilfred 82, 85

Patchwork Girl of Oz, The 163, 164, 166
    see also L. Frank Baum
PeaceNet 95
Perloff, Marjorie 74, 75, 114
phonograph 2, 7, 11, 19, 43, 45, 58, 61, 113
    see also gramophone
photography 6, 24, 58, 79, 83, 107, 121
Picabia, Francis 114, 143
Plant, Sadie 3, 128
Plath, Sylvia 87, 97
Poe, Edgar Allan 8–9, 137
    'The Facts in the Case of M. Valdemar' 8–9
Pong 108
posthuman 2, 46, 161–3
postmodernism 14, 37–40, 73, 101–8, 134, 161, 162
Post Office Research Laboratories 89
Potter, Dennis 72
Pound, Ezra 19–20, 26, 51, 56, 62, 66, 114, 116, 120
Prisoner, The 94
propaganda 17, 20, 62, 65–6, 83, 86–7
Prosser, Leopold, *Broadway Evening* 67
prosthesis 16, 91, 98, 139, 145, 155–6, 161
Pupin, Michael, *Romance of the Machine* 142
Pynchon, Thomas 101, 102–5
    Gravity's Rainbow 102–4, 105

QWERTY keyboard 110

Rabinbach, Anson 141
radar 8, 79, 84, 92, 95, 98
radio 8, 9, 13, 19–20, 23, 25, 27, 33, 60–77, 79, 98, 99, 109, 120
    radio operator 92
    radio drama 66–77, 154
    see also wireless
railway 3, 4–5, 50
Railway Spine 5–6
Ray, Lester Del, 'Helen O Loy' 159
Ray, Man 143–4
Reagan, Ronald 83, 97

remediation 35, 43, 134
Rice, Elmer, *The Adding Machine* 81
Richardson, Dorothy 51
Roberts, Adam 11, 12, 13
Robocop 159
robot(s) 15, 43, 136, 148–52,
    157, 159
Rodker, John 56
Rosenberg, Isaac 82
Rucker, Rudy 160
Ruttmann, Walter 54

Sartre, Jean-Paul 90
Sassoon, Siegfried 82, 85
Scheeler, Charles 54
Schnapp, Jeffrey T. 16, 18
Sconce, Jeffrey 8, 22–3, 73
Self, Will, *Dorian* 20–1
Seltzer, Mark 110, 112
September 11, 2001 107–8
sewing machine 109, 112, 116
Shannon, Claude 43
Shelley, Mary, *Frankenstein* 8, 11, 13,
    128, 137, 148, 164
Sholes, Christopher Latham 110, 112
Shute, Nevil, *On The Beach* 97
Sieveking, Lance 63
Silicon Valley 100, 131
simulacra 21, 37, 39, 105, 134
Sing Sing 80–1
slavery 157
Smiley, George 93–4, 96
Snyder, Ruth 81
Society for Psychical Research 9, 10
Soviet Russia 86
Soviet Union 90, 92, 96, 97, 102
spy fiction 90–4
Star Trek 94
steam-punk 3
Stein, Gertrude 51, 56, 112, 120
Steinbeck, John 52
Stelarc 161, 163
Stepford Wives, The 159
Stephenson, Neal 160
Sterling, Bruce 3, 160
Stoker, Bram, *Dracula* 9, 113–14
Strand, Paul 54
sublime, the 4, 38–9
Survivor 162

Suvin, Darko 11
Sylvania Waters 162

tank(s) 83, 85
tape recording(s) 99, 119, 151,
    153–6
Tarzan 19
Tate, Trudi 83
Tatlin, Vladimir 17
Taylor, Elizabeth 105
Taylor, Frederick 15, 142, 146–7
Taylorism 15, 141, 151
techne 31–2, 33, 138
telegraph 3, 7, 9–11, 20, 49, 58, 59,
    61, 120, 167
telepathy 7, 9–10, 11
telephone 2, 7, 10, 19, 29, 58, 98,
    127, 142
television 20, 71–3, 87, 107, 109,
    161–2
Tennyson, Alfred Lord 5
Terminator and *Terminator II* 159
Tesla, Nikola 7, 8, 9, 80
Thomas, Dylan 71
Thompson, Dorothy 69
Thurschwell, Pamela 9, 11, 111, 119
Tiller Girls 148, 150
Topsy the elephant 80
Treadwell, Sophie, *Machinal* 81–2
Trotter, David 52, 56
Turing, Alan 153
Turing Test, the 153
Turkle, Sherry 162
Twain, Mark 9–10, 67, 111
    *The Adventures of Huckleberry
    Finn* 43
typewriter 2, 3, 18–19, 26, 45, 81,
    109–19, 131
typewriter-girl 112, 114, 116

uncanny, the 7, 9, 13, 28, 52, 112

V-2 rocket 92, 102–3
Vaucanson, Jacques de 137
Verne, Jules 12
Vertov, Dziga 54
Vidal, Gore 72
video art 21, 38, 161
video gaming 18, 108

Villiers de L'Isle Adam see *Future Eve, The (L'Eve Future)*
Vincent, Harl, 'Rex' 149
Virilio, Paul 18, 44, 45, 83–4, 98, 107
virtuality 35, 128
Vonnegut, Kurt 96, 101–2, 150–2, 153
  Player Piano 15, 101, 150–2
  Slaughterhouse Five 101–2

war 18, 19, 36, 38, 44, 68, 78–9, 104, 107, 108, 120
  American Civil War 109, 157
  Boer War 52
  Cold War 17, 79, 86–98, 101, 103, 105–6
  First World War 12, 17, 61, 79, 82–3, 84, 140–1, 143, 145
  Gulf War, first 18, 38, 107–8, 127
  Second World War 20, 27, 29, 30, 32, 62, 66, 69, 72, 77, 79, 84–6, 90, 92, 102, 103, 108, 109, 139
  Spanish Civil War 66
  Vietnam War 107
Warhol, Andy 81
war machines 41
war poets 17, 82–3, 84–5
weapons systems 79, 83, 92
Welles, Orson 66, 67, 69, 76
  The War of the Worlds 69
Wells, H. G. 12, 13, 51, 64, 70, 121
Wershler-Henry, Darren 118, 119
Westinghouse Electric Company 7, 80
Whole Earth Catalogue 100

Wiener, Norbert 101, 139, 150, 153
wikinovel 131
Wilde, Oscar 67
  The Picture of Dorian Gray 20
Willetts, Peter 95
Williams, Keith 51, 58, 65, 71
Williams, Raymond 72
Williams, William Carlos 14, 19, 25–7, 56, 114, 115, 120
Wilson, Sloan, *The Man in the Gray Flannel Suit* 87
Winterson, Jeanette 96, 132–3
  The.Powerbook 132–3, 134, 135
wireless 2, 63, 65, 70
  see also radio
wireless writing 18–19, 144
Wonderful Wizard of Oz, The 136
  see also L. Frank Baum
Woolf, Leonard 64
Woolf, Virginia 14, 20, 24, 28–30, 53–4, 55, 56, 58, 64
  Between the Acts 29–30
  'The Cinema' 28, 53–4, 58
  Mrs Dalloway 29, 30
  Orlando 55
  To The Lighthouse 28, 29, 53, 55
World Wide Web 21, 35, 40, 95–6, 110, 122, 133, 162
wreader 127, 130, 131, 135, 163–6

Yates, Richard, *Revolutionary Road* 87
Yeats, W. B. 65, 70

Zerograph 110
Zilliacus, Clas 73, 76
Žižek, Slavoj 107, 108